DATE DUE

08-21-08			

DEMCO 38-296

FAULKNER, MISSISSIPPI

FAULKNER, MISSISSIPPI

EDOUARD GLISSANT

TRANSLATED FROM THE FRENCH

BY BARBARA LEWIS AND THOMAS C. SPEAR

FARRAR, STRAUS AND GIROUX

NEW YORK

Farrar, Straus and Giroux
19 Union Square West, New York 10003

Library of Congress Cataloging-in-Publication Data
Glissant, Edouard, 1928–
    [Faulkner, Mississippi. English]
    Faulkner, Mississippi / Edouard Glissant ; translated from the
French by Barbara Lewis and Thomas C. Spear. —1st Farrar
Straus Giroux ed.
        p.   cm.
    ISBN 0-374-15392-2 (alk. paper)
    1. Faulkner, William, 1897–1962—Knowledge—Mississippi.
    2. Literature and society—Mississippi—History—20th century.
    3. Southern States—In literature.   4. Mississippi—In literature.
    I. Title.
    PS3511.A86Z7833513   1999
    813'.52—dc21   98-49214

To the students of Southern University,
Baton Rouge, Louisiana

To the game who fled the Plantation

To the Oiseau de Cham, or Chamoiseau,
who sings the En-Ville

CONTENTS

"Continual return is to exegesis
as Chaos is to disorder."
—Anonymous (twentieth century)

FAULKNER, MISSISSIPPI

THE ROAD TO ROWAN OAK

She calls my attention to how much (in the pictures in this magazine) the two writers look alike. Both men have an expression that is not haughty but very reserved. They stare straight at you. One is utterly calm, the other withdrawn as if into a dream of greatness. Perhaps they are looking deep within themselves at something they share, far from any onlookers. Do I really see this or is it more a writer's silent whim to bend things absentmindedly toward what he has written? I have often associated them in my books, falling into the commonplaces of the times. Both of them are authors of the Plantation; they are two men on the edge of a caste, in a space where all is about to crumble, two colonials in fact, but so marginal among their own kind, two poets concerned with the relentless question of race and the stormy connection of one race to the other you have dominated for so long. One of these two writers, leaning toward the universal, pretends not to see this other race; the other approaches it with a wise but scattered incredulity. Both of them live on a frontier of life, on a margin where it is very hard to evaluate or trace any connection with the Other; they are trying to get around the Other, to sound its depths, and they return with mysteries, visions, and things of great beauty. They remain fixed, however, in their respective distances, tormented yet condescending. Saint-John Perse's head is tilted upward; whereas William Faulkner's head is held stubbornly parallel with the ground, as if secured by some straight and unavoidable prop.

Truly, they are in harmony with each other, although geographically so distant one from the other, and involved in projects so opposite. "Lacking" poetry, the latter would even dig into the bare and ardent earth and finally pitch camp there. The former would exhaust all speakable poetry in the universal abstract phrase in which, in the end, he lives. I look at the two images. The allure is the same: the air of the Planter, returning from the task, who does not find it unbecoming to take care of his animals, which perhaps he prefers, or pretends to prefer, to humans. I am not going to pity the Planter. I sound these two minds, two minds sharpened or exacerbated by the situation in which they find themselves caught or implicated, reacting to it, commenting on and transforming the world around it. They choose to settle into this situation and to justify it somehow by this very choice, nevertheless letting their work go far out into the world beyond.

I believe it must have been this way for Albert Camus. We are talking about artists (of sensibility as much as mind) who are situated on the frontier, on the border between two apparent or actual impossibilities. Camus with the Algerians (Arabs) and the French (Whites). Saint-John Perse with the Antilleans, the Black and White Creoles. Faulkner with the North, the "so-called haven" of the Negroes, and with the White Southerners who cannot but choose to prefer their mothers (or, rather, what they take to be truth) to justice.

Would it not be contemptible to approach such important works by methods that, in truth, appear utterly secondary relative to the breadth and insight of the works themselves? How can you reduce Faulkner's pantheistic Comedy to what he did or did not say about the race question in the United States? But how can you fail to take this question into consideration?

I will not focus solely on racism or the morality of the relationship with the Other. We are living in the moment when an indivisible world harmony and the conceptions it suggests are breaking up, a time when partial harmonies arise everywhere and converge toward a generalized disharmony, something the writer feels strongly he cannot explore without first renouncing this indivisibility that established him, sovereign and seer, in his place and words. To renounce the indivisible is to learn a new way of approaching the world; in so doing the writer learns to deploy all of his works in this approach, to become accustomed to this new and generalized disharmony while trying to follow its innumerable traces.

Whatever attitude he adopts in his rapport with the Other and whatever global vision of the Other he has formed, the writer has no choice but to disturb this vision through his work, even after expressing it in the work. Because finally he must renounce indivisibility and terrifying unicity. The author's way of plumbing the universe is the mark of his relevance, no matter what anguish, doubts, regrets, and remorse he suffers "in private."

Something clicks, and I begin. We veer around the subject—Faulkner's works—which we can feel spreading out like music, "neither close nor far." We do not pretend to know how to get there, yet we think it is within reach; days go by in dreams and worry.

The click. At the turning of a note, at the end of a short story, or in a speech in the middle of a novel, the work stands up before you. That is, its landscapes, streaks of twilight, colors (mauve and tawny predominating), and especially its smells, its haze and smoke, all rise from a yet invisible countryside; its crazed and fierce animals and its allotment of people, who share, without anyone suspecting it, the same bewilderment—the whole ensemble of his work stands before you as though erected by an architect who constructed a monument around a secret to be known, pointing it out and hiding it all at the same time.

To point out and to hide a secret or a bit of knowledge (that is, to postpone its discovery): this is a great part of Faulkner's project and the motif around which his writing is organized.

We had been settled for less than two weeks in Baton Rouge, Louisiana, in a house that was too large. We still had not put in what we needed in terms of furniture and supplies. For us, the United States—what you call "America" when you dream of coming here—was a vast body of shadows and mysteries. Eating omelettes and hash browns at Louie's Cafe (fried up on the hot griddle with a hint of cayenne so pleasing to our West Indian palates) was a new pleasure. We were hardly put off by the tyranny against cigarette smokers. We had already visited some of the neighboring bayous, so we decided to visit Rowan Oak, Faulkner's house in Mississippi in Oxford (recast in his works as Jefferson), a town that meant little more to us than the one in England.

What were West Indians going to do in the home of this Southern Planter? When you come to the United States you watch television until three in the morning and your eyes are bleary, trying to learn the language, of course, or to catch something of its meaning, but also because you are fascinated by who knows what, say basketball or football (in Martinique, sports commentators talk, as though naturally, of playoffs and Super Bowls), or maybe baseball, whose secrets you try in vain to fathom (all you see are players chewing gum and spitting on the ground, communicating at a distance in sign language with their teammates). Or you watch for the violence that everyone here seems to accept as just one of those "things" or "you-know-whats": a young girl raped and killed near one of the lakes in Baton Rouge at seven in the morning (she was out jogging); a young Black delinquent arrested and beaten badly by the police. Was he the murderous rapist? No. This time it was two young and idle Whites. The sheriff was asked if he regretted having beat up an innocent person in this way. As far as we could understand, he replied, "You know, he was lucky to get out alive.

Anyway, a young male Negro"—were those not his very words?—"is always in danger of getting killed in this country." So then, Faulkner, Oxford, Rowan Oak?

Still his work remains. His sequels, his theory, the unending parade of published books, not to mention the manuscripts stuffed in drawers, the "failed" debut poems with their symbolist pretensions, the early novels with their famous "character psychology," and the short stories: so many variations, not in the style but in the subject matter of an ever-invented country, some of them like the awkward advances of a body fleeing the spoken. And then the avalanche, an onslaught of rocks leaving no precipice to stand on, or from which to launch an "opening." From *Sartoris* to *Absalom, Absalom!* From the blue-green to the notched rock. From granite to striped jasper.

The "idea" of these books followed us on the trace, the road. We tried to recall them, to estimate their worth, as we saw it. This was our first time driving on American roads, lined with encampments of Burger Kings, fried chicken places, bars, and gas stations, which had replaced small towns and settlements. They were as shabby and mundane as any roadside on earth, but their very ordinariness stunned us with an incomprehensible feeling of exoticism.

Suddenly, past the border between Louisiana and Mississippi— marked by an indistinct sign—it seemed that another "something" bore down even more heavily. Up to that point, the road had led across gentle terrain (no doubt the idea we formed of Louisiana) where the proximity of the Gulf or the stretches of salt and fresh water, sea, and river between Baton Rouge and New Orleans seemed to wash the countryside with a kind of mist. We had entered into a tragic and irremediable thickness.

We were thus controlled by Faulkner's thinking. We felt an indefinable, engulfing menace. We found we could no longer count the churches—temples designed for the rites of despair ("the shabby church with its canting travesty of a spire")—which were hardly less numerous than the houses. Such were our preconceived ideas.

We thought we saw dirt trails intersecting up in the distance, crossroads painted in whites and calm yellows, adding a sheen of dust on the dry mud. We imagined hearing the old buggies bumping along the hard crest of the road with their iron-rimmed wheels and greased axles. We imagined seeing and hearing an accursed horse or a burdened old mule seek impossible shade under a thatch of leaves. We thought all these leaves were fighting their own fight: determined not to turn yellow (as if, all by themselves, they wanted to kill the time that fell so harshly there).

Strange advance, as we pushed into an unknown oppression that seemed to rise from everywhere (which happens when you insist on going into a hostile milieu). We would leave it behind only to rediscover it at the next turn. No doubt this area was pleasant enough. Having missed the entrance to the Interstate, we followed the back roads, and this very conventional rural reality weighed on us with a heaviness we could not explain.

Almost immediately after we saw the sign for Mississippi, we passed a little mound, a hill where three crosses stood, at odd angles, the tallest in the middle. Silence fell upon us; then one of us murmured, "Did you see that?" The three crosses, made from the rough trunks of young trees, kept following us as if keeping us under surveillance, as in those portraits where the sitter's gaze sticks to your back wherever you go and ends up terrifying you. It seemed this was the calling card of the Ku Klux Klan (someone had told us that the Klan originated in a pretty little town near Baton Rouge: St. Francisville, I believe). Those crosses had been stationed there to put us on notice, to let us know that we had to be on our guard.

Ambivalence. We knew conditions for Blacks were no better in

Louisiana than in Mississippi. Under the spell of William Faulkner's works, though, we had conferred upon the latter an absolute weight of representation for the Deep South. But, in fact, Faulkner never claimed to expose, criticize, or improve conditions for Blacks in the United States.

Our ambivalence was prolonged by wandering, a strange roving yet to come. When we finally reached Oxford, we were not able to find Rowan Oak. We drove in circles. Clumps of trees, sloping fields, a few roads branching out like tributaries, but no sign. By chance, we drove onto the University of Mississippi campus, where we asked the first student we met for directions to Faulkner's house. He did not know of Faulkner. We were taken aback and confused. Was he a science major, studying physics or chemistry? It was inconceivable to us that Faulkner could be unknown to anyone here who had any connection whatsoever with literature or culture.

Our ambivalence turned to panic as the day wore on. It was as though we had to pass a test before we could reach Rowan Oak; as though, in order to enter into the meanings of Faulkner's works, to see them stand before us and cry out in the woods and fields, we had to pass the test of their "difficulty," their resistance, had to force a path into their thick wilderness, into what we could call only their "deferred revelation."

Faulkner's books have always seemed to me to work this way. Deferred revelation is the source of his technique. This has nothing to do with the suspense of a detective novel or with social or psychological clarification; rather, it is an accumulating mystery and a whirling vertigo—gathering momentum rather than being resolved, through deferral and disclosure—and centered in a place to which he felt a need to give meaning.

Suddenly, something clicks. We are delivered from our wandering. Between tall, implacable trees on the edge of a side road, a barely visible sign indicates the entrance to Rowan Oak. The place has an air of comfortable retreat and the house at the end of the road seems imposing but neglected. This is characteristic of the United States, both North and South: glitter and glamour are always side by side with ruin and dilapidation. (Tourists in New York, for example, expect to be awed.) As if even in famous places, such as Rowan Oak, the ephemeral lies in wait, as if the building were about to be dismantled only to be rebuilt and placed on view somewhere else.

The house itself is at once a Plantation manor (*casa grande*) and family home. We discover later that the stable is a pathetic little structure, weather-beaten and rusty, like the ones we can find next to the Black slave sheds (*sencillas*; the title of Gilberto Freyre's work is always relevant). The configuration of the Plantation was the same everywhere, from northeastern Brazil to the Caribbean to the southern United States: *casa grande e senzala*, the big House and the slave hut, masters and slaves. Even with its four front columns, the main facade of this house does not suggest the proud luxury and absolute power that such an architectural composition usually claims by evoking the houses and temples of ancient Greece and Rome.

We had visited Nottoway Plantation, near Baton Rouge, which is backed by a levee protecting it from the floods of the Mississippi River. (I have been told that Black and White children alike still learn to spell its name with the old song: *M-i-s, s-i-s, s-i-pea pea aaaaayeah.*) The mythic river, Chateaubriand's exotic Meschacébé, the Deep River of Southern Blacks. The grand Old Man, site and booty for so many battles in the War of Secession, a channel of life and death leading from the continent's Nordic heart to its Creole delta.

From the top of the levee we had seen the wooden pier, doubtless swept away by the river over and over again and rebuilt just as often. From there, masters and slaves set sail for New Orleans, for trade or Carnival. A scruffy convoy of seagoing and inland barges bobbed on the yellowish water, encumbered in its middle by an island of trees and brush so enormous that it blocked the opposite shore. The barges were towed by efficient and implacable tugboats, whose rigging resembles that of the container ships (with their flat prow for merchandise, their raised castle tower reserved for staff, officers, and machine room) that carry French traffic back and forth to the Antilles, with such baroque names as *Fort Fleur d'Epée* ("Swordflower Fort").

So from one shore of this Mississippi—anachronistic in some ways, demoted from its historic role as liaison between the Plantations that starred its banks, conquered, we might say, by unseeing machines—without even having to turn around, leaning your head to one side you can survey the crest of the embankment, and the "antebellum" house takes you back to the times before the war (the only one named and considered here, the War of Secession). "Antebellum": the word is used to describe a residence, a style, and perhaps even a way of being or thinking; it harks back to a time when bands of slaves on the estates took care of everything.

There is no trace of the slave shacks which would have been alongside the outbuildings and grounds. Everything has been cleaned, sanitized, pasteurized. In the main garden, gas lamps burn day and night; the gas is cheap because the drilling fields and refineries are nearby. At the entrance to the property, past the gate that opens onto the main road, there is a small building where you can buy every imaginable tourist trinket: arts and crafts, postcards, regional specialties, and cookbooks. This fits in well with the logic of the place, where a desire to inform visitors is mixed with a compulsion not to frighten them with useless memories.

Here, memory belongs only to objects. The furnishings in the ballroom, sitting rooms, and bedrooms have a provincial and solemn character that undoubtedly comes from the solid ebony of the beds and tables. Sometimes you find the light grace of a sideboard in cherry wood. The same style of furniture is found in the Caribbean. It is called "colonial." In the music room, filled with period instruments, you can easily picture young girls tyrannized by their English or German governesses. The bedrooms in an annex were once reserved for children, who would have been assigned rooms according to age, there to sort out their budding romances and minor tragedies among themselves. Today, newlyweds spend their honeymoons here, staying three days and two nights after a reception in the restaurant built on the grounds. There are portraits or early photographs of ancestors everywhere. Those in the entrance hall include portraits of a dignified and stiff Black mammy and butler; on that evidence, we are supposed to believe they were part of the family.

Here, memory is selective, rid of the whiff of slavery. Just as there are people who deny the reality of the Holocaust, there are people here who will testify that the long martyrdom of Black slaves in the United States, the Caribbean, and Latin America was truly an age of happiness and pleasure, shared between master and slave. And if you happen to compare these two exterminations, these two horrors born of the human beast, right away there are people who will tell you to be careful, not to compare apples and oranges.

We told ourselves that "Nottoway" must have meant "not-a-way": no hook, no crook, no way José, to flee this place. Not a chance to escape as maroons: not up the river, through the wild riverbanks, not over the fields, where now, in the distance, you can see the gas refineries glimmering in the fullness of day, like myriad suns and pale stars, and where, closer at hand, huge tractors and machinery now cultivate fields of sugarcane.

We paid a brief visit to one such agricultural enterprise, still in operation, although in a precarious financial state (according to the owner), where the very high yield of the machines made it possible for him to hire very few employees. He led us across the fields, where we noticed a little wood planted with plagued trees, rising like an island in the middle of the flat cane. "That's where they buried the workers in the olden days," the man confided to us, meaning slaves. We took a long moment to contemplate that clump of trees, which seemed to twist and arch into a den. A world of tragedy was borne by those trunks sculpted in a wanton stiffness, keeping memory alive.

In our countries victimized by History where the histories of many peoples are intertwined, works of nature are the true historical monuments: Gorée Island, where all those Africans were hurled into the abyss of slave ships; Mount Pelée, and the disappearance of the city of Saint-Pierre; the underground dungeons of Dubuc Castle at Caravalle Point, again in Martinique, where those same Africans arrived (at least those who survived the voyage); the Sierra Maestra and the adventures of the Bearded Revolutionaries; and the Caiman woods, where the first oath of the Haitian Revolution was taken, a wood whose trees are scarred by erosion and where the wind yawns no longer.

We learn how the house was miraculously saved at the time of the South's collapse. The colonel who commanded the Union regiment had been received very courteously by the masters of Nottoway before the war and had spent a long time there. He refused to bombard the place, and gave the order to spare the inhabitants from fire and pillage.

We were in the middle of a slave-era film set. Some movies with historic aspirations had actually been filmed in the ballroom and other parts of the house. I remarked that all incongruous traces of the past had been wiped away. Not a single dirt-floor shack with rotten siding remained, the kind you can see at the Museum of Rural Life in Baton Rouge, where the past is reconstructed in a realistic and ordinary way. There, you can find objects, tools, and the atmosphere familiar from your West Indian childhood. I went to this museum with some singers of Creole tales from Bezaudin and Sainte-Marie in Martinique. Their eyes filled with tears as they gently touched these objects from the past scattered randomly about (one of the calculated charms of this museum). There were sickles, halters, yokes and other restraints for the work animals, most of which have since disappeared from our countries. The Martinican folksingers gained a great deal from their conversations with the Cajun storytellers of the place. Perhaps there will come a day when you will hear the story of an Acadian marriage presented as a Creole show in Martinique, or somewhere near Lafayette be told a tale of a French West Indian Br'er Rabbit successfully adapted to bayou idiom.

Here at Nottoway, only the fluttering dresses worn by the young White hostesses of the era (with organdy and flounces, in the style of Scarlett O'Hara, but a little soiled and worn from use) bear witness to the fact that the splendor really has left the place after all. But the new owners, reputed to be Japanese, are doing everything they can to keep up tradition and not tarnish it with any hint of bad taste.

What fascination had drawn us to this place? Perhaps only the unconscious knowledge that it remained a spectacular theater for great tragedy whose plot we carried inside us, even those of us who had never set foot in a colonial house in Guadeloupe or Martinique.

Rowan Oak looks nothing like a film set. There is a certain deterioration about the place. The rooms are human in scale, and it feels like a house where one could quietly and comfortably get drunk or greet children and grandchildren with a distant amiability, puffing on one's pipe.

At Rowan Oak, I did not feel the absence (the eviction, the erasure) of Blacks as I had at Nottoway. Nor did I feel their presence. Gone was the groom who helped the aging William Faulkner believe he was still a centaur astride his intractable horses. Gone also was Mammy Barr from his childhood, for whom he wrote such a beautiful dedication in one of his books. But perhaps I did not look hard enough for them.

It was as though the aura of his works had elevated the building and its surroundings to a state of splendid indifference, so that they transcended their origins. Can literature make one forget grief and injustice? Or, rather, is literature, and particularly the work of Faulkner, inextricably tied to grief and injustice so as to be able to point them out or fight against them?

· · ·

She shows me the inscription in a book by Albert Camus. We are in the library-cum-studio, a small, unpretentious room, without glass-fronted furniture, just some simple bookcases, obviously homemade, perhaps by the owner himself, giving an easygoing, natural aspect to things. It is worth considering—but is it so important?—why Faulkner (who was actually partial to London) was so quickly identified, lauded, and perhaps finally even seduced by Paris.

We sit down on the narrow staircase that leads up to the bedrooms. I have no desire to go upstairs, an utter lack of interest in the personal. Faulkner was above all a man who would sit at his desk or conscientiously laze on his veranda. I choose to wander in the garden. He and I are alike in the way we focus on huge ants employed in a task we cannot define or really place, ants like the characters in our works.

Despite the columns in front and the sovereign air common to colonial houses in the southern United States (the houses of the *békés*, the master class in Martinique, do not boast these columns or this sense of majesty), at Rowan Oak you witness the very ordinary domestic life, nothing like the parade of vanity in pseudo-Southern epics such as *Gone with the Wind*.

You have to get away from this family atmosphere, ignore these unspoken tragedies and edifying misfortunes—anything that could rise, ripen, and rot in this decor—in order to understand, that is to imagine for yourself, in the extreme purity of abstraction, what led the writer William Faulkner, with such savage tenacity, to hide everything while revealing it: the deferral of the South's damnation.

Here where the grass under the high solemn trees seems both lawn and savanna, we realize that we have not come to visit the home of a writer. This happened to us once before on a trip through Basque country. Pushed by friends I did not want to displease, we took a detour to see the house of another writer. Edmond Rostand's home was solemn and imperious, but seemed to be made of stucco instead of marble. Such a vain pursuit, so far from the demands of literature. Yet we

cannot stay away from Rowan Oak and harbor questions about it as
the place where the work took form, with the place as its model. It
was unexpected and paradoxical—and perhaps even inconceivable—
that work of Faulknerian dimensions could have been created in such
a place. This most ordinary prototype of "colonial" style exuded or
presupposed narrow minds and hardened hearts.

Happily, we abandoned this line of thought even before we had a
chance to put it into words and discuss it among ourselves.

What a bias it is—inherited from the practice of the oppressors—
to suppose that a work of art cannot arise from the house of the master
just as easily as from the shack of the oppressed. That would be as
judgmental as its opposite: "Those savages can produce nothing civilized." It echoes the same old questions shouted at writers and artists
like us from countries of the South: "Whom do you write for? Do you
write for the working class? For the bourgeois? For your race? For
Whites?" These questions evade the heart of the matter: the Relation
of literature to its highest object, the world-totality.

Stretched out on the grass on the grounds as if for a picnic, we recalled
our experiences of the past two days, trying to figure out whether we
had been victims of our own prejudices, limited by our preconceived
ideas or assumed knowledge, or whether we had truly been taken in
by reality. The night before, for example, we had stayed in a motel.
Two of us were determined to spend a night in a motel. As was so
often the case, our fascination had been influenced by Hollywood films
such as Alfred Hitchcock's *Psycho* and Orson Welles's film set on the
U.S.-Mexico border. Incredibly enough, the motel conformed with the
images we had seen: a dingy place, with dirty vinyl, questionable furnishings, a dim-lit room where nothing moves.

And then the trip to Natchez on Sunday at noon. Saddened to find
nothing alive in this deserted little city in the midst of its Sunday rest,
the four of us—three Antilleans and a very slight French woman—

ventured into a restaurant. Everything stopped the moment we walked in; as if on cue, all heads turned our way, just like in the movies. The composition of our group is scandalous in a place like this. Our appearance in a place obviously reserved for Whites is incongruous on this idle, sad noon hour in the middle of an empty day in this abandoned little city. This is a White habitat, and no one else, not Blacks, and certainly not Blacks in the company of a White woman, would have the foolishness to enter here. Petrified, we order food and drink, as little as possible so as to be able to leave as soon as we can. At such times, self-restraint is better than notoriety.

The crosses on the road, the motel, the restaurant in Natchez: each of these experiences leaves an impression, not really of danger but of a perfect conformity with our preconceived ideas. Were these not signs that we were unconsciously projecting into our "vision" of Faulkner (a representative U.S.-American) a whole passel of conventional images (despite what his books say), even if most of these images turn out to be true?

Situationally, the White racist (can we say this, or is this reverse prejudice?) hates the Yankee invaders. He is the inveterate individual caught in a storm of splendor and made to witness the hopeless grandeur of the South. He is the landowner, always strapped for cash, consumed by the struggle to maintain his property. These images seem to have little to do with literary effort—except when we consider that Faulkner's work raises troubling questions about the very phenomenon he was so bent on supporting and confirming in his "civil" life: the legitimacy of the South's foundation.

In life, Faulkner tirelessly took the side of the South, with its prejudices, its limits, and its unbreachable silences. One could even say that he wrote gloriously of the South's losing battle in the War of Secession. Even so, he posed questions in his works.

Let us pause here for a moment.

Epic literature seeks to fortify a community's identity and sense of destiny. Much more than from definite triumphs, the epic is engendered naturally (or obscurely) from questionable or ambiguous victories (the artifice of crafty Ulysses as told in the second song of the *Aeneid*; the way the *Iliad* ends with Hector's funeral and does not even depict the final victory of the Greeks). Or it responds to the defeat of the community (Roland in Roncevaux, Charlemagne using disguises and deception). Into the stone of the Valley of Kings, Ramses II engraved the epic song of what was probably one of his defeats. Victorious in the Civil War and profiting long and greatly from the victory, the American North never saw the need to sing the epic song of this war. That fell to the vanquished. The epic may be literal or artificial, concerned with appearances or the look of things (as with Margaret Mitchell's *Gone with the Wind*), or it may be erratic and disturbed, touching on veiled or buried questions, as in the work of Faulkner.

Observe how American cinema, while relatively indifferent to the country's conquests (the War of Independence, the Mexican-American War, the two World Wars), is bent on sublimating, through epic, the country's crushing defeats: the Alamo, Little Bighorn, Pearl Harbor, Vietnam—analyzing the temporary and precise reasons for the defeat and magnifying the eternal reasons that, out of defeat, have led and will lead to new and enduring victory. Actually, it was film that developed the legend of Abraham Lincoln, the conquering but scarred President, the man of action and of the people who epitomized the country's highest ideals, perhaps much more than George Washington, the founding father par excellence but also an aristocratic Planter and slave owner.

On the subject of Vietnam, there is a book by Jonathan Shay, *Achilles in Vietnam: Combat, Trauma and the Undoing of Character*,* which is significant in that it connects the Vietnam War with the epic (as in the title). In his works, Faulkner never evoked a victory at the end of

* Sebastien de Diesback brought this book to my attention.

a war without immediately referring to "the no less valorous defeat," "one giving glory, the other erasing shame."

And in a letter to a friend, dated June 12, 1955, he wrote, "Sometimes I tell myself that it takes a disaster, maybe even a military defeat, to wake up America and allow us to save ourselves or what remains of us."

Defeat as an appeal to epic passion: "His voice had the proud tranquility of flags in the dust."

Terribly beaten in 1918, Germany produced *All Quiet on the Western Front* (just as it produced the aberrant phenomenon of Hitlerism, vector of a false, fatal, and bombastic epic). Arguably neither *The Wooden Crosses*, by Roland Dorgelès, nor *Fire*, by Henri Barbusse—embarrassed as they are about the idea of (their) final victory—ever attained the dense and somber grandeur of this first work.

The epic encapsulates and expresses the instincts of people brought together in one place by a shared threat or a common defeat. There is another kind of epic, less engaging, more solemn, expressly intended to magnify a triumphant Empire or a universal Spirituality.

On the one hand, we have works that question: the pantheistic (despite its monotheism) and tormented epic of the Old Testament; the problematical works (where is the East, where is the West?) such as the *Iliad* and the *Odyssey*; the inductive epics (the Frankish, and subsequently French geste) such as *The Song of Roland*; and epics like *Tragiques* by Agrippa d'Aubigné, insanely fatalistic sagas, illuminated by bonfires. On the other hand—and from other places—we have the sovereign machinery of the *Aeneid* or *The Divine Comedy*, where it is no longer a matter of questioning and destabilizing. These works are at once wandering and immobile, and the intent is magnanimously to illustrate a Universal.

If all these books in effect are about wandering, we observe that only the first type really follows the traces of danger. In the second, the wandering is definitive (by nature the definitive stays away from the tortured rigidity of the quest), taking the paths of triumph and con-secration, even if these paths are full of traps.

Faulkner's work follows the traces of danger.

His works are unique. They magnify the geste of the lost fight, as all epic does, but they also investigate the unforeseen outcome: the ab-sence of "eternal reasons" that could have allowed the defeat to be sublimated into a future conquest. The absence is unspeakable. Even in a work of fiction, no community can consciously justify its own lack of sublimation, its incapacity to get past moments of defeat and trans-form them into reasons for hope. All of Faulkner's works are built on this lack which they would never openly declare. This is where deferral plays out and builds up; speaking the lack without proclaiming it.

In the United States today, we can see how citizens would interpret getting beyond lack by sublimating it. This would mean thinking of the Civil War as an episode in the global national history, one in which both victors and vanquished would embody and represent the virtues of the nation and the future of its power (since here, as throughout the West, grandeur is thought to depend on power), whether the pro-tagonist is Stonewall Jackson or Sherman, Lee or Grant or, in another arena, Sitting Bull, Cochise, or Geronimo as well as the Seventh Cav-alry. The many reconstructions of the decisive battles of the War of Secession and of the settlement and conquest of the West (and those of the wars of Independence) all illustrate this. So do the videos and films made on the subject, as well as the growing number of novels and historical studies devoted to the war, and now to the North as well as to the South. *The Great Battles of the Civil War* and *Gettysburg* are documentaries, *The Blue and the Grey* romantic fiction, *Andersonville* a grand televised dramatic spectacle about a camp for Northern prisoners in Southern territory. These epics are of the defeated and the hopeless who can be seen in the midst of the conquerors.

But for the South—for white Southerners—this rite of passage and this consent to a community at large are both gratifying and painful and cannot be achieved without crises. They first require a renunciation, not of the identity of the Southern community (which after all was maintained in the unified nation) but of its very legitimacy as a dignified community capable of sublimating its very real defeat into a victory no less real. Here, legitimacy means more than identity. The failure or absence of legitimacy is deemed intolerable.

At the same time, reactionary attitudes characteristic of the South have spread to the North (for example, the desire to transfer federal prerogatives to the states), and there is a new kind of sameness nationwide. The paradoxical opposition between the Democratic Party's progressive orientations in the North and the extreme conservatism of its members in the South, for example, will be resolved as the latter enroll more and more into the ranks of the Republican Party, perhaps, or even become members of a new, conservative party (a constant temptation, but one that would break with the country's traditional bipartisanism).

This typical political analysis stresses that the United States naturally breaks up into many archipelagoes, making the states truly autonomous regions through a movement of centrifugal diversification, neither progressive nor completely reactionary. And we do not know if this movement is irreversible or if, rather, it sets the stage for central, imperial power.

When Faulkner was writing, what he put at risk was the supreme institution of this Southern community. He questioned its very legitimacy, its original establishment, its Genesis, its irrefutable source. All his works are shaped by an unsurpassable a priori, a question putting everything in vertigo: How to explain the "beginnings" of the South—

this monopoly of the land by Whites from Europe, actually from no-where, all of them (in the writing) prone to violence? They clearly had no right to buy these "Big Woods" from the hands of the last Indians, guardians of the earth, who themselves clearly had no right to sell it.

To all this, a gaping wound is added, lacerating as it must have been for the Puritan that Faulkner never wished to be (but which Joanna Burden is so dramatically in *Light in August*): How can one understand, or at least envision, the South's "damnation"? Is it connected to the South's dark entanglement with slavery, inextricable from its roots and its tormented history?

To these basic, primordial questions the work makes no reply. They remain implicit and unresolved. On the one hand, the work is revealed as infinite, not locked in by any "answer" or solution. On the other, the characters in the work are not "types," determined in advance by possible answers as conceived by the author; they are people prey to this gaping wound, to a suspension of being, a stasis, an unhappy de-ferral acted out through wild exuberance or repressed within. Whether savagely racist, pathologically antiracist, or morbidly indifferent, these people are not compelled by such questions, but they inhabit the ver-tigo.

The inconceivable and impossible situation of the country (its fail-ure to respond to basic questions) has become an absolute. This is a place of contradiction, where the human situation is not to be studied but should be given a chance to ask the questions. For these reasons, there is no study of character in Faulkner, no so-called narrative weight; rather, we find a vertigo of striking, irremediable people.

The techniques of this literature, its prose and its architecture, also serve to defer. Faulkner suspends the rigorous narrative rules that have dominated Western literature. Through this gap, this suspension, for example, he gives depth to his characters' "interior monologues" and explorations of conscience. Traditionally, the monologue leads to a kind of global truth that its unfolding designates, or else the monologue is carefully distributed through the text to give the feeling of immediacy or at least a lack of constraint. With Faulkner, monologues deny the validity of every answer in a way more effective than global truths or careful distribution.

Even though he arranges his work in the shadow of questions to which he gives no answer—that is to say, nothing didactic or definite—nonetheless, in his life as well as in his convictions, he keeps faith with the reality so questioned, even if doing so will cause injustice, and even if this injustice is what makes the reality unacceptable.

If Faulkner had disassociated himself from the reality of the South, if he had passed judgment and come to conclusions, the a priori question no longer would have made any sense, and his works would have been reduced to a "realist" manifesto with no repercussions. Had he put his life as a Southerner into the cause, he could not have offered an objective view on the quivering question of the South's legitimacy. Had he abandoned the South, in his heart or mind, or simply in everyday life (for example, by leaving it to travel the world), then the question would have died out, having received his answer. As it is, the epic questioning of the Genesis of the South, of its identity and legitimacy, can be found neither in a triumphal certitude nor in a detached indifference.

The Faulknerian whirlwind gathers breadth from this articulation, tirelessly debated at high pitch or fostered through innuendo. Such bootless daring, such useless majesty, such tragic, miserable, and small-minded lives: whence comes the South's absolute legitimacy?

Landscapes (ravaged woods, barren cotton fields, teeming waters), wars, dynasties and exactions, scattered herds, and great masses of people appear in this whirlwind. They cannot be described as "characters in a novel." Everything is brought together in this whirlwind to testify to this questioning, to signify it, perhaps to wrench some disturbing answers from it while deferring their formulation indefinitely.

William Faulkner pursued this work stubbornly. Without giving it a thought, it seemed he separated his work from his daily life. For him, that was the only way to survive. With his family and in his milieu, he would be a hospitable archipelago. As a writer, he is an unapproachable island. He *must* participate in the life of the South, he *must* elucidate its problematic. However necessary they may be to each other, the two roles are incompatible. William Faulkner enters silently into a severe schizophrenia. He also takes to drink, coldly, dully, like an overly lucid machine.

He needs to be pitiless with the South, yes, to scrutinize it with seeing eyes, in order to be able to ask the question regarding its own reality—in a question that, in the final analysis, is the essential question of poetry and literature: Can we tolerate the individual Being (the absoluteness of Being), can we get close to it and know it, merely by summoning together all the different possible Beings? Is it wise to approach an essence—a pure possibility that would guard against dissipation and despair—from the standpoint of so many suffering, irreducible particulars? Or can we dismiss Being in the way we shake our heads to chase away a momentary confusion?

The language of a used-car dealer from Jefferson or Oxford, a bootlegger in the nearby woods, a lawyer in Oxford (or Jefferson) with an office across from City Hall, or even of an old woman telling children the legend of General Stuart, the Confederate hero, all would resonate with this demand: How to be, how to behave, how to think or at least act instinctively and in harmony with the land? After so many inexplicable misfortunes (nothing extraordinary, just the run-of-the-mill misfortunes that struck most of those who suffered), there is clearly a secret in this difficult association with the land.

This inexplicability, this secret. Faulkner holds on to it. In doing so, he begins to broach what is inexplicable in all literature.

As for the Blacks, if the question of the South's legitimacy ever comes up in the work, it never concerns them. (When he was young, Faulkner

often called them "niggers," perhaps not as a Southerner on automatic
but as a deliberate provocation.) He made their role emblematic. In
the last line of the dazzling summary called the *Compson Appendix*,
after retracing the relationship between the Compson family and the
county that bore their name, he mentions Dilsey, the old Black woman
who all her life had "taken upon herself" if not the honor, at least the
virtue and balance always threatened in the Compson house. He writes
simply, "They endured."

This is one of the most famous sentences in Faulkner's work. Here
is how I interpret it: These Negroes "counted." They were representative in and through a suffering that assumes and knows things instinctively and "takes upon itself." They took on meaning but not from
any decision to deliberate or act.

Once on the streets of Oxford, Mississippi, you easily figure out how
to get around, how to find the main square. It is as though you are
following in Benjy's path, his trace, described at the beginning and end
of *The Sound and the Fury*: "Post and tree, window and doorway, sign-
board, each in its ordered place."

This order, the Southern order, may be provincial, but you have the
sense that it is the perception of an idiot who was profoundly capable
of describing its characteristics: There is so much sun, lethargic, weighing down on the square, which I suppose is very modern now, compared
to what it once was. Certainly, it is less wide-open than in the days
when Lucas Beauchamp, the Black Intruder in the dust who remained
calm when accused of murder, mounted the stairs to the office of the
lawyer, Stevens, where he counted out, cent by cent, the two dollars
this man of the law claimed his services were worth. (Afterward, Lucas
asked for his receipt.) And there is no more dust. Perhaps we no longer
feel for the fatal misery of the Blacks and the downfall of the McCaslin
and Compson families. It seems, however, that time passes here just as
uneventfully as it did in the pages of *Sartoris*. We understand that it

took the utter innocence of an idiot to perceive or to at least sense—in and under the slumbering appearance of this reality—the inescapable path (a path leading *to the right* of the Confederate monument) to damnation and fatality.

How to say it: you recognize the place, in the way you never fail to recognize, in certain landscapes near Anjou, the only possible setting for Balzac's *Lilies in the Valley*. At that moment, I recognized the similarity between places like this, so suitable to Faulkner, and so many other town squares in the world of the Americas. There is the same feeling of intimacy (and infinity), a feeling of silent pleasure or of hard times and injustice, endured. . . . As if following the faintest of traces, the sun ushers a silence into the flow of traffic and the small streams of passersby.

You cannot fail to come upon the Faulkner bookstore, so rich in books, translations, documents, cards, autographs, portraits and photographs, albums, calendars, and ashtrays, all having something to do with the author. It also contains the publications of the Center for the Study of Southern Culture, affiliated with the University of Mississippi. (It is familiarly called Ole Miss, as if one were talking about an old maid— I suddenly remember the Louis Armstrong song with that name.) William Ferris is the Center's director. Among its publications are the *Encyclopedia of Southern Culture* and a quarterly journal called *The Southern Register*.

This "book boutique" was the first of its kind we visited. You could eat a simple lunch of soups and sandwiches, and drink coffee, hot or iced tea, or mineral water, right there in this room, surrounded by the works. I was later to rediscover this wonderful practice in some of the big bookstores in New York.

Faulkner's presence is everywhere, ritually so. The student who did not know who he was should be here. We begin to think that when we talked to him earlier, perhaps we mispronounced Faulkner's name.

He must have heard "Falnay," or maybe it came out "Vouklare." In the United States, you hear so many different accents, and often you are not understood (in places far from cities) unless you pronounce the simplest words with that cutting accent that rolls them on your tongue, shortens them, draws them out or rushes through them. It is just the same for the French who pretend not to understand anything said by Cajuns or people from Quebec.

In the Faulkner bookstore (that is what we decide to call it), we learn that every year there is a conference of pastiche devoted to "Faux Faulkners." A winner and a runner-up is chosen, and each given a prize, as in a television game show. Contestants in the Annual Faux Faulkner Contest imitate what are thought to be Faulkner's tics or obsessions. *The Best of Bad Faulkner* contains the winning entries. The contest has several precedents such as the Hemingway Write-Alike Contest and a publication called *The Best of Bad Dashiell Hammett*. These "bad" examples are almost always titillating and irresistible to read, even if a bit mechanical and forced in their construction. Is this not really a fine way to get into literature, having a good reason to produce imitations, to copy and exaggerate a writing style and be compensated in the process? It seems that certain people—doctors and lawyers as well as academics who are aficionados of Faulkner's work and students inspired by it—have become specialists at this.

We leave the bookstore only to stumble (our own fault, certainly) into another lengthy debate. We decide to visit William Faulkner's tomb in the local cemetery. As with the house, we cannot find it. We roam from row to row through a vast enclosure where all the tombs, in either granite or marble, are elevated. This is the rich people's cemetery, as we say in the Antilles, a little village of small mausoleums like those you can see around New Orleans. The reason, we learn, for these elevated tombs—if one discounts family vanity—is that floods often wash up and carry away the dead who are buried in the ground, sweep-

ing them down into the canals and littering the streets with coffins. In
Martinique, the cemeteries sparkle and All Saints' Day is practically a
children's holiday with its hundreds of lights glistening like galaxies in
the night.

It is a singular experience to lose your way in a cemetery. You feel
as though anguish sticks to your very bones, and as though your wandering life will brutally come to an end right on the spot. Can you
imagine that wandering does not end in the land of the dead? We read
a lot of plaques bearing the name Falkner, but we do not see William
Faulkner's tomb. We finally find it in a back part of the cemetery, to
the left on a downward slope away from everything else. We do not
find, however, the section reserved for "colored people," where it is
said Faulkner's Black nurse, Mammy Barr, is buried.

Mississippi was the second state to secede, following South Carolina,
which had some priority in the matter of slavery. However, Mississippi
was the last of the old Confederacy to officially abolish the slave regime. True, this was long before Brazil and certain countries in the
Middle East abolished slavery, but only after a long Civil War forced
it into compliance.

From the moment we missed the highway going north into the state
of Mississippi to the time we arrived in Oxford (where, without knowing it, we had endlessly circled around Rowan Oak), digressions and
detours dogged our trip. Even at the end of the day we still found
ourselves wandering in the gray and white cemetery. Were these ram-
bles not the very signs, or their equivalent, of the lag "in understanding" which is so unsettling in our reading of Faulkner? So much so
that, absorbed and transfixed by his works, we delay piecing together
so much of the implied vertigo, so much of the scattered and hidden knowledge, yet we all know that, in the end, we will have to add
things up.

·   ·   ·

The trip back to Louisiana is much quicker than the trip out. You could say that we distance ourselves from a sense of place and allow ourselves to get caught up in activity, in the city, in shopping. We already know that, in many respects, Louisiana is close to the Caribbean and especially to the Antilles: the plantation system, the thrilling persistence of Creole languages, a linguistic background of French, and, most blatantly in all of these slave societies, the insistent suffering and the Negro runaways.

Later, I would remark that whites from Louisiana generally refuse to admit any such connections.

"Do you really think there's something in common between Louisiana and the Caribbean?"

You tell the story one more time: Families that fled the Haitian and French revolutions settled here with their retinue of slaves and all their belongings; they are still here in the descendants of the Jaham and La Houssay families, and in so many other families as well. And this is without counting all the Blacks who for a time came to New Orleans in pursuit of their liberty and equality, only to come face to face with their former servile status. The cooking—the spices, the hearty vegetable soups (Lafcadio Hearn's *gombo zheb*), red beans, and pork—and the music are principally the same in the culture of this whole area. The African trace was kept alive, reconstructed according to the inspiration of a particular place. But the same architecture, furniture, and rows of slave shacks, the same instruments of torture are found everywhere in the old slave order—the whipping bar, the stake, the collar restraints, and the suspension poles—you cite a whole list for a skeptical audience that does not wish to know that its history travels with the seas.

On our return, coming back from Mississippi and moving toward the bayous once again, toward the mouth of the river, toward the Cajuns,

Black Indians, and zydeco (Acadian music with a jazz and rock rhythm), I realize that this is what Faulkner recorded in the far reaches of Yoknapatawpha. Into this fictional county Faulkner put his whole native land of Mississippi, and the entire South as well (one emphatically says "the South," with a capital "S," as though it represents an absolute, as though we other people of the south, to the south of this capitalized South, never existed):

. . . it begins on the first bus a lost person boards, leaving behind this part of the world and heading for the nearest city, Memphis, for example;

. . . it lingers menacingly at the county's horizon;

. . . it has a name, Creolization, the unstoppable conjunction despite misery, oppression, and lynching, the conjunction that opens up torrents of unpredictable results;

(like a tumultuous and boundless Mississippi);

. . . it is the unpredictability that terrifies those who refuse the very idea, if not the temptation, to mix, flow together, and share;

. . . at the deepest level of meaning, Faulkner's work has never stopped investigating both the curse of this "menace" and the damnation of those who fight it;

. . . in this way he was a prophet of the fundamental defects in our world, the massacres between different tribes, ethnicities, peoples, and nations that can agree only in regard to the urgency of the mass killing;

. . . that Faulkner, who actually began writing—his first novel, *Soldier's Pay*—in New Orleans, the land of Creolization (a commemorative plaque is tacked up in his honor on a narrow wooden house where he lived for a short time on a little street running past the Cathedral, a house with balconies stuck between some more imposing buildings on the site of an old Spanish prison), finally gave himself, at the end of his career, the task of sounding the world of the county, recognizing that such a universe fights vehemently—at the price of so much violence, theft, rape, insanity, infirmity, misfortune, and a taste for misfortune in the people who live there—against the unbearable idea that the world can invade the pure county and turn it inside out.

His works operate in that troubled place where everyone in the world feels threatened by outrages from something oddly amorphous and de-naturing, and we think it is the distorting shape of the Other. The inhabitants of this country Faulkner scours are tortured by the same "undesirable" label that we give to any intrusion from outside. They prefer the torments of withdrawal into self and the damned solitude of a refusal that does not have to speak its name.

It remains to be known—and this is a literary question, not a psycho-logical or moral one—whether William Faulkner, who so coldly yet passionately approached the infinite limits of his query, announced his answer (as I define it: "to maintain the county at a distance from the world, in order to signify the whole world") or if, at every moment, he suffered its discomfort and torment.

THE FAULKNER DOSSIER

He was born in New Albany, Mississippi, in 1897, into a truly exceptional family "ruined by the Secessionary War." For historians, this family could stand in for the great Southern families of slavery: a great-grandfather who was an officer in the Confederate army, probably a colonel (a most prestigious rank in these matters; a colonel in charge of his own regiment of troops, even though later he had to test his troops' valor on the battlefield, that is, prove their collective valor rather than his own personal, always certain, courage, before he could aspire to the rank of general). This grandfather, or perhaps one of his sons, made a fortune from the railroad, or in some remunerated occupation with little risk of social regression (but he may have started out as a small shopkeeper—a most strategic position to occupy in that postwar period—or rented out horses, a role conferring an almost noble status). Then he, or perhaps one of his sons or descendants, floundered once again. From one generation to the next, the males in the family—fathers or uncles—distinguished themselves in all kinds of eccentric professions: as mad duelists, disappointed lovers, outraged husbands, murderers (as if by calling), while the martyred maiden aunts—those who took care of the children and gave orders to the slaves and, later, the Black servants—placidly watched the collective disaster and told stories about it.

"He" is William Faulkner. The Anglo-Saxon habit of using first names and nicknames is foreign to me as a speaker of Creole. At first, I could not understand how, all his life, his friends and family could refer to William Faulkner as Bill. Nor could I imagine him using this diminutive when signing letters to his close friends and family. I had thought Bill a nickname limited to barrooms and beer halls and that, even if Faulkner could down his drink with the best of them, Bill in no way suited the great tragic poet he had become. I could not imagine Faulkner as Bill even though I knew tragic greatness is never as powerful as when it is on intimate terms with simplicity and has the common touch.

One day (when he was ready for the only real work of his life) he decided to add a "u" to the Falkner family name, as if he were uncertain of the import of the familial model and knew that he, William Faulkner, must shape this model and give it legitimacy. It was as though he told himself that the members of his family, from the old to the young colonels, from his great-grandfathers and his mythic grandfathers all the way down to the least of their descendants and cousins, would not truly have lived their tormented or dull or peaceful lives until the patronymic cast was delineated and illustrated. Unless, on the other hand—it happened differently—while pondering one afternoon on the veranda of a friend's house (sipping one of those indeterminate Southern drinks that might be cane liquor, mint, or burned alcohol), he decided that this family deserved to be "transposed" or sublimated in some way through this variant, through this "u," swollen with epic novelty. From then on, he could make the family enter into what he literally and symbolically was going to reveal as the Southern cast in his works: inalienable, at times grandiose, but always miserable and fatal.

And, from this moment on, he dedicated himself to this other family that he had finally chosen for himself—marrying a woman who had at first rejected him to marry another man and thus sanctifying his failure with a quiet and official revenge. He may have given up any idea of male descendants (after the death of his first daughter, Alabama, and in spite of the affection he bestowed upon his second daughter, Jill). It is not clear that he was not convinced, as were most of the people in Yoknapatawpha, that sons were the only legitimate descendants. Perhaps he was also trying to include the notable members of the Falkner line within the tragedy of the Faulknerian vision, spending all his strength to scrape together the wherewithal to make his world live. Nevertheless, with a ferocious yet tranquil resolve, he sundered his "civil" life from the realm of his creation, he who, in his youth and even into a rather advanced age, had pompously or preciously dedicated ream after ream of affected, symbolist poetry to the beauties he had courted; he had even gone so far as to bind, trim, and decorate by hand these volumes in which the art of poetry competed with the art of seduction.

So he abandoned the lyric, its pretensions and conventions—since it had become clear he had no gift for it—instead devoting himself to the difficult task of divining the real and what he saw within and beneath it, assembling this whole, atypical, and very lively population into a space he reorganized (an atypical population merely because we, the readers, share with the author who creates them the characters' lack of knowledge about what makes them act in such incomprehensible ways—incomprehensible at least as far as any apparently human logic goes, or according to any rules of the novel). Faulkner proved to be impermeable to the vexations he had to endure, precisely because of this dedication, accepting with an apparent—and, in any event, intrepid—constancy the rebuffs and criticism about (or against) his work: cut-rate contracts, jobs paid at almost insulting wages, suggestions that he rewrite and shorten his texts. Patient and stoic, he would put up with these quarrels from friends and literary agents, from editors and publishers of both books and magazines (he probably holds a record for the number of novel excerpts and short stories refused by both popular and lesser-known magazines): disputes over trivial, picayune questions and absurd problems that were unimportant to him but which people made every effort to ask him: Didn't this character lack "depth"? Wasn't there a contradiction between this scene and that one? Wouldn't it be better to prune this or that passage that stood in the way of the story's "action"? Diligently and conscientiously (except for the occasions when he would get all worked up, as, for example, when someone frankly asked him to "restructure" *The Sound and the Fury*) he would argue, and stand up for his ideas. He would take the position that no one who had not first "entered" into the totality of his work could even get close to making sense of what he meant in the passage. Showing an apparent humility (or perhaps out of an obscure wish to be praised for the same things as others), he would go so far as to affirm that he, too, was "profitable"—that is, as capable as anyone else of writing best-sellers to earn money for their author and publishers. Supposedly, this is what he tried to do with *Sanctuary*, in the rape scene that caused such a scandal in the United States (where the lynching scenes apparently went unnoticed), and because he boasted that he had written the novel in a careless, expedient manner. Knowing, perhaps, that he was the greatest writer of this century (despite Proust and despite Joyce, or because of them), the one who had the most to reveal about one's own, unavoidable locality *at the same time* as the Relation of this locality to the world-totality, he did not any less slave away at his work, get smashed on booze, and barely manage to get by in this life of hell and anguish which he no

doubt needed in order to endure secretly (that is, very simply, unbe-
knownst to and sheltered from every living being who was near him
in time and space) and to bear the enormous choice he had made: that
is, to forgo literature's favors and luster in order to carry literature even
further.

Still, he never stopped hoping—always in secret and with the cold
and incredible self-absorption of builders and inventors—for the recognition he had officially (from his point of view) stopped expecting.

During their honeymoon, when she fearlessly and absentmindedly entered the tragic and mundane daily life that was to be hers, his wife
attempted suicide. Their first daughter, Alabama, died nine days after
birth. His youngest brother, Dean, as if a damned duplication of *Sartoris*
or *Pylon*, killed himself piloting an airplane bought as a gift principally
with William's funds. And he, William (a modern Isis), helped to
gather his brother's broken body. As a couple, the Faulkners would
begin the only habit they would ever really share: drinking themselves
into a deadly stupor. And Faulkner would write, delivering blow after
blow in these confusing books; his most enthusiastic admirers (from
the beginning, a silent mob) were incapable either of analyzing them
or of standing up for their disconcerting innovations. It took quite
some time (in France, for example, he was considered very important
by many writers, a group that lavishly praised him from the outset but
with such hollow arguments) before Faulkner finally would no longer
be seen as simply a novelist of rural America, as a textual experimenter
in the Joycean tradition, or as a "Southern writer" variously likened
to Caldwell, Steinbeck, or Hemingway: a mix including the Far West,
the Deep South, the Midwest, and so many other mythic and remote
places in the United States of America.

He founded Yoknapatawpha County, bordered on the south by a
river of the same name and on the north by the Tallahatchie River
(Indian and primordial names), an imaginary county that could be set

against its double in reality, the county of Lafayette, Mississippi, just as Jefferson stood for the McCaslins, the Oxford of Ole Miss for the Compsons, and the Sartoris family for the Falkners. He scoured this compost, mixing the past with the present, and the wild, "big Woods" with cultivated lands. On this site he engendered poor Whites, Blacks, and families of the dying aristocracy, collected tales and legends of origins, glorious stories of the Civil War that could not be won, and depicted monstrous results from countless crossbreedings and simple-minded fools running through the countryside. He mixed these stories with figures from slave registers, details from Plantation store ledgers and rat-eared Bibles that would always fall open to the same page, and shameful letters hidden away in secret corners of storage chests in the great mansions. Not only did he bring forth a world from all of this; he bestowed upon it (paired it with) an utterance that he perhaps knew would reverberate with so many other utterances in the world.

Not only did he describe the reality given to him and refashion it; but he persuaded this reality to yield to a higher (or more hidden) meaning and a sense of becoming.

His writings can be organized as I have done in the chart below. This schematic is generally accepted, even if many connections can be drawn between the different categories, deliberately clouding them, and even if three or four other possible classifications could be suggested. The entries cross one another horizontally, flow from one another, and are mutually informative and revealing:

"PREPARATION." "LITERATURE": ("Afternoon of a Faun.") *The Marble Faun* and *A Green Bough*. The first novels: *Soldier's Pay*. *Mosquitoes*. *The Wild Palms*.

BEGINNINGS. THE OLDEN DAYS: *Go Down, Moses*. ("The Bear.") ("Big Woods.") And the corresponding short stories (particularly those in *These Thirteen*).

THE COUNTY. THE CURSE: *Sartoris. The Sound and the Fury. Absalom, Absalom! Light in August. Compson Appendix. As I Lay Dying. Intruder in the Dust. The Unvanquished.* The "Mississippi" tales and short stories. (*Knight's Gambit.*)

THE EXTENSION. MONSTROSITIES: *Sanctuary. Requiem for a Nun.* And corresponding stories. (In three short-story collections, particularly in *Doctor Martino and Other Stories.*)

FARAWAY PLACES. AMBIVALENCE: *Pylon. A Fable.* The "European" tales and short stories.

THE SNOPESES. THE END OF THE EPIC: *The Hamlet. The Town. The Mansion.*

And: *The Reivers.*

(It is not long before she points out to me, with a reticent resolve, that there are inherent contradictions in this scheme and that the Faulknerian mix does not allow for such methodical separations. I insist, repeating what I have said regarding cross-referencing and, for example, how some of the county works can be linked to those of the faraway places, via the European wars. In short, this general outline still argues for the inextricable, visibly stemming from a central knot—the county—whose individual cords spread out to a great distance in every direction without stopping or choking off a single one. She counters that you could correctly put forth many other structures or divisions: for example, a distinction between those in the county who accept their curse and those who refuse to accept it or fight against it, those who escape it, etc. I concede that there are several different trajectories to follow. The pattern I have sketched out, however—and the one that is most widely accepted—seems to work, on several levels, following the path of Faulkner's works as well as of his life. She smiles serenely.)

To further clarify the list, you can use several different themes:

Mississippi. Under this designation—not by chance—there is a whole series of poems as well as a draft of an autobiography.

Jefferson, Yoknapatawpha.

Oxford, Lafayette.

Faulkner, Mississippi.

The remote sketches: "Father Abraham," where one can find a pre-figuration of the Snopeses, and a prose poem, "The Hill," where Faulkner alludes to a "seasonal migrant" character. Wandering as strength, and as weakness.

"Sherwood Anderson and Other Famous Creoles." In Faulkner's amusing introduction, he tries, perhaps, to escape the very unsettling charm, or grasp, of the Creole world.

Then there are the prefaces, letters, and speeches and the innumerable "first drafts" of his works that leave one astounded by his prodigious energy.

Short stories unpublished during his lifetime, or not published in collections.

Film scenarios: less innocent, or should one say less "professional," than they first appear. Reading them evokes a certain admiration for the discriminating Hollywood producers who for the most part wanted nothing to do with them.

So it is possible to follow the path of this life for no other reason than to sound these creations (books) through which Faulkner rushed headlong, from one to the next: so many moving roots of a single flaming network. His works have been examined with great intelligence in detail and as a whole (by Frederick R. Karl, among others, in his biography of Faulkner, and by Maurice-Edgar Coindreau, one of the eminent translators of Faulkner into French), and by means of varied theories that, in order to connect his life with the generation of his works, little more than commonplaces remain. But from these commonplaces, a world-thought emerges.

Faulkner as a young man (the first category of my chart, the first of the transversal periods) was willingly unkempt and provocative and would pretend (that is, he would take on the laziest yet most contrived appearance possible) to be drunk before he had downed his first glass: a young and ersatz dandy. I should not exaggerate, however: he sank into drunkenness in the very same way that he went into his silent funks, locking himself up with his project as "the writer with a Bohemian reputation" and all the rest of the hoopla, including as expected the initiation tour of Europe (Italy and France, as German Romantics and Russian novelists would travel to Rome and Venice), immersion in New Orleans, his first relationships with literary contemporaries: Sherwood Anderson and the others, all very "Southern" but surely more amenable, diffuse, and agreeably featherbrained than this Mississippian, "student, house painter, migrant, day-worker, dishwasher, bookseller, bank employee," in short, all the conventional indicators of an artistic presence according to the blurb he wrote himself—and this, after he had already invented a completely imaginary résumé listing armed service "in the RAF during the war." "Afternoon of a Faun"—knowing what these words meant for symbolists from Verlaine to Mallarmé and whose greatest merit would be to instigate the development of "Afternoon of a Cow," perhaps the only text where a Mr. Faulkner appears, as well as Mr. Faulkner's cow, replacing (in the self-parody in which Faulkner excelled) the most stilted literary convention by the bellowing of the craziest animal at once the most real and unreal. *The Wild Palms* is therefore included with the novels of beginnings, even if it was written after many of the works of the county. These early novels could be called analytical novels; they try to persuade their readers; they have a tendency to "explain," which is not worth exaggerating, however. Ultimately, readers will not find these works so very different from those that follow. From the beginning, ruptures and brutal implosions fill his texts, the first works already full of the narratives and short stories that will form the primary subject matter of his works.

The obsessional Faulkner (the third category in my chart) fills Yoknapatawpha County with an atypical and unpredictable population that nonetheless signifies what the author already knows (without knowing): the curse at the source of all earthly things. Many of Faulkner's characters will try to escape this curse. But some of them, the graced as well as the damned, will face it directly, with a silent, raging stubbornness. A curse that is a question before it becomes anathema.

Sartoris tells how a family that based everything on attaining aristocracy will irrevocably decline from one generation to the next (from a John to a Bayard Sartoris, the latter a cursed echo of the former) until it has practically died out, under the calm and jaded (lucid) eyes of Aunt Jenny. The novel focuses on the character of Great-grandfather Falkner, who, in the story, becomes truly larger than life. He was a Confederate colonel stripped of his regiment who then started a new one, a writer (*The White Rose of Memphis* sounds like a rather precious reworking of a Faulkner short-story title; but it is well worth the search to read it), a murderer who founded a railroad company first, then a bank and perhaps a law office, and finally was assassinated. But is it really a Falkner in question here, or is it not John Sartoris who was stripped of his regiment by his deputy, Sutpen—in *Sartoris* and *The Unvanquished*—and who was killed finally because he was tired of killing? In *Sartoris*, the theme of the cursed twins (John and Bayard)—to which I will certainly return—is woven throughout the story, unfolding in the narrative's murky lethargy (the first readers could only see this as a structural flaw since they did not yet have a sense of his entire work). The narrative's violet hue also exudes, more than verbena, a scent of lilac, or magnolia.

The Sound and the Fury: In this novel, the Compsons end up owning the land but knowing full well that their possession of it is neither legitimate nor definitive. Absurdly geometrical, almost unreal in the surrounding proliferation of wilderness, the land concession, later broken up piece by piece, is what the first Compsons to arrive had obtained from prosperous Choctaw Indians (so passionate and skinny when the first Whites encountered them, by then they were cunning, lazy, and slave-owning). Jason Compson's father continues to siphon off sections of this property. (The Compsons' first names alternate between Jason and Quentin, male and female, just as there are Johns and Bayards in the Sartoris family or—the same tragedy—as in the great Icelandic founding sagas, first names are repeated from one generation to the next, rhythmically accompanying land seizures, abductions, rapes, and murders.) And the last sale of land was to build a golf course. It is this land that Benjy (brother of Jason, Quentin, and Caddy) will distort, in his retarded outlook and language. This is the setting at the book's beginning: a story of sound and fury told by an idiot. Caddy's flight, Jason's slow autism, the faraway suicide of brother Quentin, the far-off disappearance of niece Quentin (Caddy's daughter), Benjy's castration and sequestering . . . all this suppressed fury of the South: the breaking up of the concession of land. The geometrically artificial straight lines that mark the property decompose into a wild, mixed-up degeneracy, like putrefying vegetation no longer in regeneration but in steady annihilation.

Absalom, Absalom! Echoes of the Old Testament—Faulkner's most common point of reference, along with Shakespeare and Greek tragedy—are heard throughout this endless and aborted progress toward the "foundation," or settling, on the new land. At the center of the story is Sutpen, but he lacks Solomon's wisdom. In fact, he is the opposite of Solomon, who was able to entertain the idea of an alliance and *métissage* with the Queen of Sheba; Sutpen will see all of his children struck down. Filiation (the intergenerational relationship between a father and his sons, and its continuity) will collapse irreparably. The book also extends the contagion (contamination) of this disaster to the umpteenth Quentin Compson (Jason and Caddy's brother), who shares the revelations about the Sutpens' story with his

Canadian friend, Shreve, and commits suicide shortly thereafter. Thus, a "stream of consciousness" is set up and developed here; it runs throughout Yoknapatawpha County as one of the objectives in all the work, as well as a recurrent technique of exposition.

In a parallel but much less systematic or constrained way, *Light in August* develops the stories duplicated in *The Wild Palms*: the search for Lena Grove—an innocent and one could say invulnerable woman who wanders from one state to another (Alabama, Mississippi, Pennsylvania)—and the double curse of Reverend Hightower, who is prey to demons as well as to a hallucinated fury that causes him to re-create the entire Civil War (where he sees, or imagines, himself among Confederate troops, "boys riding the sheer tremendous tidal wave of desperate living"), and of Christmas, the mulatto (since he believes he is one), who rebels against himself. Joanna Burden is another one of the damned, tormented on her cross, divided between her passion to defend the Negroes and her repulsion to come near them. These are examples of the burning gloom of puritanism and racism. The novel covers all of these subjects, showering us with them in no ideological order. It is a dim, transparent light of a land steeped in tragic torpor, almost as impenetrable as that of *Sartoris* and, in the case of Lena Grove, serene in a way one could almost call pastoral.

Then the marvelous *Compson Appendix* intervenes, a text coerced out of Faulkner like an exercise pulled from an author who has been asked to furnish some explanations. A dazzling genealogy with dizzying concision and shortcuts—one cannot but regret that he did not produce an equivalent for the Sartoris, Sutpen, or McCaslin family (although he did include one in a more "narrative" form within the story of *Requiem*)—the *Compson Appendix* is an absolute success: drawing from the legends of Scottish mountains as his source, and ending with a close-up on the face of Dilsey, the Black woman servant of the Compsons: "They endured."

At the same time, we can see that, while accumulating narratives and short stories, patiently constructing some novels from his short-story material, or writing others in fits and fevers, Faulkner "sweeps" the county's horizons, particularly aware of what he must say about two generic types (for whom he takes narrative responsibility): poor White farmers and Blacks. He is also profoundly aware of what he must say about the event that, like primordial truth (actually a looming embodiment of it), precedes his investigations of the real and obsesses him: the War of Secession.

As I Lay Dying. His poor White farmers are prone to wandering, are stoic before death, accustomed to natural disasters, and desperately fight against something that they cannot even name but which has the face of the destitute. At the same time, they are raised to the level of epic heroes, or, rather, they are naturally given that status by the use of their interior monologues in continuous discontinuity, each with his or her own, and each, in turn, in a connected series. This is done in such a way that the novel is broken up like separate clods of earth while, at the same time, it flows like a river. The language of these interwoven interior monologues does not abandon the realm of peasant speech or relinquish the grandeur of epic interrogation. How is this possible? These monologues fit into a single framework and yet in them one can distinguish variants according to the characters who express themselves: stubborn, violent, devious, innocent, or inspired by the gods (that is, simply mad), escorting the dead mother's casket through this land riven by nature's excesses. Do these people seem like worker bees buzzing around the queen mother? In the end, the mother is carried to her final resting place so each of the others can attend to his or her own destiny. Then again, does the landowning energy of these poor Whites foretell the anger of present-day Rednecks? Or, prophetically, does it go even further? Still again, it is worth noting that there is not a single Black (who counts) on the horizon of this "pastoral" epic.

. . .

Intruder in the Dust. Movies have made such cases familiar: a Southern Negro (Lucas Beauchamp) is accused of a crime (murdering a White man), is imprisoned, and then lynched after a few well-meaning people (Gavin Stevens, for example) try to save him. Faulkner includes stories of lynching in several of his works—in one of the short stories in *Knight's Gambit* (where this same Gavin Stevens reappears) and in the short story "Dry September" in *These Thirteen.* In the case of *Intruder in the Dust,* we know that lynching is merely a threat and Lucas will be saved. There is another subject operating here, perceptible from the opening section of the book. It is not a matter of knowing what happened, because everyone knows that Lucas Beauchamp knows, but rather of finding out why he does not want to tell. How can he consider himself a silent and omnipotent protagonist when he risks an imminent, ignominious death? Must he show off that he fears nothing and no one? *Intruder in the Dust* tells of a moment in the education (the initiation) of a young White male, the narrator and decisive player in the story. It is also a picture-perfect portrait of a Negro's opacity, an opacity that, until the end and despite the explanations and a return to everyday life, never swerves from its course. Readers pretend not to appreciate this troubled simplicity, not of the text but of its principal "subject," and so the work has been found wanting aesthetically.

In *The Unvanquished* (known in French both by the plural title, *Les Invaincus,* and, in the first editions, as the singular *L'Invaincu;* the English title lends itself more easily to ambiguity), the swaggering bravery of Southerners lies like a layer of dust over the occasion of the War of Secession and, after the war, over the Sartoris family, all through the entire initiation of young Bayard Sartoris (one of several Bayards in Faulkner's work). Faulkner cannot free himself from his rather conventional view of that war and, for that matter, war in general. The Yankee armies appear to be somewhat innocent when they encounter the Confederates' crazy initiatives. Even so, Faulkner portrays them as chivalrous from time to time. At the beginning of the story, a Yankee officer refuses to lift the hooped skirts of Miss Rosa Millard (grand-mother of young Bayard Sartoris); two little children (one White and one Black) are hiding there. The children had set up a very clever trap for his regiment of troops and had killed one of his mules. The officer right then decides against burning down their house and scattering its inhabitants. In general, *The Unvanquished* is a sublimation of the South: the most symbolic, facile, and perhaps even conventional ide-alization of the stubbornness of the people in the county and, moreover, of the (utopian) good relations between Blacks and Whites. It is also one of the rarely obvious examples of the temptation of incest, between this so-called Bayard and Drusilla, the young wife of his father, John Sartoris. The title of the novel refers to the epic principle—that is, that defeat itself brings about another victory—called forth in Song.

Faulkner the visionary (the second entry in my chart) focuses upon a time now lost once and for all—a time of unanimity, of indivisible nature, and a time of origins, that is, before property, slavery, and profit, a time that hunters ritually try to revive at a certain season each year— and situates it in a particular place (the big Woods, the land conces-sion, Jefferson County). Without looking at this visitation of original innocence, one cannot really understand the underlying links between the rest of his works. Variously personified, the county as a whole can be seen as an example of suffering for the loss of this time (or, using Claudel's expression about the act of creation as it relates to God, "not to be what is"). If the novels in my third category or classification are the opened shutters of his works, *Go Down, Moses* is the ever-offended frame.

A Puritan despite himself (my fourth category), Faulkner tries to draw a conclusive lesson—not a moral but rather a metaphysical les-son—from the story of the county.

Two books that are centered on Popeye, Temple Drake (who be-comes Mrs. Gowan Stevens), and Nancy Mannigoe call attention to this theme of malediction: the curse of monstrous births and awkward deaths (Popeye), the temptations and misfortunes that befall descendants (Temple), and the expiatory victim who dies leaving no descendants (Nancy).

In all these examples, we have a dizzying dramatization, a *mise en vertige*, of the question of bloodlines and the issue of descendants.

It is no coincidence that *Sanctuary* and *Requiem for a Nun* take their titles from religious ritual and the place of performance. This brings us to the idea of the sacrificial victim, a victim always matchless in both good and evil: Popeye leads to Temple, who leads to Nancy Mannigoe, whose solitary tragedy seems a fruitless effort to make up for the ambiguities and failures of the communal epic.

A meticulous archivist, Faulkner has gathered, in the meantime, a great many narratives and short stories whose most immediate goal (often frustrated) seems to have been financial. Even so, I will show how these narratives are one of the mainstays in his work. It is difficult to sort them into the categories of my chart. Different short-story collections, for example, mix "Mississippi" tales with "European" ones. *Knight's Gambit* is the sole collection to assemble only stories of the county, all of which concern Gavin Stevens (young Stevens or Uncle Gavin). Faulkner did not assemble his other collections of short stories according to a "geographical" theme; no doubt he wished to preserve the integrity of his works as a whole as well as diffuse the confusion (in time and space) they provoke.

In *Pylon* and *A Fable* (my fifth category, that of "external" information), Faulkner concentrates on two of his three great passions: aviation and the anguished scrutiny of war (Faulkner's other great passion is hunting or horseback riding)—looking at the Great War, the period setting for *A Fable*. Some of his major short stories, such as "Turn-about" in *The Faulkner Reader*, deal with the Second World War. In *Pylon*, airplanes become the site of fate and death.

All of Faulkner's passions reveal a powerful intention toward mastery, to subdue the noble beast, to control the awesome machine that takes to the skies, and to triumph in the battle. More often, however, we find a bitter resignation to personal and collective defeat.

Biographers and historians have suggested that, after the repressed complexes of his fragile adolescence, these passions were a way for Faulkner to attain in his own way the proud and hardy virility of his father and the other men in his family.

In fact, he catches up to his ancestors by the end of his life. Thrilled by the hunt, he would insist on conquering the great and nobly named horses that eventually broke his body. In a photograph in the Pléiade *Album* on Faulkner, we see him in the background at a hunters' meet. One wonders what kinds of worried or supercilious thoughts run through his mind in this gathering of placid, earthy farmers with whom he could vie only in drink.

Pylon and *A Fable* take us into the far-off reaches of the county. Even the people who live and struggle there cannot escape distress and damnation; they exemplify the same relentlessness in times of misfortune as the protagonists of *Sartoris* and *Absalom, Absalom!*: a steady, unyielding relentlessness that is the last remaining thread of their dignity.

Having covered the entire county, questioning people everywhere, listening to storytellers, scrutinizing, imagining, creating from life, making guesses as often intuitive as rational, and projecting the county into its far-off limits, Faulkner finds himself not at the end but at the confirmation of his writing project, the moment when he begins to suspect that his works have created Faulkner, and not vice versa. What he has implicitly assumed for such a long time in the writing is hence-forth imposed upon him by the writing he has realized. Knowing that the epic has dried up, it is from this very drought that his work has been born.

The Reivers is a comic novel. I am using "comic" in the sense of the comic diversion that intervenes in a trilogy of Greek tragedy. Faulk-ner's words are always graced with humor but this is the first time, except for a few facetious narratives or short stories, that it unleashes such a sustained rustle of familiar laughter. A young man goes on an outing (first to a whorehouse, then to the racetrack), accompanied by Boon Hogganbeck, one of his grandfather's employees, and an animal-bewitching stableboy. First, they steal the patriarch's car for their ad-venture, and then trade it for a lame horse (foolishly bypassing the more professional horses of the place). Victory is theirs thanks to a strategy (a package of rotten, or almost rotten, sardines) which allows them to transform what is clearly an old nag into a fantastic racehorse. After this escapade, they return to the family mansion, where the grandfather's genuine leniency takes precedence over the father's weak and mechanical inflexibility.

This is a novel way (owing, in part, to the boy's innocence) to connect the big House, the estate, the outside world, and the city—all the vexed places; to force a transition, as restive as a racehorse, between the tragic and the comic; to imagine or suggest that the distant reality (as though one has broken in during an absence of things) is not so corrupt that it cannot welcome and tolerate naïveté, childhood, and an adventure posing no mortal risk.

The Hamlet, The Town, The Mansion: Faulkner is now obliged to meticulously trace the road corresponding to the expansion of the Snopes family, not because he is especially fond of them but because the rule he has drawn up (which I would express as "take nothing away from the real, maybe even add to it") forces him to cover this ultimate space. He admits that he has been pounding out this saga of the Snopes for thirty years, as though working toward an ending that has already been given, inevitable even at the beginning.

The Snopeses' world is one of clever, conscientious scheming conducted with an instinctive and adaptable precision. Its greatest strength is patience. Once these perverse and mundane people have appropriated the entire county, does this signify its demise, from Faulkner's point of view? Is Faulkner's world pessimistic to the very end? The question (whether a work is pessimistic or its opposite is not a crucial issue in literature) would be meaningless were it not to include a consideration of the writing itself. After all, the writing—or at least the lessons it provides—is what remains after reality has dissolved into malediction, then into epic and tragic failure, finally giving in to the triumph of vulgarity. The Snopeses may have conquered the county, but they cannot take away from what the writing has given to it. They are described in language that is flat, the only cadence suited to them. They will never know tragic torment or the broken flight of the epic.

One must also include the screenplays, written when Faulkner was slaving away in his Hollywood chains. Ridiculed and scorned in the movie industry for his obstinate attachment to "literature," he put his nose to the grindstone, tied himself to his typewriter, drank himself stiff, and kept plugging away. There is something doomed about his endeavors; Faulkner cannot imagine a single subject, synopsis, screenplay, or bit of dialogue without immediately broadening the subject (he is often reminded), without blowing it up into gigantic scale, without making a world-subject out of it when he is merely being asked to be direct, precise, and quick (which he is very adept at doing but which always seems insufficient to him). A "seasonal migrant" in the world of cinema, he was never really interested in film adaptations of his own works. He was happy struggling with other people's stories. Even when he is approached, after unexpectedly strong sales of his books, it is with a certain distrust. None of this bothers him. He lets them change his name, or delete it from the credits altogether. Sections of his scripts are simply eliminated or the whole piece reworked by others, and he is paid peanuts. In such a world, a writer is someone who knows how to score with the first draft, who never gets bogged down in murky complexities, and who is always his own best agent. How could Faulkner, who had raised the art of deferral to such sinister and sparkling perfection, ever find his place here? In fact, he hardly found subsistence, the opposite of earning a living; it was as if he had to pay this arid tribute to his profession as writer.

Having (almost) completed his life work, he finally has the time to enter secular life, to actually enter reality and the century. For him, this means giving in to the life of the South, whose secret threads he has spun into so many stories. He becomes obsessed with owning large estates (as if compensating for the deprivations and uncertainties of his youth, like Sutpen but in a calmer and more peaceful way), living the life of the gentleman farmer, trying to reconcile within himself the Ike McCaslin of Go Down, Moses, a hunter and nothing but a hunter, and the great landowner like so many others in the county. He who has so loudly condemned property and the very idea of ownership (demonstrating their uncertain and improbable results) will go so far as to write on the bottom of a map he has drawn of Yoknapatawpha County, "William Faulkner, sole owner and proprietor." You can tell that it is not simply a question of literary property—unless he was trying to stress the fact that this latter property is the only one that engenders rootedness and permanence. He seems to think that the impossible situation of the county as well as the misery attached to it have been defeated (despite the clearly predatory habits of the Sutpens) and that he has earned his legitimate right to live there (in reality) as landowner, hunter, horse trainer, and great drinking buddy. Faulkner gives his works the status of truth, convincing himself that his writing has exorcised damnation and that he can henceforth live easily in the daily life of his country.

He wants to discover the world. I have been told that, during his trip through Northern Europe into Scandinavia and Iceland, he would only thaw out and agree to talk (suddenly launching, as he could do, into excited and affable conversation) once he had had plenty of time to partake of the local liquor, a schnapps called Black Death. There is a trip South, to Venezuela. In the East, he goes to Japan, although he may consider this a trip West (the preferred direction for all of his epic journeys, recalling *Those Who Always Go West* by Saint-John Perse). It is as though he wanted to exhaust all these cardinal directions in record time—the time remaining to him—surprised, perhaps, by the international resonance of his work. Except for extending the county by implication into the European wars and taking a few treks into some nearby hamlets in Mississippi, Faulkner's writing did not cover the world, as Hemingway's had, or explore the city and the megalopolis (what we now call "suburbs"), as Dos Passos's did.

Once he has become famous, thanks to the great number of characters he has created (and with whom he continues to associate), Faulkner begins to receive requests to do nonliterary work. He accepts a State Department assignment (perhaps encouraged by his primal but rather lax anti-Communism) and occasionally accepts protocol visits, such as to West Point and the U.S. Military Academy (certainly more a Southern than a national impulse). He delights his audience of cadets with funny stories (no doubt hunting stories or others taken from his books); it has been reported that during this trip Estelle Faulkner remarked that they were traveling in a plane staffed with an all-Jewish crew. Some invitations he turned down—for example, President Kennedy's invitation to a Nobel Laureates dinner in Washington, D.C. (an anti-Yankee response, unless this is the Scottish Protestant reacting to an Irish Catholic, or even the graceful hesitation of the man who secretly believes he has earned recognition later than it was deserved).

To race around the world. Did he ever try—hooked as he was on the minutest detail (an accent, a scowl, a greeting, a shout . . . feelings about a horse race)? Did he have the time to see whether his investigations of the county and its preexistent double, the state of Mississippi, were relevant *elsewhere*, anywhere, even nearby? Further on, I will suggest that, despite the "total" character of Yoknapatawpha County, presented as a world in microcosm, Faulkner may have thought (or felt) that the subsidiary roots from elsewhere—the innumerable relations with other places—too obviously risked appearing absent in his work, or actually were absent; and this is what he needed to discreetly compare, looking in every direction. He needed to see whether he had been right to keep the county apart from the rest of the world in order for it to represent the world in its entirety.

It would thus appear that his famous bouts of silence are actually filled with unspoken, or rather impeded, words that, rather than concurring with his works, were the beginning of a different commentary. These are difficult words because it was not in Faulkner's nature to offer commentary. He had produced too much and was doubtlessly tired of the great struggle and the great success that, nevertheless, he could not refrain from comparing with the fullness he had dreamed of saying. All he could do was bear or worsen (by his stubborn resistance to any serious medical examination) the deterioration of his body. He was no longer able to ride a horse.

The date of his death (July 6, 1962) was recorded in a hospital that was not qualified to treat the illnesses he suffered from. He had been taken there in an emergency (not thinking he was going to die). It is said that he gave up his spirit with something like a hiccough that, in one motion, sat him up and knocked him over forever on his hospital bed.

It is certainly offensive to talk at length about anyone's death, but it seems to me that William Faulkner died as a storyteller; yes, he died of an overflow of tales and a passion to expose. But what could he still have to say, after having created the Snopeses? In his dying moments, had he returned to a communion with the Big Woods?

This is how this dossier ends, in a straight duplication of the *Compson Appendix*.

•   •   •

Among the award-winning samples from *The Best of Bad Faulkner* of 1991, I found a text by one Allen Boyer (second place, honorable mention), who has also made a pastiche of the *Compson Appendix* but in a much more amusing manner than I. His *The Sound and the Fury, Appendix II* ends as follows: "long before then, in that year which marked the midpoint and balancing fulcrum of his century, [he] had achieved his own apotheosis (a medal, a speech: accolades of a Nordic capital) and long since had abandoned his tales of aerial combat and silver plate and in their stead declared that he was just a farmer who wrote. 'I'm just a farmer who writes,' he said. That sentence was his simplest fiction." (*The Southern Register*, Summer 1991.)

Inspired by his huge ambition, he had also elevated his works to a level far above his own person, far above his own individual self (no doubt he thought of himself as a Southerner, a horseman and aviator, and an authority on good drink). As a joke, he composes his own epigraph: "He wrote books and he died." This is proud humility from a man who wished to efface himself in the greatness of what he had created.

Henceforth, members of the Falkner family will be called, or could call themselves if they so desire, by the name of Faulkner.

The demands that William Faulkner's readers have made know no limits. In my conversations with several of them, I have heard some of the most enlightening opinions—and some of the most far-fetched—concerning his works. His readers have never held themselves back from excess and extravagance, carried away by the drift and dizziness these works breed and inculcate. One person in particular, who will remain nameless, told me one day—in a far too unreasonable tone to allow analysis or full appreciation—"Now we know that we're all going to die, since Faulkner died."

IN BLACK AND WHITE

I do not know whether it took courage or a certain ignorance on my part that day in 1989 to insist, before an audience of African-American students and professors at Southern University, in Baton Rouge, Louisiana, that there is room for a reconsideration of Faulkner, for a fresh reading and study of his works. Certainly they knew this. It was not my place to play the expert on the subject. If they refused to "recognize" this author, they had many reasons to do so. In their brief lives, these students in particular had piled up a wall of arguments to justify their keeping clear of Faulkner. Likewise, Faulkner had no interest in associating himself either with them or with their future when he was writing his books.

To put it differently: Faulkner's oeuvre will be complete when it is revisited and made vital by African-Americans. Already this process has begun, Toni Morrison being perhaps the first to do what I am trying to do here.

And this completion will be achieved by a radically "other" reading, not simply because Faulkner's novels are peopled with Blacks. With Mississippi as his chosen setting for "the question," could he have done otherwise? He reduced Mississippi to the limits of an imaginary county so as to exalt it, enlarging it to universal dimensions. Blacks lived there and, at the time, were more numerous in rural areas. They were servants in the Falkner family, or perhaps workers for the railroad company founded by his great-grandfather (was he the one? Or was it the elder Sartoris?). They were surely mule drivers or farm laborers, or they were sharecroppers, isolated in the woods and fields and thus more vulnerable to the madmen of the Klan. Or they were stablemen, handymen, idlers, or vagabonds.

They were just beginning to profit from the experience of the factories and big cities where a segment of this population would soon scatter and often be lost. Slavery was recent enough (at least in the atmosphere of his works), the Civil War even more so (and White Southerners tended to hold the Negroes responsible for it). In any event, the Whites had seceded to protect their right to maintain the slave system; if Abraham Lincoln began the war to preserve the Union, he ended it under the banner of abolition.

Faulkner could not have done otherwise than to include Blacks among the people who inhabit the lands of his novels. The role he gives them is so specific and particular, however, that it must be scrutinized by a criticism in which they themselves take part before it can be recognized as part of a poetics of the real.

There is another conventional literature of the South (while there is also an incredibly large number of good authors and, moreover, an impressive group of writers with no apparent link between them—none, perhaps, other than Faulkner himself as interlocutor—from Sherwood Anderson to Eudora Welty and Flannery O'Connor to the new Black writers, many of whom, interestingly, are women). This other literature being one of "realism" or nostalgia while remaining always provincial (unconsciously moored to a Center it denigrates so as to suit it better): a literature sketching Black characters that resemble those we used to see in the movies or in musical comedies, always

rolling their white bug eyes in the air, strumming a banjo or tap danc-
ing, singing ballads or nonsense rather than speaking.

No heroism or legendary figures, neither courage nor fortitude (Harriet Tubman, or the Black infantrymen, or the Maroons, or the mar-
tyrs) were yet appreciated. At the time (in the early thirties), Jesse
Owens had not yet won his Olympic gold medals in the heart of Nazi
Germany and Joe Louis had not defeated Max Schmeling. The jazz
geniuses played for pennies, and they were stuck in segregated motels,
restaurants, and buses in an apartheid state. The bars where they once
performed are now legendary places, and Billie Holiday's tragic song
resonates in our ears forever.

Faulkner may not come anywhere near these stereotypes, but neither
does he render the "real" situation of Blacks. Rather, he describes
Blacks in a situation that suits his purpose. This is why their presence
is so important: as a generalizing "signified" (*signifié*), they embody a
position (as people) that is weighty and substantial.

In no way whatsoever does the "situation" sketched in his works— as
in the books of Richard Wright, Langston Hughes, and Chester
Himes—predict the direction the Black community would take: not
the Black Panthers, not the Black bourgeoisie (as covetous as any
other), not the middle class, not Martin Luther King and civil rights,
not Malcolm X, not Muhammad Ali and the Vietnam era, not anti-
colonialist solidarity, not multimillionaire athletes and entertainers,
not free jazz or homelessness, not Black sitcoms or Black talk shows
(as engulfing and vapid as those of Whites), not the Los Angeles riots,
not sensationalist trials, not Black generals or Mr. Farrakhan, not rap
or poverty or murder or drugs in the cities, not even those on death
row condemned to die in the gas chamber or in the electric chair or
by hanging: it takes all these struggles and all this hell in order for the
Black portion of the population of the United States of America to
outlast its circumstances and enter completely into the nation's life,

without giving up its particularities. None of this can be found in Faulkner or predicted from what he wrote. One could say that, on the textual level at least, the prospects of Black life did not interest him.

We know how reductive objectification "removes" a community from its context in order to make a meaningful picture, both true and false, magnified and abstract: the Antillean Creole community in Saint-John Perse's *Eloges*, for example. With their long, amber-colored legs and their dizzying speech, that of "black witches" performing their ritual (the rituals of the kitchen, that is), his "black servant" women have a charm that is contagious. But we never enter into the *drama* of their place in life, or their struggles to be seen as sympathetic, or their fight with a history they could determine for themselves in the end. This is not to be found in Saint-John Perse. One could say that, at least on the textual level, the future of Blacks did not interest him.

Faulkner's depiction of Blacks is "rural." It claims no perspective or verisimilitude. Rather, it stems from one absolute source: the moment when the land suffered a split between the Indians, its first inhabitants, and the Whites who appeared from Europe (or from nowhere). To this, the Blacks, introduced into this land as slaves, were silent and suffering witnesses. The "situation" of Blacks is thus emblematic of this beginning: they were but living witnesses, not a responsible party, to the original sin of the South (whether or not you call it expropriation). This "situation" will not accompany them throughout History, for they do not make History. As for the Indians, they have almost completely disappeared, at least from within the county borders (through the murderous exodus to Oklahoma). So it is only to White people that the question—the nagging question of original responsibility—is addressed.

But Whites have changed; they "get into" a story, even on the textual level.

Much has been said about the way they invade the county and slowly take possession of its wealth (its land and commerce), the way the various members of the Snopes tribe—these newly rich social climbers—push the Sartorises, and others such as the Compsons, into a void that confirms their original damnation, or forces them to expiate it by becoming like the Snopeses. Thus, in 1866, Colonel Sutpen is reduced to opening a cheap little store on the edge of his property, and Jason Compson, by 1950, has long since withdrawn into his bitterness and his sick, miserly obsessions, secretly guarding his stash. It is not the Snopeses who are responsible; they are too mundane for that. They never lived in the Big Woods, they never signed any treaties, they never fell from any upper class. In all of his works, Faulkner waxes prosaic in a Snopesian proliferation, consummately merging epic and interrogation.

Yet again, the Snopeses signify this: Whites have changed.

In the works themselves, Blacks are the only ones who have not. Since they were not held responsible for the original damnation, and could not be, their absolute function was to put up with it, to "take it upon themselves," and to testify (by their very social rank) to the impossible conditions of the county. You cannot change absolutes.

Descriptions of Blacks cannot be other than immobile: Blacks are permanency itself. The rural life that confines and signifies them is the site of the absolute. The Bundrens, the poor Whites in *As I Lay Dying*, for example. This ruralness is not that of the author describing a country setting. It is the painful and sacred astonishment of the chorus of chosen peasants.

In this hidden inquiry into origins (of the county and its maledictions), to which his works always give (or rather propose) answers that are forever postponed (into the infinity of Time and Death), Blacks are and represent the unsurpassable point of reference, those who remain and who assume.

Here, we find that the extended African family has no claim to constitute a family lineage. So it never meets with failure. Even if this family has no history and takes no responsibility (and we know that

the young Faulkner considered Negroes wayward children), it continues to exist after the extinction of the Sutpen line, the putrefying
consumption of the Compsons, the vanishing of the Sartorises, the
resignation of Ike McCaslin, and the morbid madness of Emily Grierson. On Faulkner's agenda, the only means of change for Blacks would
be miscegenation: the advent of the mulatto, some sort of genetic and
cultural Snopes. That, at least, is what we read between the lines. Let
us leave it aside for the moment, however.

"The impossible situation of the county made it an absolute: a place
of irremediable contradiction where the human condition is not studied, it is questioned." This questioning "speaks" only if it is conjectural
in nature and if its essential cruelty or relentlessness is tied to a boundless love of place and of its actual inhabitants, regardless of their origin.

The text is not a "Deed" that could validate a report and give a
truthful account of things. Nor is the author the "attentive observer"
so often found in Balzac. Rather, if the "observer" is important, "attentive" is even more so. Balzac seems to threaten his reader in this
way: if you do not pay attention, you will miss something. For Faulkner,
"attentive" seems to mean "involved" as much as "detached." The
dizzying tension of disclosure comes into play here. One needs a sense
of contradiction, a questioning of the storyteller, a sense of this impossibility, and yet a passion for the impossible.

"They endured." They used to endure. They have endured. Many
critics (but perhaps I am thinking only of Michael Mohrt) have drawn
a link between the verb "to endure" and the length of duration, a
relationship that is more obvious in French: *ils en-duraient*, they lasted
through the hardness of it all. Faulkner's poetics shows that, if Blacks
can achieve duration (it is said cats have conquered eternity by stillness
and sleep), it is because they do not master history. They do not play
with the devil or damn themselves in order to establish a domain; they
do not kill merely to safeguard their filial ties (as others—White peo-

ple—kill or are killed for such "serious" reasons). Let us not assume that Blacks lacked the means to do so. They keep getting killed only because they stubbornly endure. We can contrast their behavior to that of Jason Compson, who brought his niece Quentin to her ruin and had his idiot brother Benjamin castrated, then violently withdrew into scornful and anguished days and nights, into the pitiful yet estimable stature and splendor of the Snopeses.

Could duration, sufferance (fully accepted, without calculation, without premonition, with neither plan nor project, borne as completely as Blacks bear it in Faulkner's works), be the best and surest way to vanquish Time and its torments?

Another "reason" for the emblematic presence of Blacks in Faulkner's work is that they form a link between the land and the animals that inhabit it. When Faulkner wanted to name a particularly unusual animal, most often it would be *"the one niggers call* this or that," as though the name given by Blacks added clout and descriptive qualities and stemmed from some arcane knowledge. This ability to link the land and the animals was also the privilege of the legendary White forefathers and their immediate descendants, the "Uncles" who went on epic hunting expeditions, crossed rivers and creeks, felt the bite of early morning cold, slept in freezing shacks, and bootlegged bourbon. All of this was lost, however, for subsequent White generations. Communion with nature, which could have established legitimate ownership of the land, was frittered away through the melancholic ruin of the Sartoris family, the sickly consumption of the Compsons, and the wild downfall of Sutpen. It was literally shipwrecked in the relentless, wicked and victorious hustle of the Snopeses. For Faulkner, the Black man has kept this communion. As a character type, he is the most meaningful witness to the former order of things. Perhaps we eventually understand that he is destined to reshape it.

• • •

He is not the only one. There are others who also have neither power nor mastery over events: women (the Black servants or the White maiden aunts) and children, instinctively close to the fatalistic and confused reasoning that derive from the county's burdensome past. Women and children sense this past; like the author, they have incorporated it more or less directly into their hearts and minds. They seem to act in unexpected, even baffling ways because their point of reference is instinctive, a knowledge that others cannot possess but can only trace in the patterns of vague thought. When these women and children talk about some part of this history, a bit of the past, they never pinpoint the knowledge or say why. Otherwise, for the spinster aunts, by definition barren and without heirs, mention of the past always leads to a premonition of a fate and a damnation they accept with pain. For the children, this premonition is the decisive element in an initiation that will send them off to a destination that is sometimes fatal. Their stories always delay the disclosure—that is, they hold firmly to a presupposition which neither the author, the people of the county, nor the reader can grasp with certainty but which indeed dictates what everyone considers real.

Because of their innocence, women and children suffer more acutely than the others the force of what has gone before. They are amazed to be still standing, alive and talking, after so many staggering misfortunes. Their amazement is tragic. Step by step, it takes over and proceeds through a kind of *contamination*, whose causes and effects I will discuss at length below. And it is rooted in and obscured by this presumption—this historical antecedent, this primordial "avoidance"—while simultaneously ordering the disclosure.

Unlike White women and their children, Faulkner's Blacks—that is, those Blacks who "count"—do not speak of the past. (Not even the Black servants, Dilsey and the others, who have so much responsibility.) They do not speak of the past: they suffer it and perpetuate it through suffering. By carrying on in this "role," they re-create the past. With rare exceptions, they cannot contaminate anyone or make any decisions for change. One such exception is Clytie, the daughter of Sutpen and a Black slave, who at the end of *Absalom, Absalom!* sets fire to the place and, through this apocalyptic destruction, ordains the end of the story.

Several autobiographies of former slaves were published at the time Faulkner was starting to write.* Through education, the ex-slaves had gained the ability to pass judgment on the system and those who had profited from it. At the beginning of the century, several organizations documented the numbers of emancipated slaves still alive and recorded the testimony of these survivors. When published in the thirties and forties, *Native Son* and *Black Boy*, by Richard Wright, depicted the true situation of Blacks. Obviously, in none of these instances would one find the trace of a supposed communion or solidarity (not even a hidden one) between those who had been slaves and those who had been their masters, even though many house slaves (never the field slaves) stayed close to their masters and helped them during the Civil War. Richard Wright's denial of this communion is total. He does not allow austerity or mitigation to creep in, not even the stirrings of pardon.

William Faulkner no doubt consulted these works. It seems that he was neither troubled nor influenced by them. Perhaps he was convinced that the cry of revolt logically should come from Blacks and decided it was not up to him to sound it in turn. On the whole, he

---

* Barbara and Philippe Artières provided me with memoirs, newspapers, and autobiographies of various kinds, including, among others, the following slave narratives, first published in the late nineteenth and early twentieth centuries. (Some were in print during Faulkner's lifetime. Others were published more recently.) *Incidents in the Life of a Slave Girl Written by Herself* by Harriet B. Jacobs (Harvard University Press, 1987); *Shadow and Light: An Autobiography* by Mifflit Wistar Gibbs, with an introduction by Booker T. Washington (University of Nebraska Press, 1995); *The Life and Adventures of Nat Love* (University of Nebraska Press, 1995); *The Memphis Diary of Ida B. Wells* (Beacon Press, 1995); *The History of Mary Prince, a West Indian Slave, Related by Herself* (University of Michigan Press, 1996); and *All God's Dangers: The Life of Nate Shaw*, by Theodore Rosengarten (Random House, 1974).

had contradictory opinions on the subject—including his statement in favor of school integration and inscribing the names of Black soldiers (on a "separate" list) on the monument honoring the dead of the two World Wars—which finally placed him in a very uncomfortable position in Oxford.

Faulkner was neither a civil rights activist nor a social reformer. His writing was not a platform for the reform of society. By nature and by profession, he was conservative rather than simply a reactionary. Clearly, he was not blind to the iniquities of the South, even if he did no more to relieve them than anyone else. He was more a Unionist than he realized. We have remarked how some citizens of the United States can brutally criticize their own society but heaven forbid that a foreigner should gaze disapprovingly at the same wrongdoing.

Moreover, Faulkner cannot detach himself from the South, which is his caste and country. Of Albert Camus, he writes, "We share the same anguish." What anguish could he be talking about? Certainly not the anguish that motivates an existential thinker, but the anguish of having to conceive justice and not utter it (even if you must separate it from the truth), since to do so would be a betrayal of your own people.

There is another reason Faulkner "suspends his judgment" about the South. He needs ambiguous disclosure as the basis for the development of tragedy. An emphatic statement about the "decadence" of the South would have interrupted forever the itinerary of disclosure in the work. It is in and through the articulation of the mysterious (in any event, unspoken) disclosure that the first possible iniquity proves to be damnation; error brings forth tragedy. Literature matters more than making testimonies or taking sides, not because it exceeds all possible appreciation of the real, but because it is a more profound approach and, ultimately, the only one that matters.

Because of this, Faulkner will treat Blacks in a straightforward way, describing them bluntly (as he does everyone else), conventionally, without the slightest stylistic precaution, and with the consideration he thinks they deserve: a pitiless impartiality.

The conventional. Conventions are dispersed, liberally, throughout the descriptions: "A young black horseman, skinny as a rabbit, superbly . . ." A man who laughs "with the grave and simple pleasure of his race" or who moves "[w]ith his race's fine feeling for potential theatrics," and so on. These passing remarks are drawn from a global perception of Blacks as gangling bodies and naïve souls, from a whole theory about the Negro form that is never openly admitted, yet comes across without emphasis in these portraits, which are not really portraits so much as silhouettes.

True, it is said more than once (someone will repeat) that Whites are incapable of understanding Blacks. We do not hear the parallel implied that "Blacks are incapable of understanding Whites." It is as if only the Whites feel the need to understand.

In any event, Faulkner's Blacks are conventional silhouettes, as though invisible as long as they remain a group. Is this a way of respecting the opacity of the Other or is it a beginning of a system of apartheid? A freethinking depth of identity or disinterested negligence? It depends upon which character in the text is speaking.

Pitiless impartiality. There is almost no work in Faulkner's oeuvre in which Blacks do not appear or are not referred to by Whites who either despise or scorn them or calmly state their inferiority. Faulkner does not shrink from the harshest cruelty in his portraits. Some of the county residents exude a bestial racism, which Faulkner suggests incidentally, apart from any formal presentation, and in such a way that one can never tell whether he condemns this racism or accepts and applauds it.

To express his surprise before an unexpected situation, one of the characters in the short story, "Ad Astra," nonchalantly begins: "When I came to this goddamn country . . . I thought niggers were niggers." Turning down Narcissa's offer of help, old Miss Jenny says, "I need little; nothing the Negroes can't do." These are the kinds of offhand remarks that leave you numb.

Brutality. One single example, taken from a passage that summarizes the attitude toward Blacks in all of his works, will suffice: "Afterward, Uncle Buck admitted that it was his own mistake, that he had forgotten when even a little child should have known: not ever to stand right in front of or right behind a nigger when you scare him; but always to stand to one side of him. Uncle Buck forgot that." Even a little child . . . Because this reductive objectification of Blacks is not a matter of ideology. It comes instinctually. Racism is in the depths.

These remarks, these conventional observations, and this brutality all apply to ordinary Negroes. ("Without changing the inflection of his voice and apparently without effort or even design Lucas became not Negro but nigger, not secret so much as impenetrable, not servile and not effacing, but enveloping himself in an aura of timeless and stupid impassivity almost like a smell.") There are the Negroes who leave but fleeting traces in Faulkner's works and there are those who take on meaning, who "take it upon themselves." They are exceptional in their destitution and misery. Their masters and subsequent bosses silently respect them and even, in their giddy private thoughts, admit that they are perhaps the *only* witnesses. So it is for Roth Edmonds, the distant white relative of the Negro Lucas Beauchamp, with whom he will have such a difficult relationship: "He thought, and not for the first time, *I am not only looking at a face older than mine and which has seen and winnowed more, but at a man most of whose blood was pure ten thousand years when my own anonymous beginnings became mixed enough to produce me.*" The dominant race in Lucas—the Black race—remains pure whereas Roth Edmonds, who is White, reflects upon the fact that he is the product of mixture. Is this one of the reasons why it has been said that Faulkner, in an unconscious and unacknowledged—but no less racist—manner, advanced the idea of the superiority of Blacks over Whites?

Sam Fathers, Lucas Beauchamp, Dilsey, Nancy Mannigoe, and a few others.

Even if the "final" story of the Snopeses is written in a flat style (without the flashbacks, complications, and hesitations that characterize the county's fabulous chronicle), that is, realistically, in a way that allows no place for the uncertain, that does not "defer" or aim at "deferral," still, in Faulkner's work, Blacks occupy a very specific role.

The county's two "finalities" are the Snopeses and the Blacks, as identified by Régis Durand in his introduction to *Yoknapatawpha, Le pays de William Faulkner*, a volume of photographs by Alain Desvergnes:* "Faulkner's world is one of the tragedy of descendants. The only ones who endure are those with the ability to adapt and the greed of insects or rats (the Snopeses, for example), or those for whom endurance, waiting, and survival have become second nature through the force of circumstance (the descendants of slaves, they are the ones who 'endure')."

Let us look at how the latter are treated in the writing.

The range of narrative technique in Faulkner, it has been said, comprises three "moments" or modes that are relatively easy to describe. There is the objective narrative (the carriage bumped along the roads), the subjective narrative (he didn't want to go into these woods, he told himself that he would only circle around them), and the interior monologue (it isn't that he wanted to make me believe that he was going to sell that mule, he only wanted . . .). These modes not only become complicated or problematized under the impulse of the deferred in direct or "objective" narrative (the carriage seemed to go forward by itself toward something that one could neither foresee nor figure out, in such a way that you would have said that it bumped on

---

* Editions Marval (Paris, 1989).

this road). They can get mixed up in the same paragraph or sentence, in which case the typographical conventions (I refer to the ones used in the French translations) distinguish between them. The second mode (subject narrative) is sometimes placed between quotation marks; the third (interior monologue) is always italicized, put between quotes and sometimes, in addition, between parentheses.

The use of the second mode is rare for Blacks; the third is almost never used for them.

Rather than think that Faulkner's techniques of narrative and disclosure concern only Whites (those who act, own, make war, exploit others, and decide things) and that, as a result, the latter two modes (subjective narrative and interior monologue), which are sites of interiority, depth, disturbance, and vertigo, are exclusively theirs, I prefer to think that this choice of technique shows a clarity and honesty (in short, a natural and systematic generosity throughout) in one who knows, who admits in effect, that he will never understand either Blacks or Indians and that it would be hateful (and, in his view, ridiculous) to pose as an omniscient narrator or to try to penetrate these minds that are unfathomable to him.

The "pose" of Negroes in the Faulknerian narrative (I am speaking of those who "count") is phenomenological in nature—that is, it does not assume any "depth" which would be imposture. These eyewitnesses are cut in silhouette against the dark background and heavy air of the Southern country. But these silhouettes are not the author's puppets. They are massed disconcerting shadows whose outlines—all the unexpected carvings, the odd scraps they attract to themselves—speak louder than shouts. It is in the consciousness of White characters that the attitudes and behavior of Black characters are reflected and, every now and then, translated into moral debates. Not only do the Whites *manipulate* these Negroes, confirming them as Negroes, as inferiors, but they sometimes try to express why their behavior, which appears so chaotic, can and should be clarified or justified, and even, sometimes, why this justification must be made.

"[H]e . . . Sambo [Lucas, the Negro] . . . will even beat us there because he has the capacity to endure and survive." "[B]ecause he had patience even when he didn't have hope, the long view even when there was nothing to see at the end of it." "[T]hey can stand anything."

There is no question that these remarks show an idealized view of the real if one compares them with the narratives of former slaves and black sharecroppers, who challenge almost all sense of complicity between the two social segments in the South, flying in the face of the myths created by Southerners subsequent to the "Lost Cause."

Among the historians of the South, especially the antebellum period, there are still those who attest to a real and indisputable cultural interaction, an "interchange," between Whites and Blacks, in social mores, art, music, religion, crafts, work, and leisure. There are others who add nuances to this observation. The question is this: Is the South a society with two intertwined cultures, one dominant and the other dominated, or a society that combines two separate and distinct cultures? But "interchange" can exist without cooperation. So the question that remains unanswered is essentially this: Is cultural interaction or "interchange" a harbinger of intermingling, miscegenation, and finally Creolization?

Faulkner is not alienated from the situation of the South, he is not caught up in dreams of a racial panacea. Using everything at his command, he wants only to ground the enigmatic relation between Blacks and Whites in a kind of metaphysics. Why? Because in the enigma of the foundation of the county, there is the damnation which cannot be expressed or consciously resolved. Everything is done as if for him the flaw of slavery was moral suffering, in what we would call Being, an irreversible decline (absence from History), much more agonizing than physical suffering. But also, for the slave owner, this is an irremediable lack.

He rarely describes an overseer bullying a worker or whipping a slave to death. The evil is elsewhere, it goes much deeper. (Nonetheless, in *The Mansion*, we find Clarence venting his violent emotions: "[H]e and his gang had beat up Negroes as a matter of principle. Not chastising them as individual Negroes, nor even, Charles's Uncle Gavin said, warring against them as representatives of a race which was alien because it was of a different appearance and therefore enemy *per se*, but—and his Uncle Gavin said Clarence and his gang did not know this because they dared not know it was so—because they were afraid of that alien race.") In rare didactic discourses in his works, specifically those of Gavin Stevens, Faulkner sometimes exposes what he perceives as the "fault," but then right away recoils with a burst of pride. " 'No,' his uncle said. 'I only say that the injustice is ours, the South's. We must expiate and abolish it ourselves, alone and without help nor even (with thanks) advice.' " And Uncle Gavin adds: "We owe that to Lucas." (That is, Sambo, the Negro.) This is the epitome of racist snugness, but certainly Gavin Stevens does not know this, because he would never dare realize that this is the truth.

The Faulknerian genius, occupied with deferring and at the same time revealing what torments the consciousness of Whites in the county, instinctively chooses to treat Blacks as if they had opaque, impenetrable minds, even the most important Blacks in his works.

I find myself speaking about characters, but this is merely from convention. In the county there are only people, and they precede his work. A metaphysics of confusion conceals the Faulknerian people, placing them outside the conventions of storytelling and the novel.

Sam Fathers is one of the people whose "idiosyncrasies" seem decisive here.

He is at the beginning of all things, the special guest in the "great Woods" where no primitive scene is played out, for these woods and their inhabitants seem eternal and sufficient unto themselves. (The women, temptresses and mothers, are absent from this place, except in the misogynist tales of the hunters.) Sam Fathers, as though he

was never born of woman, is said to be: "himself his own battleground, the scene of his own vanquishment and the mausoleum of
his defeat."

He is half Negro by his slave mother and half Indian by his father,
Ikkemotubbe, Chickasaw chief.

His father is a usurper who publicly poisoned his nephew, the legitimate heir of the Chickasaw empire; as soon as he became chief, he
immediately sold (alienated) some of the land to the Whites, while
trading openly in Black slaves. In this, he followed the practice of his
predecessors, even outdoing them.

Sam did not speak any more than he had to, and he lived alone in
communion with the bush and his animals, especially Big Ben, the
fundamental bear. Crippled but very much alive, Ben limped, like Vul-
can or like Boon Hogganbeck, who also came from the Big Woods and
would be there when the story of the county was all told (a number of
notorious people in the county were lame, and we know that Faulkner
feigned a limp to make people believe that he had been wounded in
the war).

Nevertheless, Sam readily forgoes his habit of silence around children (the children of others, those of his masters), young Ike McCaslin
and, much later, young Compson. It is as though he knew that innocence is the ephemeral kingdom of truth.

He has no children, having renounced all procreative ambition, and
was never so inclined. Likewise, Big Ben, the bear, who outlived all
his wives and all his sons. They are "Chief" and "Grandfather" to all,
but no one's father.

Sam: "the old man of seventy who had been a negro for two generations now but whose face and bearing were still those of the Chickasaw chief who had been his father."

The bear: "the old bear, solitary, indomitable, and alone, widowed
childless and absolved of mortality—old Priam reft of his old wife and
outlived all his sons."

And again: "the old male bear itself, so long unwifed and childless
as to have become its own ungendered progenitor."

.   •   •

Accepted into the McCaslin and Compson clans, Sam Fathers lives
among the Blacks, dresses like them, but does not abandon his Indian
heritage. Slave and property of these families, he takes orders from no
one unless he has agreed to do so. His behavior seems unpredictable,
until we see its motives in deferral.

"Did you ever know anybody yet, even your father and Uncle Buddy,
that ever told him to do or not do anything that he ever paid any
attention to?"

"In the boy's eyes at least it was Sam Fathers, the negro, who bore
himself not only toward his cousin McCaslin and Major de Spain but
toward all white men, with gravity and dignity and without servility
or recourse to that impenetrable wall of ready and easy mirth which
negroes sustain between themselves and white men."

He initiates at least two McCaslin generations in the hunt and in
the knowledge of the forest: first the nephew-cousin Edmonds Mc-
Caslin and then Ike McCaslin, the true legatee of the estate, "heir
through the male line," whose narrative of upbringing in the rites of
the bush covers most of the stories in Go Down, Moses, as well as
several others published in Thirteen Stories. The child Isaac turns into
old Uncle Ike, almost without a pause. Although the legal heir to the
estate, he has no direct descendants or actual property. He never claims
his inheritance (leaving the estate and the land in the hands of his
nephew-cousin Edmonds McCaslin, fifteen years older than he). For
nearly twenty-five years after that, he stays close to the hunt and the
forest, his real home, irreparably encroached upon by civilization:
slash-and-burn farmers, speculators, automobiles that drive better and
better, and commercial centers that are more and more appealing.

Most of Faulkner's readers know this. This is no secret; it is a clear and
undeniable truth. Too much so. Because we finally must ask why Sam

Fathers (this plural meaning is taken from his other name, Had-Two-Fathers) is half Indian, and if he is, why is he half Negro, and if he is, what are these two halves doing together in the same body and soul? For, no more than Lucas Beauchamp, Sam never represents the half-breed, the mongrel we suspect Faulkner did not appreciate at all.

In several places, he emphasizes the "decline" or at least the disruption and suffering that slave blood—slave blood but not illegitimacy—has introduced into the bloodline of the son of the Chickasaw king. What matters is not that Sam's birth mother was not the chief's wife, but that she was an inferior. Sam Fathers is not a bastard; he is a Negro slave. But because of his Indian blood, he refuses to think of himself as a slave. (We remember, however, the runaway slave, at the death of Issetibbeha, and the Indians who chased after him. "They were both on a footlog across a slough—the Negro gaunt, lean, hard, tireless and desperate; the Indian thick, soft-looking, the apparent embodiment of the ultimate and the supreme reluctance and inertia.")

All this questioning about blood and race would be pointless if we did not think that Faulkner really means something other than race, despite the overriding importance of race to the county and the South. First of all, he wants to draw attention to the stunning and apparently impossible connection, which in poetics we call the Relation, between all these people—Whites, Blacks, and Indians—caught in the system's trap, and also the sustained honor, courage, and will, whatever their race or condition, of those who oppose the system, for whatever reason. We understand this when we read these words of an Indian:

"This world is going to the dogs. It is being ruined by white men. We got along fine for years and years, before the white men foisted their Negroes upon us." In several places, Faulkner puts forth the idea that the Indians, once they are slave owners, become even lazier, fatter, and more cruel than the Whites. This is an unusual observation, intended, perhaps, to share the sin.

If we correctly understand the allegory, slavery is what distorts human nature, affecting first those who profit from it. Thus marked by what he has not done, by what has almost been done, why does Sam come so close to the absolute? Because he represents a pure beginning with no "progeny" who never deigns to express himself, except to children?

Faulkner does not try to enter "into" the mind of Dilsey, the Compsons' Black maid, or "into" the mind of Sam Fathers. Sam Fathers is present at the beginning of the tragedy that embroils the people of the county. The story ends with Dilsey examining the photo of Caddy Compson at the side of a Nazi general and refusing to acknowledge it, delaying the realization of what could be called the remote regions of Yoknapatawpha: the incomprehensible world, where, like Caddy, the people of the county get lost and become zombies.

Sam Fathers is Black and Indian because he must epitomize multiple aspects of the same fault. Ikkemotubbe, his natural father, not only killed his brother and nephew (an act which we could have excused, even if we did not understand or condone it) but after and because of this, he also appropriated the title of king and bought and sold both male and female slaves. With one of them, he sired this hybrid being (Sam). His actions cast a bad light on legitimacy, which is the guarantee of all stability, and then on family lineage, the visible envelope of legitimacy. This is the whole story of the tragedy of the county, of the Sartorises, the Compsons, the Sutpens, and those who keep them company.

For a long time, based on my readings of the *Compson Appendix* and *Go Down, Moses* ("He probably never held it against old Doom for selling him and his mother into slavery, because he probably believed the damage was already done before then and it was the same warriors' and chiefs' blood in him and Doom both that was betrayed through the black blood which his mother gave him"), I thought that this

Ikkemotubbe-Doom, baptized Du Homme by a French knight during a trip to New Orleans (in "Red Leaves," we learned that his name was Chevalier Soeur-Blonde de Vitry, and we imagined him looking like an old and dying Voltaire), thus crowned as "Man"—that is, Head Chief of the Chickasaw (or Choctaw?) Nation—was really and truly Sam Fathers's father.

"Red Leaves" (as well as "A Justice," a story I had read long before) tells how "the one Sam called Papa," an Indian in Ikkemotubbe-Doom's entourage who may have answered to the name of Crawford, vied for the attention of a black female slave with the slave she lived with, and profited from his relative power (over the slave, certainly not over Doom) to arrange some meetings with this woman, and that this was how Sam was born. In this version, then, Ikkemotubbe was not Sam's father.

These short stories also confuse the histories of Doom and his immediate successors, Issetibbeha and Moketubbe, so much that I took care not to remember (as a reader, I am especially fond of vertigo) the precise narrative of Sam Fathers's double paternity. Which version was primary, and why should it be accepted as such? Faulkner critics have undoubtedly addressed, discussed, perhaps even resolved the question. I wanted to debate it for myself, to test if I would survive this whirligig.

It is said in the *Compson Appendix* that this same Doom ended up selling the mother and child to the Whites. From that, I formulated a fragile but plausible view of how paternity (or filiation) is perverted under slavery, which essentially turned Doom into a crafty, inverted equivalent of the Planter Sutpen (who also abandoned mother and child in Haiti) and cast Sam as a Joseph figure sold in Egypt. Having two versions contradicted this viewpoint. Not being the father or, rather, the sire of Sam, Doom did not sin against his bloodline by selling mother and son, but simply made a decent profit from merchandise that had cost him next to nothing.

• • •

I reread "Red Leaves" and, even though I was close to abandoning my
hypothesis, I remained convinced that Doom's countless mysterious
ways of putting distance between his companion (and subject) and this
slave woman could mean only one thing. While he was affecting to
act with justice, protecting this Negro, piling up the obstacles between
the woman and her fellow Indian, he actually profited thereby so that
he, too, could make his rounds and visit this woman. More than he is
cunning, Doom is inscrutable and indifferent to all. He likes to possess,
even at the cost of misery. Why did he so stubbornly side with a slave
against one of his subjects? No. He hides one of his secret possessions
by trying to dispossess another, his companion. At no moment can
anyone determine (not the reader or any of the people appearing in
the story, with the possible exception of Three-Basket, another member of his entourage) that he has his sights set on this woman and that
he has attained his goal. True to his nature, he has fooled everyone:
the Negro, a man from his tribe, and the reader. Only this woman
knows the truth, but she has no right to speak.

The two stories reflect, in a *mise en abyme*, in a microcosm, the story
of Sam Fathers's paternity. He has not two, but three fathers: the official and very frustrated Negro slave father, the man who claims to be
his father and apparently is recognized as such in the end ("the one
Sam called Papa"), Ikkemotubbe's subject; and finally, his real but
hidden father, Doom himself, secretly enjoying this victory, which really meant nothing to him.

This narrative of three men—a slave, a subject, and a king—fighting
over a woman as if she were an inanimate object, is certainly confirmed
in the Plantation registers (where rape was the rule), even if Doom's
estate had only the remotest connection to those belonging to the
Compsons, the Sutpens, and Major de Spain.

All this collapses in confusion, falling ultimately into the derelictions where Faulkner leads us, daring to hide as much as he discloses.

In "Red Leaves," you catch a fleeting glimpse (in the space of half a line) of Had-Two-Fathers taking part in the pursuit of Issetibbeha's runaway slave (who will be sacrificed on the latter's tomb). He is a participant, but his role is unimportant. He acts as an utterly anonymous member of the Choctaw nation, mentioned only because he was present and not because he has a secret or a cause. In "The Bear" and "A Justice," it is said that this same Sam Fathers was sold with his mother to the Whites, and that all his life—if we exclude the seasons when he hunted for bear, opossum, and deer, "the last week of November," when he went along with General Compson, Major de Spain, McCaslin, and Boon Hogganbeck on the quest, rather than the hunt, for old Ben—he lived in the Negro quarters, where he spent his time making wagon wheels and plowshares. How could he appear, at the same time, to be an ordinary member of the Chickasaw nation who never left the tribe?

Similarly, in the short story "Wash," it is expressly stated that Sutpen's son—this can only be Henry—died in glory in the Civil War, but we know from *Absalom, Absalom!* that he kills his half brother Bon (in 1865) at the entrance gate to the homestead (Sutpen's Hundred) and then remains in hiding there until 1909. Did Sutpen lend credence to the idea that Henry died as a warrior? And did the people in the county decide to maintain his honor out of consideration for Sutpen?

Actually, these are differing, although not contradictory, moments, which appear to be at odds but are not in terms of the "continuous stream of consciousness" that runs through the county. The same event can be experienced and interpreted in different ways by different people at different times, or by the same person, who in the interim has had a change of opinion, interest, or belief. For this reason, Faulkner did not concern himself much with what some readers and critics would call "contradictions," but which were not so for him. Sam Fathers (Had-Two-Fathers) is a Negro and an Indian. He can be in several places at the same time. He is a Choctaw hunter and a Black slave, depending on who is looking or who thinks he has "figured him out," and when. He escapes all contradiction, and so does Faulkner, and perhaps the happy reader who can do so as well. Keeping it to myself, I maintained this hypothesis of perverted filiation and achieved legitimacy.

The quest for legitimacy and the assurance of filiation promise that we can conquer the ephemeral and the everlasting at the same time, whether by trying to establish an estate and a family or by trying to make people believe we are destined for a new creation of the world and therefore become "founding fathers," archetypal or first men.

Ikkemotubbe (who chose his own name, Doom—damnation or curse—deriving it from the name he was given, Du Homme) vaguely knows he will not be this first man, this founding father of truth.

Certainly, when established traditions—races—come into clashing contact, there is a great temptation to get beyond nettlesome crossbreeding by retreating to primordial unity. We seek truth in Being, trying to insure ourselves against the risks in Becoming. That is, we try to return to a source that would legitimize everything. And we strive to pass down this legitimacy without error or interruption. So Ikkemotubbe is obsessed with the worry that haunts usurpers: the legitimacy of their bloodline.

When he sells Sam and his mother, we can assume that he is trying to save himself from error or possible patricide. We recall that many conquering heroes, mythic or historical, were the illegitimate sons of kings or gods, who forged in blood and pain the legitimacy of their dynasty or immortality. They all had much to fear or suffer in their filiation. We have Hercules, hero of ancient Greece (never king of anything), and Tantalus, the Lydian king, according to one of the most ancient Greek tales an ancestor of the Atridae (both sons of Zeus), and Chaka, bastard son of the king of a small nation who became emperor of the Zulus. Under the spell of the insanity visited on him by the goddess Hera, Hercules killed his wife Megara and their three sons; Tantalus killed his son, Pelops, and served him as a feast to the gods, who, outraged, punished him forever; and Chaka had a male child killed (the only one his wife dared bring into the world) for fear of having to confront his heir later.

We remember how transitory the triumphs of these princes were. Their immortality (after Hercules is received on Olympus, history hears no more of him) comes from their ultimate defeat, and is limited by death but even more by the absence of any descendants (or else their children are damned from birth), a fate worse than death.

Through their vague coming together in a vague corner of the earth—Indians, Whites, and Blacks—tragedy unfolded. Ikkemotubbe lived the real and symbolic role of usurper and founder, an impossible role. Sam Fathers takes the place of all fathers and all ancestors, a role likewise impossible. Instead of the triumph of a bastard conqueror, all that was left to him was silence and self-effacement. He and his father prefigured the destiny of the Compsons and the Sutpens.

In these moments of trouble, confrontation, and inconclusive conflict, should we go back to a redemptive essence and resolve to be "Du Homme," *the first man* (announcing "Being")? It is not without hesitation that I note that this is the title chosen for the unfinished work about his childhood and adolescence that Albert Camus had begun to sketch out shortly before his death. Algeria at the beginning of this century is certainly not Mississippi in the middle of the last century, but we find the same question: What must be renounced, and what must be accepted?

And should we not, can we not, start humanity on a fresh, completely new path, all over again?

.   .   .

We admit that Sam Fathers is not mixed, but both Indian and Black. The slave blood that is his downfall is also necessary to him. Without it, the inextricable would not exist. (In "King Light's Settlements" by Saint-John Perse, there is a section called "To Celebrate a Childhood," and at the beginning of *Eloges*: "where the too big trees, sad with an obscure design, drowned an inextricable pact.")

It is this inextricable that creates the text of the poem and orders the disorder in the world, accumulating it marvelously.

Sam Fathers existed in a thick, silent, and constant fog. His purpose is simply to exist, without plan or hope, so this inextricable can *exist* again, this agreement that the Indians, Whites, and Blacks established at the very beginning, where there was no hierarchy between position (the Indians), action (the Whites), and passion (the Blacks). The long habit of slavery has ended up undoing this pact, which will have to be established all over again.

Dilsey is there at the end of this tragedy when the Compsons finally waste away. We know this traditional character from Plantation literature: the bighearted slave or servant, bound to an impossible task without knowing why, silently sacrificing herself, day after day, for the master's family. She is one of the family's pillars; without her they would never be able to make any decisions. The domain of the everyday belongs to her: "She rules as mistress in the kitchen and on the floor where the bedrooms are." We also know, for example, that Molly, Lucas Beauchamp's wife, nursed and raised one of the Edmonds children who had lost his mother. We can examine the troubled face of the Negro Lucas for signs of his relative, this Roth Edmonds. It was Molly who was responsible for "teaching him his manners, behavior— to be gentle with his inferiors, honorable with his equals, generous to the weak and considerate of the aged, courteous, truthful and brave to all." A Black woman teaches a White child the ideal behavior for a needy gentleman, as Mammy Barr had done for Faulkner, as he has admitted.

The character of the Black female servant is common in Caribbean and South American literature. How many times have we railed against her conventionality, judging her so much more unbearable, the more she corresponded perhaps to some part of the truth of the real?

Faulkner dedicated *Go Down, Moses*, the book of beginnings:

TO MAMMY

CAROLINE BARR

Mississippi
(1840–1940)

Who was born in slavery and who
gave to my family a fidelity without
stint or calculation of recompense
and to my childhood an immeasurable
devotion and love

Such emotion and sincerity from Faulkner (note that under Barr's name he did not write Oxford or Caroline Barr's birthplace, but a name that sums up everything for him, Mississippi). Still, this "devotion" bothers us, as have so many books inspired by similar situations, such as *Youma*, a novel by Lafcadio Hearn set in Martinique. In this book, a Black female servant (a nurse, a *da*) saves a White baby at the cost of her own life. She holds the baby in her arms while, underfoot, a poisonous serpent bites her savagely.

For these "risk-free Negroes" (who pose no threat to the master), slavery is not a downfall. It is suffering. These people do not express the past (the family's past); they suffer it, much more so even than the Whites, who are tormented by their own obsessions and follies.

• • •

Dilsey (whom Jason Compson, her enemy, calls the "Black Woman") is not a conventional character; she is tough and inscrutable, representing the end of this lineage and the ruin of this foundation, all the while extricating herself from the everyday. Her function has always been to die each time the death of this family. She alone is feared by Jason, the almost Snopes. She is a sign without hope that the inextricable persists. She is not the bighearted servant; she is the indisputable witness. I would say she represents Sam Fathers's real mother; or rather, that through Dilsey the genetrix of Sam Fathers has finally become mother—even if Dilsey seems to let her own children, Luster, Frony, and T. P., run loose.

For those of us who are Caribbean, our prophetic vision of the past makes us hear ("the eye listens") the cry Black slave women would shout to each other: "*Manjé tè pa fè yich pou lesclavaj*" ("Eating the earth saves a child from slavery"), which refers to the belief that eating dirt could make women abort when they had been raped by their masters or those sent to do their breeding for them. What suffering there is in this one cry! A suffering as stubborn as Dilsey's.

Perhaps this suffering (probably a widespread but futile kind of resistance) only rarely led to sacrifice since the suffering of these Black women servants, like Dilsey, was rooted in endless patience?

Besides, we know that in Martinique, and probably all through the Caribbean, the *mulâtresse* (the offspring of a White man and a *négresse*) would be set up and kept practically as an official mistress when her turn came. I believe that in Mississippi she would have answered to the name of Belle just as the bighearted servant was called Mammy.

The erotic literature of the tropics, so plentiful in Haiti and Martinique in the seventeenth and eighteenth centuries, complacently introduced this "creature" who does not appear in Faulkner. We find a number of Black whores, of course, but never any kept *mulâtresses*. The creature that Horace Benbow visits (actually his wife) and who acts so much like him is named Belle but she does not fit this category at all. These Belles are the White ornaments of the elegant erotic garden of the South; they have nothing at all to do with *mulâtresses*.

In Faulkner's work, the Blacks represent a tiresome moral rectitude. Yes, they are moralists. Otherwise, they never would have known how to be legitimate witnesses or "endure." They can be Uncles or Mammies, certainly not Belles.

In this universe of the county, we will not find the exact opposite, a character of primitive revolt, not an eminent, dyed-in-the-wool Negro revolutionary like Nat Turner (whom William Styron, so much like Faulkner, tried to portray). One of the black servants of the Sartoris family in *The Unvanquished* wickedly runs away, but Faulkner's portrait of him quickly turns generic and conventional. Faulkner is not a contemporary of liberation struggles. A Lucas Beauchamp and a Dilsey are withdrawn and headstrong only in terms of their opacity.

Surprisingly, quite a number of these Faulknerian Blacks have mixed blood. Interracial relations were customary in the South, although never acknowledged, but we are astonished that Faulkner insisted on this point. Lucas Beauchamp is a direct descendant of old Carothers McCaslin, and Elnora, the Sartorises' Black serving woman (the text describes her as "café au lait"), is the old colonel's half sister. Clytie, who is almost white, is Sutpen's daughter. White and Black lines overlap in the extended family, just as they do in Louisiana. But there is no chance whatsoever that these relations will be mentioned or take on "greater meaning" or lead to the slightest disturbance. We see instances of Black women who "pass" and escape the ghetto, or at least try. Usually, however, all mixing is mortally despised in a servile regime. When Creolization (which is not the same as *métissage* or miscegenation) is afoot, the first principle is to condemn it.

Creolization is the very thing that offends Faulkner: *métissage* and miscegenation, plus their unforeseeable consequences.

How then to catch hold of the immemorial he interrogates, if that is *what* is constantly changing? The Caribbean, land of Creolization, would not attract Faulkner. The inextricable is not the same as mixture. Sutpen encounters his first failure to found a dynasty in Haiti (let us not forget) where he is dumbfounded to learn that he has been tricked: his wife has Black blood and his son is a mixed breed. But when Sutpen first settles in the county ("a total slave of his secret and furious impatience"), the Negro savages he has brought with him still do not know one word of English: "doubtless there were more than Akers who did not know that the language in which they and Sutpen communicated was a sort of French and not some dark and fatal tongue of their own." Doubtless this "sort of French" is Haitian Creole, which the people in the county think of only as a "dark and fatal tongue." Sutpen speaks Creole, as do all Planters in Haiti and Guadeloupe. This represents the very thing he wants to kill in himself.

Two travelers landed in Martinique at the turn of the century in search of a fundamental truth. Charmed by the country, Lafcadio Hearn wrote several novels and a number of other books about it (in particular, a precious little collection of Creole proverbs from Louisiana, Guadeloupe, Haiti, and Martinique, called *Gombo Zheb*) and then left for Japan, where he completed his literary work and became other, was transformed. Paul Gauguin lived a year or two in Martinique before going to Tahiti, where he reinvented his painting. Both were too embarrassed to catch the changing radiance of this Creole reality, which must have struck them as a variant of lightness, a parenthesis of being, without much intensity. At least this is what I believe. The bliss and the suffering in their almost alchemical transmutations—Hearn in Japan, Gauguin in Tahiti—even if they were conscious of doing nothing but slumming at the limits of an alterity they hoped to influence (to accommodate, to appropriate for themselves), that was the sign that they could neither live nor tolerate the bliss and suffering of Creolization, all the more since, appearing in the Antilles out of a history of oppression and obvious renunciation, Creolization must have seemed to them capable of leading only to affectation, deterioration, and the degradation of the authentic. So Hearn and Gauguin went looking for sultrier places with thousand-year-old traditions. The time had not yet come to give serious thought to "what is changed by the exchange."

Faulkner understands this rhythm of change-exchange, but he summarily rejects it when it comes to the county. When he dreams the situation of the South, he invents a surprising synthesis; in the view of his biographer Frederick R. Karl, he pretends that what should have been realized there was a unique, Black-and-White race. It is clear that he did not use the term "miscegenated."

This Black-and-White race resolves unbearable hate and absolves injustice, but preserves all absolutes. Black and White are absolutes; the half-breed is anathema. Still, Sam Fathers was not a half-breed, but Black and Indian. I sense that for Faulkner the Black lineage of the McCaslins and Sutpens is not mulatto, but truly Black. ("*Old Carothers got his nigger bastards right in his back yard and I would like to have seen the husband or anybody else that said him nay.*") This lineage is confirmed by the Plantation. In this universe, the mulatto is the half-breed who is corrupted by the advance of civilization, just as the Big Woods are ruined by slash-and-burn cultivation.

To raise the question of the absolute, Faulkner needs Blacks as absolutes. The apparition (in the terminology of miracles) of a race that is Black-and-White concedes two absolutes while avoiding the hated miscegenation, and leaves the South intact as a whole. This recalls my oft-repeated assertion that Whites in the South detest the Black race but love Negroes, and Whites in the North love the idea of the Black race but neither like nor associate with Negroes. It affirms, as Faulkner did, the (obsolete) solidarity of the Black-White polarity in the time-space of the South but ignores the franchised "future" of the Black segment of the population. The Faulknerian Black-and-White is already outmoded; it neither accepts nor resolves the racist contradiction in the United States, where there are Latinos, West Indians, Asians, immigrants from Eastern Europe, all differing from each other in some respect, and different from both Whites and Blacks. Peter Brimelow deplores this unchecked flow, in his work *Alien Nation: Common Sense About America's Immigration Disaster*, to which Lydio F. Tomasi, executive director of the Center for Migration Studies in New York, has drawn my attention. Brimelow observes that Blacks will perhaps soon lose their "first minority" status.

Creolization is unavoidable.

In contrast to Brimelow's work, Francis Pisani told me about an Internet site, New York Online, saying that its motto is: "The Mix Is the Message," an expression that emphasizes language and race mixing. This slogan brings us before all the clumsy, lumbering horrors that show us how backward we still are. For example, what could the son of a Jew and a Black American woman do, except sink into the sewers of dereliction, or what could the daughter of an untouchable from India and a Scandinavian woman do, except make up this kind of message?

One of my closest friends, the late poet Jacques Charpier, whose humorous spirit soared just under the skin with the wild and ribald gaiety of a tall story or a thoroughly pagan feast, once told me that while teaching at Bryn Mawr he came across one of his colleagues stumbling through one of the college gardens in a fit of consternation. This normally dignified professor spilled his secret in one breath: "It's extraordinary, I have just learned a terrible thing, a colored man can be Jewish!" And (without even making a reference to Sammy Davis, Jr.) Jacques consoled him: "But, my good man, you are forgetting the Queen of Sheba and all her descendants!" All this happened long before the Ethiopian Jews, the Falashas, were taken to Israel and were treated so badly there after having hoped for so much.

In the surreal metaphysics of the South, miscegenation truncates the family line. Mixing would establish an extended family, which would not "include" patrilineal descent and, therefore, would not allow for the founding of a dynasty. When miscegenation and Creolization have been thrust aside with revulsion, misfortune and damnation are the only possible results.

Someone told me an amusing tale—embroidered a bit after public wags in Louisiana got hold of it, but surely the tale was inspired by what people believed. It was said that certain archives in New Orleans were closed to the public after some honorable people in high society (such as those who preside over the Carnival Ball) discovered while researching their genealogy that an ancestor had gravely sinned with someone from the "other race." (Paul de Montigny, in the short story "Elly," is reputed to have Black blood. His name is obviously French, and he comes from Louisiana, no less obviously. Louisiana was considered dangerous—contaminated—on this question, no doubt because of the reputation of lust in the former French milieu, much more so, at any rate, than in the other states of the Deep South: Alabama, Mississippi, or Georgia.) This anecdote from Louisiana, tripping a little on the fantastic, testifies no less to a convention, an obsession that we do not know how to erase. In many films, for example in a television series (I think it is *North and South*), we find the character of a White female who is really a *négresse* and who has the weakness (or misfortune) to marry a Planter who cannot stand by her when he discovers her secret. This is what happened with Sutpen in *Absalom, Absalom!*, but this misfortune occurred not in Virginia, Louisiana, or Georgia, but in Haiti.

Haiti, the Caribbean, the elsewhere, in any event, is a place where, one suspects, the stain of miscegenation marks every corner of the Plantation. There, mixture is a threat and a menace. It certainly signifies an intention that Faulkner "displaced" this first sin (which was involuntary for Sutpen, since he learned of it only after his son's birth, just as Oedipus did not know at first that he had done what he had done). Does Faulkner imply that such a calamity would have been impossible in the South? We have seen that this is not the case—that "mixing" occurs as often there as elsewhere (and perhaps even more often in Louisiana). Actually, there is an intuition that what surrounds the county assails it, but the county does not know this. Faulkner points to this elsewhere that is menacing, misunderstood, and charged with everything problematic. He sets up the premises of a truth: the Plantation system is corrupt, wherever it is found, and it is useless to consider it a valid foundation. He qualifies this corruption outrageously: inevitably sanctioned, it is the mix, even if paradoxical, of violent appropriation with the iniquitous law of slavery.

The county is linked with its immediate surroundings, the Caribbean and Latin America, by the damnation and miscegenation born of the rape of slavery—that is, by what the county creates and represses at the same time.

There is another relationship between the county and the *Toutmonde*, the Whole World, much farther away, on the other side of the ocean. The two World Wars fascinated the writer almost as much as the Civil War, all the more so as he only experienced the first through a distant echo, in a training camp for pilots in Canada.

Even if we fully understand that Faulkner speaks most of all about the misery of the soldiers, and the curse of those who survived (like Alec Gray in "Victory," which was about the 1914–18 war, or Weddel in "Victory in the Mountain," which was about the Civil War—antithetical and sad titles—both men flattened and destroyed in the aftermath of war by its solitude, imprisonment, and fatality), we deduce that for him there is grandeur in this misery, which is a prelude to the exasperated but implacable silence of the damned. These distant settings continue the damnation of the county: the trenches, the warships more fragile than butterflies, the ditches where a whole regiment is swallowed up, the desolation of field hospitals.

To escape from all that, to leave the mud behind, to tarry no longer *in the dust* where the flags lie and where the Black Intruder marches.

To rise. To the stars. *Ad astra*. The heroes make the dangerous, precarious machines their servants, using this very precariousness to trans-
form them into instruments that redound to their own misfortune. At
least here, all we have is the damnation they carry with them, the
disgust that arouses in them the cowardice and injustice of men. We
find neither the inextricable nor the mask. We do not have to submit
here to the temptation or the kind of trouble that comes from racial
entanglement. Negroes were not yet part of the war effort (at least not
in great numbers; their technical and mental skills were not trusted).
Especially not in aviation.

Today, we can watch a film that follows the odyssey of the first corps
of Negro fighter pilots in 1944–45, segregated in "colored" squadrons.
The film details the iniquities and injustices they had to overcome,
and gives the full record of their heroism and sacrifices. Fifty years after
these painful ordeals, General Colin Powell became chairman of the
Joint Chiefs of Staff. No doubt, Whites did not dare challenge him,
nor did all Blacks claim him.

Lucas Beauchamp stands apart. We find him in *Intruder in the Dust*,
in which, although fathered by a White man (one of the McCaslins),
he represents the essential Black. His hard-and-fast silences serve to
deepen the mystery of what has happened. But the reader never believes that he is guilty, that he will be condemned, or that he is at
risk of being lynched. The suspense is not there. Lucas is not a victim;
he is the Intruder who disturbs the order of things. Lucas's silences
do not conclusively deepen the mystery; rather, they emphasize his
implacable personal opposition to all attempts at explanation, assis-
tance, comprehension, and reconciliation. The silhouette (not a pup-
pet but a person viewed perspectively) is Faulkner's distinguishing
feature. He does not pretend to offer an opportunity for exploration,
at least not in depth.

In *Sartoris*, Faulkner assumed that no Whites (no doubt meaning no

Whites in the South) would admit they understood Blacks. This statement labels any attempt (any temptation) to mix the races as illegitimate and deserving of condemnation. Is this not clearly apartheid?

For Faulkner, it is true that, although sired by a White McCaslin,
Lucas is not mixed, and he is certainly not a mulatto. Especially not a
mulatto. Actually, he is a Black-and-White. Thus, in *Go Down, Moses*,
Faulkner, who never enters "into" the minds of the Blacks, runs the
risk of circling this other consciousness, without ever really substituting
his own. This is an incidence of one of those incomprehensible Southern obsessions: the search for buried treasure.

In the countries where the Plantation system held sway (a circle
radiating from the Northeast of Brazil to the Guianas and the Caribbean coast of Colombia, Central America, and Mexico to the Creole
South and the arc of the Caribbean islands), this is a constant in the
collective imagination: the belief that the family fortune could have
been buried before or in the wake of a catastrophe. For example, the
French Revolution reaching the Antilles, the victorious Haitian Revolution, and the Civil War in the American South were occasions for
secret burials of gold, jewels, and silver. Add to that the penchant for
mystery, in a *buena suerte* manner, and for West Indian *quimbois*. The
hysterical search for buried treasure is like the quest for Knowledge: a
deep search, an effort that cannot be shared, and indubitable. Lucas
succumbs to it for a moment ("the three-hundred-dollar mule which
he had stolen from not only his business partner and guarantor [Roth
Edmonds] but actually from his own blood relation and swapped for a
machine for divining the hiding-place of buried money"), before wisely
renouncing it. It is to this madness that Flem Snopes reduces his nem-
esis Armstid, at the end of *The Hamlet*. Armstid, a levelheaded White
man, is no longer anything more than a blind machine, compelled to
dig his trench in quest of a treasure that has taken possession of his
mind and is destroying his body.

·   ·   ·

Here is Lucas Beauchamp, he who was "already alive when their father, Carothers McCaslin, got the land from the Indians back in the old time when men black and white were men."

Here is how his White relative, Roth Edmonds, sees him when a child: "He listened as Lucas referred to his father as Mr. Edmonds, never as Mister Zack; he watched him avoid having to address the white man directly by any name at all with a calculation so coldly and constantly alert, a finesse so deliberate and unflagging, that for a time he could not tell if even his father knew that the negro was refusing to call him mister."

Then, when Roth Edmonds was a teenager, he saw "in his father's face that morning, what shadow, what stain, what mark—something which had happened between Lucas and his father, which nobody but they knew and would ever know if the telling depended on them— something which had happened because they were themselves, men, not stemming from any difference of race nor because one blood strain ran in them both."

Then, "toward his twenties," when he was almost a man: "he even knew what it had been. *It was a woman*, he thought, *My father and a nigger man over a nigger woman*, because he simply declined even to realise that he had even refused to think *a white woman*." (Molly was the cause of this conflict, and Lucas the offended party.)

Then, in the prime of his life, Roth Edmonds thought about "the face which was not at all a replica even in caricature of his grandfather McCaslin's but which had heired and now reproduced with absolute and shocking fidelity the old ancestor's entire generation and thought—the face which, as old Isaac McCaslin had seen it that morning forty-five years ago, was a composite of a whole generation of fierce and undefeated young Confederate soldiers, embalmed and slightly mummified—and he thought with amazement and something very like horror: *He's more like old Carothers than all the rest of us put together, including old Carothers. He is both heir and prototype simultaneously of all the geography and climate and biology which sired old Carothers and all the rest of us and our kind, myriad, countless, faceless, even nameless now except himself who fathered himself, intact and complete, contemptuous, as old Carothers must have been, of all blood black white yellow or red, including his own."*

Let us dispense with the audacity or incongruity of bringing together or "synthesizing" all these young racist Confederate soldiers, even indirectly, in the face of one Negro. I will conclude with the observation that Lucas, like Sam Fathers and old Ben, the basic, irreducible bear, definitely "gave birth to himself." Without direct parentage and without descendants that count. Without a bloodline and without legitimacy.

Roth Edmonds grows old and sees Lucas differently over the years, and finally realizes that the latter's major attribute was the eternity of the model he incarnates. Lucas does not age.

The only way to live the inextricable while escaping damnation is to extract oneself from "History," to remain self-sufficient and petrify oneself, without hope and without illusion. That is what the Faulknerian Negroes do.

And Lucas Beauchamp does just that in *Intruder in the Dust*, by means of shrewdness and a ruse, but also with a determination that impressed Gavin Stevens's young nephew.

It is time to speak of the closure that Nancy Mannigoe (in *Requiem for a Nun*) represents, coming near the "end" of Faulkner's career. For a long time, I put off reading *Requiem* in its entirety, annoyed by what seemed to have been a metaphysical and puritanical appendix to an exploded work. In a limited way, I saw the novel as the theatrical play—Nancy's passion—which it includes. Some people have complained that this "play" is full of scenes in Jefferson; others have regretted the barely theatrical character of the "play," saying it "lacked action." Eventually, however, I understood the totality that such a work suggests and brings to a conclusion.

Like her mistress, Temple, Nancy had been a boarder in a Memphis brothel. Now she is approaching sainthood. Yet she accedes to that level, if one can call it that, by a terrible act: murdering Temple's child. This murder is intended to keep Temple at home and somehow prevent her from slipping back into the torments of the "bad life." This is the improbable thread of the story, which we intuit much more than know. Only in the light of the absolute can the improbable be acknowledged. Nancy represents this absolute, which is, once again, metaphysical. Her act is intended to set off, like a spark, the music that Temple Stevens plays for herself, and the meandering ways of her tortured mind. Nancy Mannigoe is not self-sufficient; she lives and dies so that Temple will suffer the passion of her redemption. She "endures," so that Temple may fully exist and speak.

Nancy is named in and by silence (of the absolute). Only once do we hear her not engaged in conversation with Temple but pursuing her own monologue in the margins of Temple's remarks. Apart from that, she is ecstatic, quiet, and suffering. She completely manifests what Faulkner (in his work) expects from Blacks: bearing the unbelievable delinquency of the Whites.

It is even more impressive to reflect that Faulkner "surrounds" and "informs" this absolute episode with a whole historical, relative, and related chronicle of the county, which participates in the myth of beginnings (as described in Go Down, Moses), in the nomenclature of families (as sketched out in the Compson Appendix), and in the city records (as recounted in the other novels and stories). The various episodes of Nancy's passion answer to the divisions in this chronicle, and vice versa.

In Requiem, what is it that exists in common between the narratives that patiently summarize the history of the county—the arrival of the

first Whites, the relationship with the Indians, the epic construction
of the prison, courthouse, and City Hall, the genealogical outline of
the families (the Compsons, Sartorises, McCaslins, and others); in sum,
the constitution of a civil society—and the "final" (present and contemporary) deed of Nancy Mannigoe? Not only the proof that this
prison, courthouse, and governor's receiving room form the setting of
the drama, but also the idea that, from the very beginning, such a
drama (the murder of a White woman's child by an obsessed Black
woman) was inscribed in the order, or rather the disorder, of things.
At length, Faulkner links the county's epic beginnings to the tragic
outcome of Nancy and Temple's solitude.

What is tragic is the ascription of responsibility to the individual for
everything that epic disruptions in the community could not endorse.

As if *Requiem for a Nun* could summarize "the whole history." As if
Nancy Mannigoe was not "the first man" but the ultimate person, at
least among those who did not act with the opportunism or the "rel-
ativism" of the Snopeses.

This *négresse*, this absolute person, is a good example of what Faulkner would offer as a contrast to Blacks generally, in the name of the
conception he has of them—seeing them in his works as keepers of
the suffering, guardians of the temple of the unspeakable, but not as
an oppressed population that has the simple right to rise up against
oppression.

Between these two absolutes—Sam Fathers and Dilsey, or Sam Fathers
and Nancy Mannigoe—we have the long, sterile, and often grandiose
stubbornness of the McCaslins and the Compsons, the palpable decline
of the Sartorises, and Sutpen's demented assault; and, as if by extension, the calm but menacing threat of the poor Whites, the Bundrens,
for example, and the example of some monstrous phenomena, such as
Popeye; and finally, in the dissipation of the epic model, completely
beyond the space-time demarcated by Sam and Dilsey, we have the

relentless prose of the new realists, the Snopeses, who do not have an army of slaves or Black servants at their beck and call, but who are undoubtedly members of the Ku Klux Klan.

The principle of the whole work is indisputable, and we must not forget it: what is founded on slavery and oppression cannot last. Still, it is not enough to be satisfied with this kind of affirmative statement. If we were, if Faulkner had been, there would not have been these works to mark out for us a new path through the maze of the world. The tragic heights and the damnation and the minor misfortunes of those in the county issue from those who would fight this principle to the end, to the point of depleting their need to exist (their determination is stronger than they are). It is through sounding this damnation, this denial, that the work draws, not a lesson, but a new vision.

About Zachary (or his son Roth) Edmonds, we read: "Then one day the old curse of his fathers, the old haughty ancestral pride based not on any value but on an accident of geography, stemmed not from courage and honor but from wrong and shame, descended to him."

And after that: "So he entered his heritage. He ate its bitter fruit."

And Jason Compson, the "last" of his race: "In 1865, . . . Abe Lincoln freed the niggers from the yoke of the Compsons. In 1933, Jason Compson freed the Compsons from the niggers."

And Bayard (any one of them) Sartoris, thinking about the Blacks and Whites in Yoknapatawpha: "two opposed concepts antipathetic by race, blood, nature and environment."

In each of these four texts, and without Faulkner having to say it explicitly, we witness the playing out of slavery and its repercussions—what these wreak in the loneliness, anguish, damnation, prejudice, and blindness of the former masters. Under the conventions of this society (unmitigated belief in White supremacy) there exists this fault, which is not interesting except in one sense: it measures what reversals must occur in sensibilities before new alliances—the new experience of the Relation—can become deliberate. Faulkner's work struggles toward this change of direction, not through moral lessons, but by changing our poetics.

It seems strange, on one hand, that this change has been undertaken in a realm destined for perdition (that is, "damned"), in a society that actually displays the mundane characteristics of institutional slavery: technological stagnation, a single-product economy, racial blindness, and compensatory paternalism—in short, the very elements present in any place, Caribbean or continental, that is part of the Plantation universe, possessing subject matter that lends itself to specificity as well as sublimation. On the other hand, having mercilessly accused the avatars of this damnation in his work, in life he rigorously defended this "model," even if in many instances he could do nothing but offer a few adjustments to satisfy the simple wisdom of things. I have already discussed this question and will not stop debating it throughout this book: the question of the total perspective proposed between the place where a literary work is born and the work's very organic necessity. This necessity moves in an entirely different direction than analysis or proposed "solutions," both of which are no substitute for what we could term the "resolution of the dissolute."

Blighted Thebes requires Oedipal disclosure to expel its plagues and stop its lamentation, and the kingdom of Denmark needs the vigilant and heroic asceticism of Prince Hamlet so that what is rotten in the state can be evacuated, and so that Fortinbras, its legitimate king, can gain entrance. The "reasons" Faulkner cast the South as a plague-ridden Thebes or a rotten state of Denmark—worthy, like them, of tragic and epic disclosure—are also strong: the perversion of legitimacy and the bloodline, which weaken the right to possess land and challenge the possessor's very equilibrium.

These "reasons" belong to tragic opera. If they were real "reasons,"

Hamlet would have known how to resolve them, and Oedipus could have eluded their fatal outcome. The sacrifice of a Hamlet or of an Oedipus is necessary for equilibrium to be restored at the site of the word.

The gap left open in Faulkner's work is that for him the sacrifice that was the Civil War has already taken place. The defeat is complete, yet equilibrium has not been restored. What war is this that presents every aspect of epic struggle, yet has no redemptive effect? Roland dying at Roncevaux opens the hills to the voice of the Franks (soon to be the French). But neither Stuart, Lee, Stonewall Jackson, nor Bayard (one of the Bayards) Sartoris encountered the Song that would bring them into agreement and nearer to redemption. What defeat is this, so valiant and heroic, and as great as victory for the opposite side, but which still did not allow any "resolution of the dissolute"?

Faulkner organizes the sequences in his work according to these questions. Can we correct the original sin of the South? Where does its legitimacy go? Was the war not enough, since it was neither won nor profitable in defeat? To these questions, the tragic view answers: "usually," but not here in the South. Then (in this lack of response) we find a summation: "What is this Time that does not begin, what is this Death that does not assume Life?"

Is he the all-powerful novelist who evaluates truths or raises preliminary questions, and then, on the basis of these questions, decides the conduct of the characters he puts onstage? In truth, not at all. The preliminary questions are not "reasons" but sheer intractable forces: they intrude both on the writer and on the people he has gathered together in the work. The writer is not an omnipotent novelist, but a Pythian and unfathomable poet, staggering before the chasm of Knowledge accompanied by those he has brought with him. The "presupposition" in the Faulknerian work is not mastered either by the people in the county or by the poet who gives them voice.

We can conclude that he has refurbished, from bottom to top (or rather, from shack to big House), the principles of the epic and the tragic.

Epic song and tragic disclosure have traditionally had as their purpose a restoration of a lost unity. Through their intervention, we are guaranteed to regain it. The Faulknerian intervention accepts the impossibility of a return to equilibrium. This is the source of its originality and force.

Endlessly pointing to the flagrant lack in which epic catharsis and tragic disclosure culminate, this intervention extends into multiplicity, into what we would call the suspension of identity. Into the inextricable, which is its boundless home.

For these reasons, the people in Faulkner's county are almost always outside the limits of the common and the ordinary; they are extreme and monstrous. Thus, it is risky to speak of Faulkner's "psychological understanding," his penetration into the secrets of the human heart. In his Nobel lecture, he asserts that the task of the writer can only have bearing on "the eternal truths of the human heart," but adds "in conflict with itself." It is out of this conflict that the eternity of the word is born. Faulkner's "psychology" operates only in obscurity and malediction. This is a prodigious deviation at the crest of the unnamable. In his life as in his work, it is not study, knowledge, or psychological attention that interests him. In the work at least, it is the abyss. The refusal of Creolization leads toward this new abyss: the ramblings of the Southern world as well as those of the world as a whole are wrought by the same refusal and the same disturbance—namely, that of the Other.

Neither Sophocles nor Shakespeare lived in the place and period of the tragedies they chronicled. We can suppose they wrote for the edification of their peers, although, in all probability, it was because they were beset by scruples of legitimacy, or because they contemplated the stupefied face Victor Hugo describes in relation to Aeschylus. Faulkner, on the other hand, lives the moment of this tragedy that he assumes the responsibility of expressing. For him, the vanquished South he examines is not outmoded, and besides, by the end of his career, he wants to relive it. Plantations, horses, fox hunts, "everything in its proper place." Already in his youth, long before conceiving the entirety of his work, *ad astra*, with his head toward the stars, we have seen that he invented an aviator's pedigree for himself. Wanting to be a war hero, he pretended to limp and carried a cane, to affect a mythic wound. He was ready for the asceticism of the work. He relished the flush of heroism, wanting to attain the height of this lost epic he was going to sing. It is as if, instead of acting in this play within a play that, onstage, he directed, Hamlet had, in Shakespeare's place, written the whole play, making himself the hero.

Faulkner's "objective" cruelty with respect to the people he evokes and convokes (he describes some of them as if he were imagining them in accordance with the inspiration or the spirit of the place, others as if he were re-creating them from nature, and still others as if he were executing a kind of synthesis, but he never *invents* them, for they all have their prior necessity, in relation to the entirety of the work) is the most obvious sign that Faulkner is furious that he inevitably has to accompany them on this path of damnation. At the same time, it is the sign that he reserved for them once and for all his whole store of tenderness and compassion, from which there is no turning back.

This is how I would trace this path. First, he assembles the people in the county so that, through them, he can try to signify an original abyss which he senses in advance. In this abyss, there stirs the mystery of the configuration (the difficult aggregation) of the South. He sings the epic song, hoping to redeem the original sin that seems tied into this configuration. Then, suddenly, he feels that neither this song nor its first occurrence (the defeat that ended the Civil War) can resolve the disturbance, get rid of what is rotten in Elsinore, or reestablish the Theban calm. He has to accompany these people to new depths.

Imagine a kind of epic literature for which no "resolution" could be conceived. It would leave the dissolute dispersed. It would lead through the Big Woods to the wandering people, whose worth would be that they wander. A road that would trace an uncertain route, not a beaten path. It would be an unsuspected and unpredictable opening, not at all systematic; it would be fragile, ambiguous, and ephemeral, but would shine with all the paradoxical splendor of the world. It must be that way; otherwise, the drying up of traditional epic would have caused a death much colder and harder than even death itself.

Deep down—that is, in the reality that is the South—Faulkner acquiesces at the conclusion of the epic by sanctioning the elevation of a class of parvenus, the Snopeses, who conform to the "Americanization" of the county. In formalist terms, it is in the realist prose of the Snopeses that epic interrogation is extinguished and erased. Faulkner has been chided for the "prosaic" tone of his last books. But how could he have "forced" his imaginary relative to a reality that he only felt obliged to summarize? There was nothing to "defer." And so, there was no suspension of writing that had to be put into operation. Everything remained to be said, plainly. The only suspense here was pathetic, treating the twists and turns of the Snopes family's machinations. Faulkner's last books are not weak; they are logical in terms of their goal: presenting the quagmire of meticulously calculated profiteering and the extinction of epic tension. This is how he explains and ratifies, first of all for himself, the uselessness of this epic passion and, consequently, the tragic and sterile reduction of the South: what the carpetbaggers, then the Snopeses (perhaps a matter of the same "race") have chewed up and swallowed.

The failure of the traditional epic engendered, before settling into the ultimate prosaic, this other, Faulknerian epic. The presumption underlying the South, intuited but never consciously formulated, has led to modes of writing where the convention of disclosure is the principle.

Questions to which one anticipates finding the answers, the inklings, and the sense that these first questions, and the answers that follow on their heels, are not relevant. You must assume that there are others, not the one spelling out impossible victory, for example, but rather the one about the uselessness of defeat, and so forth.

This gradation in disclosure (not to be confused with the progressive revelation of Oedipus's quest for himself) introduces a suspension of being, a shattered conception of nature as well as human nature. Through this continual process of a diffracted writing, endlessly projecting deferred answers.

What is unique in Faulkner is that he harmonized the modalities of this stream of writing with the rhythm of tragic disclosure (which is my subject); he made this writing of the deferred necessary (Frederick R. Karl, and no doubt others with him, thus thought that this was "oblique" writing), and we have not yet exhausted its splendors or visited all its chasms.

This is not a style (style can sometimes survive its material), but a renewal of the very modes of writing that can take weight in every language except Anglo-American. The most beautiful translations into French, even if they lose the grain of the language spoken in the county (by the country folk or the police), forcefully highlight the structures and intentions of the work. The art of translation has entered into the circle of literary creation like a transversal, a diagonal, that reveals, from one end to the other, poetic intentions that are diverse but convergent today. When it comes to Faulkner, we must realize that the pattern of the deferred transcends language. The more these works are translated, the more they are "understood." A poetics can "pass" from one language to another, from now on, for the sumptuous yet complicated reason that today we juggle all the poetics of all the languages of the world. We think and write in the presence of all the languages of the world.

If we can convince ourselves that what happens to these people in the South does not touch us in a special way after all (there are so many oppressed people in the world; besides, we already know there is so much injustice in the situation of Black Americans), if we can smile at the heroic solidarity between Faulkner and the White South yet take offense sometimes at the injustices he is led to *think* about the subject, we nevertheless realize that his writing on the subject corresponds, prophetically, to the current disorder that looms in the contemporary sensibility.

He has shown that the uncertain, the questionable, the deferred, the pattern of the ambiguous, and the threatened finally engender some unsystematized couplings where the tangled realities of our world irrevocably explode (as the surrealists hoped). The inextricable. Thanks to this writing of the deferred, the people thus described and presented have taken on such an enormity of vertigo, attesting to such a suspension of being, that we forget the real characters they incarnate or represent: the racist Plantation owner, the Black with the fixed stare, the preacher tortured by the idea of sin, the nameless Black maid, and so on, in order to allow only this suspension and vertigo, the measures beyond measure of contemporary humanity.

Yes, Faulkner is a moment, a beat in the world-thought.

Faulkner writes fully and freely, disengaged from the secret restrictions that act upon the Southerner. In his works, he can mistreat niggers, blame Whites, and revile Indians without having us think that he has given in to racism or to the conventions of the place. In "private," there are these contradictions, agonies, sorrows, and regrets, all this smothering flurry of excuses, this search for an impossible balance, in short this hesitation bringing to the surface the latent racism he no doubt shares with his fellow Whites in the South, but from which he suffers no less surely.

And even if we do not factor in this kind of personal misery—which is a discomfort to some extent, although minimal compared with the sufferings that Native Americans and African-Americans have suffered—we still have to evaluate it in order to judge the measure of injustices that he was charged with denouncing.

These injustices, these *thoughts*.

They bring us back to the Blacks *in the works* of Faulkner. They cannot be removed from this context. Any attempt, not violent but simply intended to suddenly change their real fate, would provoke the writer's anger. He denied having made the blusterous declaration that he would not hesitate to go out into the street and shoot down Blacks if it were necessary (to defend his own). We choose to believe that he was not sober when he made this statement. He hides his embarrassment in a formula: "I would choose Mississippi." But he wrote a very significant essay on the subject, "If I Were a Negro" (reprinted in a 1969 issue of *Ebony*, which, in excerpts, cites another of his remarks dating from 1955: "To rail against the equality of race and color is like living in Alaska and taking offense against snow"). This is a text remarkable for its cautiousness and especially its coloration, if we dare say such a thing.

He recommends that Blacks practice passive moral resistance to gain their freedom; in addition to this Gandhian nonviolence, which is a very acceptable position, he advises them to have decency, dignity, and correct deportment (probably referring to proper attire, posture, and conduct!), and moral and social responsibility. The text ends in a tangled rhetoric that tries to counsel Blacks to *earn* their liberty before receiving or conquering it, arguing that this is the best way of keeping it.

The Blacks he is talking to in this way have never left Yoknapatawpha, have never known the ghettos of New York or other large cities in the United States. They have never lived with drugs or assassinations, with dilapidated shelters or homelessness, or with degeneracy and constant danger. Faulkner, who assigned Blacks an absolute function in the absolute interrogation of the South, absolutely could not have foreseen the Los Angeles riots, and, besides, he definitely would not have gone down into the streets to shoot down the niggers.

He tried pathetically to maintain a solidarity between Whites and Blacks that did not exist, for the United States had already become something else that was not the least bit hybrid. Everywhere else in the world a proposition such as this (of this kind of hidden, murky, and subliminal solidarity) would very simply have appeared ridiculous.

In the fifties, Faulkner supported integration of the public schools; this alienated him from the Whites in Oxford. Prior to that time, one hardly ever found his books in the library at Ole Miss (they were considered scandalous, and so was he). However, we are stunned to find that he advises Blacks to make themselves indispensable to Whites! Through education first of all, and without upsetting society. There are perhaps no words more smugly racist and paternalistic than these. Even if you can indeed say that education—as almost all associations of men and women of color, religious or lay, have understood—is the first step to better conditions for Blacks. This whole history is complicated.

There is his response to the venerated Black leader W. E. B. Du Bois, who invited him to a debate on the subject of integration on the steps of the courthouse where the Emmett Till case was going to be tried. (It was after this that Faulkner, in an article, asked or counseled Blacks *to go slow, now.*) "I do not believe there is a debatable point between us. We both agree in advance that the position you will take is right morally, legally and ethically. If it is not evident to you that the position I take in asking for moderation and patience is right practically, then we will both waste our breath in debate."

But would we not have admired the grandeur of such a Socratic exchange taking place on the steps of a courthouse in the midst of a national crisis?

The "man of the South" had no intuition of this grandeur.

This was April 16, 1955. In March 1956, he publishes in *Life* a "Letter to the North" and in September of the same year a "Letter to the Leaders of the Black Race." He multiplies his declarations. Faulkner apparently hated the Blacks who never engaged in the epic and tragic interrogation of the South by becoming complainers and loudmouths, like the Snopeses.

So the students at Southern University in Baton Rouge, Louisiana, were right to balk when I boasted of the importance of William Faulkner, and I was right to try to make them believe it. They had not "endured" a function of any kind in the Faulknerian universe. They taught me that no kind of literature was worth the price of thingification.

I tried to tell them (on the basis of which science?) that we were free nevertheless to look Faulkner in the eyes, to go with him wherever we want to go—that there was, in his work, an upheaval of the unitary conceptions of being, a deferral of the absolutes of identity, and a vertigo of the word, all of which perhaps constitute the work's revenge on the genial Puritan who gave birth to the ensemble of the work.

"I speculated on time and death and wondered if I had invented the world to which I should give life or if it had invented me, giving me an illusion of greatness."

4

THE TRACE

Faulkner's landscapes are suffused with a fragrance of mauve, with a power of melancholy that makes you feel like painting your own countryside, whether near or far, when you see what Faulkner has evoked. Whether the Big Woods in the cold, early morning mist, the feet of hills caught midway between the fates of drought and flood, fences of faded white birch edging the farms, a simple water barrel behind a cabin (with water dripping from the tin roof through a bamboo-shaped gutter and a zinc spigot for drinking directly from the barrel), fields of cotton running as far as you can see from the sheds in rectangular flight, or the pretentious, Versailles-like flower beds of the great Houses, this landscape evokes for me an unpleasant smell: the "cold perfume of magnolias." It is easy enough for me to differentiate this smell from that of *vezou*, the scent of fermenting sugarcane that bathed the countryside of my childhood which I can call up at will even now, when the distillery boilers no longer exist in the country.

The two smells are similar enough to become superimposed, one in memory (*vezou*), the other in imagination, without their becoming confused.

The fragrance of magnolia is heavy and vaporous, giving the air an amber quality, confining or rather clustering the air around it. The smell of *vezou* (a few vexed and finicky minds have reproached me for changing the French spelling, *veszou*, but the "s" seems too light to me) is also thick, but joyously so, the burnt-corolla smell indiscriminately finds its way to the most faraway hills. Apparently only the sea can block the smell of *vezou*. On the other hand, the fragrance of magnolia remains concentrated, hiding behind the thinnest wall of acacias.

In long-ago woods once intact, there was no smell of *vezou* or magnolia, here in the Caribbean or there in the Deep South. And when the history of the South began—that is, for Faulkner, when White people arrived—let us take a look at and observe the newcomers who settle and who, over time, will replace the harsh and humid smell of the great Woods with whorls of magnolias whose melancholy trails will linger under windows that are ajar.

These settlers—pioneering adventurers, of course—have nothing in common with those who stepped off the *Mayflower* at Plymouth Rock, the armed migrants, bedrock of Yankee capitalism, the White Anglo-Saxon Protestants who landed with their tools and skills, and developed a highly industrialized society. Nor do they resemble the waves of domestic migrant workers who followed, scouting out the terrain in advance for their families, who little by little would form capitalism's middle class, both vulnerable to and dependent upon the first group of migrants (for example, in South America). These arriving settlers often come weighed down by their pots and pans and cooking utensils, and, hidden in the bottom of their old suitcases or in their bundles of belongings, they have a painted portrait, or later a formal photograph, of the family they left behind. Of course, they do not resemble those who were deported here, the Africans stripped of any vestiges of their former establishments, *dispossessed migrants*, whose genius will be to reconstruct, from the few traces remaining available to them (in palpitations

of the unconscious and surges of memory), voices and accents—jazz
and reggae music, for example—that speak to the whole world. And
finally, we can see that they do not resemble the heroic pioneers that
settled the Far West; those dispassionate Indian butchers, bandits as
much as settlers, whose passions were organized (and little by little
brought into check) only by the a priori and all-powerful laws from
the East. Even today in the United States, this country of every possible
illegal extremism, we can measure the force of the expression "It's
against the law" by the response of the idealistic and individualistic
expression "Just do it." These pioneers, however, were already migrants
from within.

The first to arrive in Faulkner's world, the new ancestors of the great
families, are not of these types. They have no technological skills and
are not future capitalists. (Some of them—the Whites but sometimes
the Indians as well, who are not migrants but atavistic to the land—
are "splendidly comatose" and will profit enormously from the oil rush
"they had not foreseen.") They are neither bound to family nor dispossessed. They are not domestic pioneers, neither refuse nor surplus
(excess) from the East pushed West by need. No. They are adventurers,
willingly gentlemen but always fallen from a former standing, more
often Catholic (the minority) than Protestant. In any event, they are
branded with two characteristics that we could say are immeasurable.
They are marked with misfortune, bad luck, a destiny that is secretly
contrary, and, like heroes of Icelandic sagas, a vocation for failure. And
like heroes of all epics, they are wanderers, pushed from place to place
toward the impossible Place where they hope to settle down, plant
roots, find legitimacy, and perpetuate the family line.

They are not obsessed with their children, not even their sons,
whom they do not exactly burden with affection. Nonetheless, they
burst with the very idea of having descendants. So Colonel John Sartoris in *Sartoris* and in *The Unvanquished*, escaping from a pursuing
troop of Yankees during the Civil War, thought of his two daughters
living in Memphis, safe and sound, but he gave no thought to Bayard,

his son, because Bayard's destiny wasn't his own but that of the Sartoris family, and it just wasn't the Sartoris way to brood upon such things.

This primal pattern—the fate of passing on the name—was respectfully observed by the two families who were without a doubt the most important in Faulkner's world, the McCaslins and the Compsons. Even if the Sartorises, because their lineage is so directly connected to the Falkners, appear to be a founding family with roots deep in the landscape. Even if Sutpen's cataclysmal relentlessness, biblical in its extremes, symbolizes this passion to establish a foundation. Even when they are crushed, weary or degenerate, they do not resemble pioneers in wagons; they still (or already) have about them something of the aristocracy Faulkner admired, perhaps little more than the privileged air of malediction that hangs over them.

In the beginning of *The Hamlet*, however, in the account of the creation of Frenchman's Bend, we find a description of migrants that seems to fit the general pattern. First, there is an "armed" migrant who builds everything; then, there are the "domestic" migrants.

The founder: "Even his name was forgotten, his pride but a legend about the land he had wrested from the jungle and tamed."

His successors: "that appellation [Frenchman's Bend] which those who came after him in battered wagons and on muleback and even on foot, with flintlock rifles and dogs and children and home-made whiskey stills and Protestant psalm-books, could not even read, let alone pronounce."

Steeped in their solitude, the founders are doomed to fail grandly. They were not, in fact, so terribly "armed," and they never became capitalists. If most of those who came after them do give some order to life, it is distinct from any memory. Bit by bit, we see how these later arrivals, now a majority in the county, were not so "domestic" as one would have thought. They would not escape the curse either.

The *Compson Appendix* summarizes the origins and wanderings—and the malediction—of the founders and gravediggers of such families, who arrive from Europe after who knows how many previous disasters, holding on to an element of the fatality that leaves its mark on Scottish warriors of yore. We learn less about the Sartoris family journeys and forebears, despite the information supplied by the "retrospective" in *Requiem for a Nun* and the indication that they had a common ancestor from Normandy. They had found shelter in Pennsylvania and the Carolinas (the Falkner family example seems pertinent here) before seeking their fortunes in Mississippi. Their itinerary is unremarkable (after all, migrating from one state to another is common practice in America; on the highways you still encounter mobile homes that people pick up and plant down elsewhere like tents). Their decline is linked with nothing other than some sort of predestined violence. Their relationships (from John to Bayard Sartoris, from one generation to another, and by a confusion-confrontation of the twin brothers John and Bayard in the last generation) mix up sensibilities and wills, steering them away from obviously edifying roles and toward more and more obscure, damned objectives.

If, in an ephemeral manner, the McCaslins, Compsons, and Sartorises were at least able to establish their lineages, Sutpen is the startling example of irreparable failure: his descendants are depraved, and his mansion is apocalyptically burned down by Clytie, at once a tenebrous Clytemnestra and a (hardly prophetic) Cassandra.

Sutpen tried to establish himself in Haiti (his choice of both country and time was poor, the Haitian Revolution had already taken place) and found himself faced with the most radical impossibility of all: that of mixed blood. It could be argued that he was formed not so much by the humiliation he put up with in his childhood (a Black servant made him use the servants' entrance to a great Mansion) as by this first death: when he discovered the bastard blood that threatened him. To accept this invisibly Black wife and son would be truly to go back to using the servants' entrance to the "establishment." His fury grows strong in this memory and his frenzy takes its force from the need to elude forever such a danger. Little by little, his obsession for a legitimate male descendant is transformed into a mania for a male descendant of any kind after the imprisonment of his son Henry (from whom he never seems to have expected very much). Sutpen tries to rape his last fiancée, Miss Rosa (sister of his second wife), and impregnates Milly (the grand-daughter of Wash Jones—his White slave or some approximation thereof). He is ready to do whatever it takes to outlive his dream. What the end of a family line would mean for the McCaslins or the Sartorises is, for Sutpen, an irreversible adventure in which his two lines of descendants, Black and White, are already becoming extinct.

In every case, the same original lack imposes its fatality. For the Compsons, it is exerted through the attrition of history and property. For the Sartorises, it is through metaphysical decline. For Sutpen, it is through the explosion of the curse.

The various dimensions of the same impossibility go back and forth until they have spun a social web. One of the Compsons, General Compson, was "Sutpen's best and only friend in the county." He and his son tell Sutpen's story—the time, for example, when Sutpen replaced John Sartoris at the head of his regiment during the Civil War, to Sartoris's great, and suppressed, fury, and on and on. *The Sound and the Fury* weaves through *Sartoris*; together, they are woven through *Light in August* and *The Unvanquished*; they originate in *Go Down, Moses*, with an insurmountable example in *Intruder in the Dust*; they continue through *Sanctuary* and *Requiem for a Nun* and complete their path with *The Reivers*.

Faulkner's vision of the "peopling" of the South both recognizes and sanctions the unfathomable energy of these settlers (who, moreover, spread out all over the United States—not yet the "United" States—and, by first devastating its landscape, changed its face). Yet this vision omits altogether the tragedy of the extermination of the Indians of the Far West, attributing to the Southern settlers a familiar, somewhat degenerate, and ultimately placid role. I have shown how this perspective willingly exaggerates the unconscious or involuntary complicity between Blacks and Whites. Still, it raises infinite questions about the Foundation's legitimacy and the durability of its works, both in the county and, consequentially, in the South as a whole: the steadfast, shimmering question of the relationship with the Other in the world-totality.

This vision does not correspond with the brutal tension that, in the rest of the "American" countryside, led the settlers forward, never worrying about malediction or bearing metaphysical angst. The "Americanization"—that is, the expansion of the United States across the plains, sierras, wetlands, lakes, and canyons of the northern continent—was of a much more abrupt violence than that which troubles Faulkner's universe.

Because of this, a primary misunderstanding has arisen between Faulkner and the reading public of his country; his readers refuse to accept the idea of this oppressive, incomprehensible impossibility-of-being that remains associated with the original cast of *settlement* players and their descendants. The industriousness, heroism, and tenacity of the founders and pioneers—accompanied by the massacre of Indians and the enslavement of Blacks—are ideas that are far more simple and conclusive for the majority of the people in this country.

In his works, traits that limit a foundation (wandering, malediction, invasions, crime) determine the size and quality of the county's population, and even its farthest geographical and spiritual boundaries.

Faulkner's idea of deferral is disconcerting yet rich. Taking stock of the county, both its nature and its people, yet never taking a prejudicial view of either the concrete or the carnal, his works tend to return to a hidden source and find a secret there (the impossibility of establishing a foundation), which from that point on determines everything—without anyone's realizing it.

This is what charms and carries us away in Faulkner's text: we know where he is taking us, but the moment of knowing is ceaselessly delayed. This is also why Faulkner's critics are right on target when they are confroned with the essentially recurring themes: family lineage, malediction, the confusion of time and memory, and so forth. The intelligent and intuitive reader is forced to reconstruct the "first causes" along with the characters and the author, sharing their ignorance and surprise. Everyone who has spoken of his work has been touched by Faulkner's stunning, prophetic finesse, particularly in his return to the primal issues in which everything is given (yet hidden).

Wandering becomes indispensable, powerfully impelling the county's chosen people. Its workings could be summarized as an almost savage impulse that moved pioneers all over the Far West and, one could say, dropping them so dramatically at land's end, the *finis terrae* of the Pacific Ocean. But at least the pioneers conquered and cleared the land; in full possession of their energies, they wanted to change its face. For them, wandering did not mean suffering.

For the Faulknerians, wandering is a person's destiny. It is superfluous to count the number of times this subject appears in his works. We know that, in one of the works of his youth ("The Hill"), Faulkner mentions a "seasonal migrant" character; this is merely an omen, a signal of what will be the inveterate wandering of the first Compsons. ("Charles Stuart . . . was not expelled from the United States, he talked himself countryless, his expulsion due not to the treason but to his having been so vocal and vociferant in the conduct of it, burning each bridge vocally behind him before he had even reached the place to build the next one. . . . Fled by night, running true to family tradition, with his son and the old claymore and the tartan.") There is the calm and happy suspension of being that leads Lena Grove throughout the country, from the beginning to the end of *Light in August*. (In the beginning: "Lena thinks, 'I have come from Alabama: a fur piece. All the way from Alabama a-walking. A fur piece.' Thinking *although I have not been quite a month on the road I am already in Mississippi*." And, at the end: " 'My, my. A body does get around. Here we aint been coming from Alabama but two months, and now it's already Tennessee.' ") We find the ontological wandering of Addie Bundren (both dead and alive) and her family, anticipating and beyond Death, in *As I Lay Dying*. Other examples include: the wanderings of Joe Christmas, the worldly drifting of Caddy Compson, and the crazy races of the Bayard (all of the Bayards) Sartorises. This tendency to wandering is not caused by a curse, such as the one that struck down Cain, nor is it the consequence of one's status in the world, as might be said of the "wandering Jew." It is not even the dazzling effect of a passion to know and to conquer, as for an explorer or colonizer. No, wandering exudes from within an individual, as though by need. It is this need that prescribes malediction. For the people of Faulkner's world—for the "chosen" few—wandering is not so much an obsession with movement or the furor to know as it is the unalterable necessity to find oneself, alone, in the frightening movement of flight.

In the idea of wandering, we sense both suspense and intrigue (not, however, in a detective sense of these terms). Faulkner's wanderer flees what is established and, consequently, the idea of any system that projects and decides upon any determination of foundation or any seizure of territory as the absolute condition of his or her (collective, familial, or furiously individual) being and pulse of life. The founding members of the county obey no system other than the wild and chaotic impulses of their own intrigues and obsessions, which cannot be shared. They have no gift for "colonizing" and no fixed address, even if these may be their crazed aspirations.

I have argued, on other occasions, why systematic violence is equivalent to territorial violence.

In *atavistic* cultures the community takes shape around a Genesis, a creation story in which there is uninterrupted lineage from father to son, with no illegitimacy. The community's ontological relationship with territory is so tight that it not only authorizes an aggrandizement of territory—as with colonialism—but also foresees *what is to come, what is going to be conquered, and what is going to be discovered*. This is the power of predictability. Just as the community tries to keep itself pure from any outside assault, so it seeks to establish its own supremacy in the outside world, imposing upon that world the future it envisions for itself. All systems, and all the power and glory of the creations they produce, derive from this double movement: to foresee and to conquer.

Composite cultures were created with western expansion and out of the mingling of many contradictory atavistic cultures. They do not generate their own creation story but content themselves with adopting myths from the atavistic cultures. For composite cultures, colonial expansion has no way of becoming naturally legitimate; it must find other "reasons."

We can make conjectures about what these composite cultures have lost—namely, a direct experience of the sacred (the advantage of being able to assume a myth, and to have an intuitive sense of the world's creation)—and what they gain by being able to choose among many different experiences of the sacred, to mix them and, if possible, syncretize them into a new form. We can also surmise that individual freedom has greatly increased in the composite cultures of today. Little by little, each person is freed to see himself as "atavistic" in composite surroundings, or "composite" in an atavistic world.

Similarly, we can accept that the sacred "results" not only from an ineffable experience of a creation story but also, from now on, from the equally ineffable intuition of the relationship between cultures.

Because atavistic cultures are inextricably bound up in Relation, they tend to become composite (to decompose), in the same way that composite cultures aspire to the ancient dreams of atavism: truth and a grounding in a Genesis.

What is Yoknapatawpha? A composite culture that suffers from wanting to become an atavistic one and suffers in not being able to achieve that goal. For example, in one of the few entirely "ideological" speeches in Faulkner's work, the uncle in *Intruder in the Dust* says, "It's because we alone in the United States (I'm not speaking of Sambo right now; I'll get to him in a minute) are a homogeneous people. I mean the only one of any size," and adds, "And as for Lucas Beau-champ, Sambo, he's a homogeneous man too, except that . . ."

A homogeneous population: the atavistic dream.

In Faulkner's world, the "impossibility" of establishing a territorial foundation is also the impossibility of foreseeing, making plans, and projecting into the future. (Only the Snopeses can see ahead.) Thus, deferred thought painfully intensifies as it reaches back into an elusive past, and wears itself out seeking a perspective on the future. (This is the "vague attenuation of time" that Régis Durand cites from *Absalom, Absalom!*) Only the Snopeses have the cunning patience to prepare (their moderate establishment).

Foundation, a series of works by Isaac Asimov that has fascinated generations of readers since its first publication around 1950, confirms the hypothesis set forth here: a Foundation's strength is determined by its power to anticipate, foresee, and draw up plans for the comet, the planet, and the entire universe. Asimov's story also relies upon the certainty that History is both singular and sovereign, and that its heresies (the particular stories about people considered marginal and peripheral) are destined to be diminished. This is a fascinating illus-tration of systematic thought and the foundation of legitimacy. Faulk-ner's works are the exact opposite of this.

In their defeat, the people of Yoknapatawpha County (that is, the "true" and emblematic ones, those who count) uproot the very idea of system and legitimacy. For the sake of order, legitimacy is commonly appealed to as a necessity in the United States—where the idea of legitimacy haunts every jurisdiction in its shadow (civil and family status, spirituality, politics)—and so the country was not prepared for Faulkner's turbulence. I am not the only one who has observed that this is a country formed virtually on the idea of ter-ritorial conquest. The myths and realities of this conquest have taken the place of a Genesis. I could argue, tongue in cheek, that practically every sporting match has an ideal and constrictive territory as a goal, where it is a question of *scoring* on the other's terrain while maintaining one's own; American football is one of the rare sports where the conquered territory is measured meticulously after each play, and this measurement either authorizes or refuses the right to advance further. Territorial conquest never suffers upheaval (except in the case of tropical fever) and is never questioned. It is systematic. It is not wandering but rather, like an arrow, a forward projection.

Wandering, on the other hand, is the capacity to maintain oneself in living suspension, far from foundational and systematic certainties. It is also the impulse of epic heroes toward other places, where they reinforce roots or compensate for their lack. How? By affirming that having roots should neither exclude nor permit a forward projection, the impulse toward conquest. Wandering is a confused setting down of roots: This is a precaution that the great, foundational works established, something their partisans forget when they focus only on the excluding elements of the works.

Can all of this be found in Faulkner's works? Yes. How? How can these works—so densely populated, so indisputably articulated around a country's specific realities, where you smell the countryside and smile at the language the people use; works that never bombard you with declarations or ideological pronouncements—how can they also derive from the most abstract and idealistic principles of Western civilization and its hiddenmost motives, while also subjecting them to criticism?

Now that we have looked at wandering, let us go back to the idea of malediction, or curse.

Did the settlers bring this malediction with them (or within themselves)? The Compson ancestors—of English and Scottish origin, as are many of Faulkner's immigrants and as was the Falkner family it-self—seem to have the same stubborn streak in the face of failure that leaves its mark on the Sartorises (and whom Aunt Jenny will attack so vehemently: " 'Oh-h-h, damn you! . . . Damn you! You—you Sar-toris!' "). The Compsons seem to be perhaps the only members of the damned among the defeated ranks in which each of them stands to be counted. Or perhaps the curse originates in the methods of new land acquisition in Yoknapatawpha County.

We recall that the settlers negotiated with Ikkemotubbe (the "dis-possessed" and "fallen American king": is it a question of the first of his kind, or the one who was snatcher and murderer?). In the begin-ning, they dealt in the buying and selling of Black and Black-Indian slaves; next they dealt with land transfers, particularly with the clearly rectangular piece of land the Compsons so pathetically squander at the end of their story (". . . the best of all talking. It was of the wilderness, the big woods, bigger and older than any recorded document—of white man fatuous enough to believe he had bought any fragment of it, of Indian ruthless enough to pretend that any fragment of it had been his to convey"). Incidentally, what does Ikkemotubbe—whom we have such a hard time identifying—get in exchange for this land? An un-beatable horse that runs the six-hundred-yard race and collapses a yard from the finish. It was thanks to this horse that the first Compson made his fortune, organizing races (whose distance he carefully regu-lated) against the young warriors of this Ikkemotubbe, who probably had not yet become Doom. This horse is one of the many fantastic animals in Faulkner's world, one with the speed of lightning but ulti-mately without the ability to go very far. The horse of the ephemeral. Symbol of a proprietary deed. An absurdly geometric concession of land completely surrounded by prolific woods, as though to signify that the land is not part of them, but merely a monstrous outgrowth thereof. An artificial property without roots. An Ikkemotubbe, if he is really the one a White man called Du Homme ("the first man"); he himself changed this name to Doom: malediction, condemnation. Like Sam

Fathers (Had-Two-Fathers, who, with his mother and the land, was traded for the horse, unless—what a contradiction—they were sold to McCaslin), some of the descendants will not deign to have children or begin anything original at all, in word or deed. A complete sterilization.

Obtained from a man who had no right to grant them, and founded on a commerce in slaves that carried in itself its own demise, it seems that all these arrangements, acquisitions, and trafficking were illegitimate (worse, damnable). All this is in Faulkner's work.

Although admittedly not obvious, Faulkner maintains throughout his works an unflagging, calm, and stubborn condemnation of property—property acquired under such conditions.

All of this can be seen in *Go Down, Moses*. Ike McCaslin, for example, "owned no property and never desired to since the earth was no man's but all men's, as light and air and weather were."

Young Ike thinks that the land belongs to the Indians and not to his family: "their hold upon [the land] actually was as trivial and without reality as the now faded and archaic script in the chancery book in Jefferson which allocated it to them and that it was he, the boy, who was the guest here and Sam Fathers's voice the mouthpiece of the host."

This is not enough for McCaslin. In a seemingly natural way, he becomes dispossessed of his inheritance, to the profit of his nephew-cousin: "his elder cousin, McCaslin Edmonds, grandson of Isaac's father's sister and so descended by the distaff, yet notwithstanding the inheritor, and in his time the bequestor, of that which some had thought then and some still thought should have been Isaac's."

There is a dizzying nonpossession, tied with passion for the Big Woods and the wilderness that will preoccupy Ike McCaslin for his whole life until the time when, a bedridden old man in his freezing shack, he cannot do much more about it than dream, mixing regret with endless racist and disagreeable invectives.

This land which man has deswamped and denuded and derivered in two generations . . . where white men rent farms and live like niggers and niggers crop on shares and live like animals, where cotton is planted and grows man-tall in the very cracks of the sidewalks, and usury and mortgage and bankruptcy and measureless wealth, Chinese and African and Aryan and Jew, all breed and spawn together until no man has time to say which one is which nor cares.

All through *Go Down, Moses*, Faulkner raises this art of repetition to an astonishingly hypnotic degree, which tends more acutely to accuse man of destructive work against nature.

". . . the surrey moving through the skeleton stalks of cotton and corn in the last of open country, the last trace of man's puny gnawing at the immemorial flank."

And again: "the old wild life which the little puny humans swarmed and hacked at in a fury of abhorrence and fear like pygmies about the ankles of a drowsing elephant."

He also sings praises to the Big Woods and the wilderness ("an unforgettable sense of the big woods—not a quality dangerous or particularly inimical, but profound, sentient, gigantic and brooding"). In essence yet without ever really saying it, he calls them the primordial Mother. What does he say about the wilderness so repeatedly (at least six or seven times in some twenty pages of "The Bear," perhaps at first without us even noticing)? That it *leans* over men and animals, like a protective guardian, yet is too vast for anyone to feel continually either its gentle touch or its reproach:

"the wilderness . . . seemed to lean, stooping a little, watching them and listening, not quite inimical . . . but just brooding, secret, tremendous, almost inattentive . . ."

"It seemed to lean inward above them, above himself and Sam and Walter and Boon in their separate lurking-places, tremendous, attentive, impartial and omniscient . . ."

". . . and in the following silence the wilderness ceased to breathe also, leaning, stooping overhead with its breath held, tremendous and impartial and waiting."

". . . it was still no living creature but only the wilderness which, leaning for a moment, had patted lightly once her temerity."

In his work, speaking perhaps for someone other than himself, Faulkner does not say that "property is theft." Here, property is seen as the death of the natural order. Ultimately, this is a condemnation, if not of the peopling of the land, at least of the original methods and future consequences of this occupation.

This is not a simplified version of Rousseau or a program such as that of Proudhon, but rather the affirmation of a pantheist reality (the invigorating solidarity among nature's species) outside of which all other human, social, political, or economic demands lose their meaning. There is a remarkable obsolescence in these words that leads, however, in a most pertinent way, to what threatens us today. Yes, all of this is in his works, but I will not (take the time to) develop these ideas here.

The curse is double: what the first Planters, the Compsons and the Sartorises, brought with them (within themselves) and what is inseminated with the rape of the earth. The wanderers' curse was intensified by the curse uprooted with this silt. Side by side, we find earth's degradation and the human greed that only hunters ("not white nor black nor red but men, hunters, with the will and hardihood to endure and the humility and skill to survive") try to resist. Leaving aside for a moment the ritual function of this return to roots that hunting season embodies, it is now necessary to ask ourselves how epic reconstruction and the tragic tension that succeeds it intervene into this context of failed foundation.

.　　.　　.

One can ask, therefore, not only why this defeat did not give birth to epic flux—the transfiguration that could have turned it into a point of reconciliation—but also why these shams (in the manner of, say, *Gone with the Wind*), inanities of pale nostalgia and wretched literalness, have taken precedence over the deep breath that should have arisen from defeat.

The first answer is given precisely in an analysis of what the works lead us to believe about the founding of the county: you cannot build a lasting foundation on appropriation and crime. This is a "confirmation" of the traditional epic principle according to which one finds community disequilibrium when there is a failure to abide by the source, a perversion of the "root." But this is the first time in the history of epic passions and their underlying motives that this perversion is tied (secretly and nebulously) to injustice and oppression—namely, slavery and the slavery system. The works are a meditation upon the impossibility of the epic in this particular time and place. Or, rather, they are a frenzied struggle against this impossibility, a heroic effort to give birth to and express it from the improbability it infers. Faulkner will magnify and construct this impossibility in Yoknapatawpha, and, later, give it a name.

He praises the courage and exalted craziness of his Southern compatriots of the war, such as the time when Bayard (one of the Bayards, Colonel John's brother) Sartoris, accompanied by General Stuart, charges ahead through Federal lines. Unbelievably elegant and charming, carefree and brave, dashing and daring—absolutely unbelievable—uselessly provocative and one could say technically irresponsible, even injuriously inept if not absurd in its ending: "and a cook who was hidden under the mess stuck his arm out and shot Bayard in the back with a derringer." These knights of another era get shot in the back by the kitchen help or, boasting after feats of war, are "on the next night . . . discovered by a neighbor in bed with his wife and . . . shot to death."

On such occasions, despite Faulkner's expression of great fervor and pity as well as his admiration, he never gives up his harsh words ("Bedford Forrest while he was still only a slave-dealer and not yet a general") or his unrelentingly clear descriptions, a testimony of his deep communion with what he describes.

Can we admit that courage and craziness were not enough? They did not suffice. Not to win a war that, in this case, was unwinnable, but to make the defeat "profitable." Something else would have been needed, something that, using terms of Western thought, I call legitimacy.

Faulkner's merciful, suffering but fearlessly lucid stroke of genius can be found in his having drawn out the failures of this legitimacy and having dared name them (confusing them with the impossibility of setting up a foundation): malediction and damnation.

The community itself (the traditional South) thus feels a secret aversion for granting any recognition to such works (except to coat them with a veneer of respectability through which no one looks very hard). Overtly and guiltlessly, it prefers to rewrite and celebrate, ignoring nuance and states of mind. Exploring cruelty at its supernatural limits, Ambrose Bierce wrote some dry tales and brief narratives devoted to the War of Secession (more than thirty years before Faulkner's birth, Bierce, a Yankee, really "covered" the Secessionist War and found nothing epic about it even if, like many of the survivors from both sides, he felt an indefeasible melancholy when visiting the old battlefields after the war; in any event, during the war he developed a strong sense of justice—indistinguishable from truth—as well as several other obsessions that prevented him from becoming the great writer he could have been). Bierce's stories never could have been welcome here (in the South) or even taken (understood) for what they were.

.   .   .

The loss of legitimacy (loss of the right to establish roots) is symbolically illustrated by the failure of the great families of the county to
produce descendants. The Sartorises finally "end up" having a son, the
child of Narcissa and Bayard (one of the Bayards, the last one), but
his mother decides to name him Benbow, after her brother, and already
you can sense that she will coddle this last of their offspring and wean
him from the Sartoris side of the family; Aunt Jenny predicts that a
simple name change (following family tradition, the child should have
been named John, since his late father was named Bayard) still will
not be enough to save him from the curse of the Sartorises.

The Sutpen family sinks into apocalypse and fire, and its last representative—an idiot and, to make matters worse, Black—disappears
into the world beyond.

The McCaslin family can be summed up by Uncle Ike, stubborn and
alone after the death of his wife, and left with no children.

The final generation of the Compsons is cursed more than any other:
one brother is a congenital idiot, another commits suicide, Candace
disappears into damnation abroad and Quentin (her daughter) van-
ishes without a trace, and finally Jason—"the first sane Compson since
before Culloden and (a childless bachelor) hence the last"—becomes
almost a Snopes, bitterly reflecting upon his defeat and swallowing his
indignity.

The patriclan—a family clan ruled by patrilineal descent—falls
apart.

For the ordinary residents of the county, or rather the (human or animal) members who represent it, the loss of all one's children and the
rupture of descent are inevitable. Consider Sam Fathers, Boon Hogganbeck (until he meets and marries a bighearted prostitute in *The
Reivers*), and old Ben.

This is perhaps where we see signs of their irreducibility, the only remaining pinnacle of which they can boast: ultimate "sterility." The roots that "survive" are usually from lateral branches: the Edmonds family, for example, or the "impartial" Stevens family, some of whom comment on the story and become conscientious debaters and fastidious record keepers. In *As I Lay Dying* we find that Jewel, a child of adultery, is the most innocent but also the most protected of the children in the Bundren family. He is perhaps the only one the future would accept.

In this universe, we find a predominance of Uncles (Jason, Horace Benbow, not to mention the usual ones, White or Black, who maintain tradition: Uncle Buck, Uncle Gavin) and Aunts, and sometimes Grandmothers (bursting with prejudice, they are all racist and calmly unrelenting: Miss Jenny, Miss Rosa, Granny Rosa Millard). Fathers are insignificant if not mediocre, except, of course, when they are colonels in the army, in which case they are nevertheless remote and indifferent. The father of the youngest Compsons is a profuse speaker of banalities (inspired at least once, surely, by the Sutpen story); he is the epitome of resignation, a portrait of what is called the absent father. The Bundrens' father, Anse (again, in *As I Lay Dying*), is perhaps the dullest character of the whole story, the one least possessed with ghosts and illusions (his only obsession is with money). Emily Grierson's father, the young runaway's father in *The Reivers* (and, even earlier, the father of Donald Mahon, the anguished hero of Faulkner's first novel, *Soldier's Pay*), and all the others appear to be either silent accomplices or enraged and powerless men, not energetic decision makers as would seem logical for the county.

To have no father becomes a kind of virtue: it is a way of being cut off from malediction.

In Lucas Beauchamp's words, "not denying, declining the name itself, because he used three quarters of it; but simply taking the name and changing, altering it, making it no longer the white man's but his own, by himself composed, himself selfprogenitive and nominate, by himself ancestored, as, for all the old ledgers recorded to the contrary, old Carothers himself was" ("The Fire and the Hearth").

In the words of old Isaac McCaslin, born when his father was over seventy years old: " 'An Isaac born into a later life than Abraham's and repudiating immolation: fatherless and therefore safe declining the altar because maybe this time the exasperated Hand might not supply the kid.' "

Efforts to create descendants and a foundation are thwarted by two obstacles: opposition and refusal by the Blacks (the extended family) and the curse of the Whites ("the exasperated Hand").

This is what Quentin Compson says about it: "The last. Candace's daughter. Fatherless nine months before her birth, nameless at birth and already doomed to be unwed from the instant the dividing egg determined its sex."

The people of the county who act against each other and against their opacity have only themselves as their point of origin, and they leave no descendants. Through this, they refuse familial inheritance and legitimacy, the indispensable base of every foundation. Among other examples, the passages I cited previously from "The Bear," referring to old Ben (*ancient Priam who has outlived all his children*), demonstrate how the resistance and uniqueness that can be found in individuals can also be found in a chosen group of animals, tame or wild.

"Lacking" descendants, these paternal failures are all the more meaningful because Faulkner suggests, throughout his works, that matrilineage is not really lineage at all since it grants no legitimacy.

We have seen how it was with Ike and his cousin Edmonds McCaslin, who inherited from women. Everyone in the county, including perhaps Edmonds himself and his offspring (Zachary Edmonds and his son, Roth), thought they were not entitled to what they had appropriated; all of the Edmondses must suffer at least when they think about this.

The Black, Lucas Beauchamp, a bastard of the McCaslin family but through a male line, never thinks of using this relationship to his advantage against this very same Roth Edmonds, who is a legitimate (White) McCaslin but through a female line. The latter is tormented by the thought.

It is said that Doom, the usurper of the Chickasaw throne, was "born merely a subchief, a Mingo, one of three children on the mother's side of the family," and that he had improperly replaced "the chief, the Man, the hereditary owner of that land which belonged to the male side of the family."

Did not Faulkner suffer? He who so symbolically named his first daughter Alabama—a daughter who died nine days old. A state that forms, with Mississippi, the other side, if there is one, of the Deep South; Alabama is such a beautiful name, and yet so terrifying for the segment of the population that is Black. Did not Faulkner suffer? He who was so attached to his other, cherished daughter, Jill, perhaps without ever understanding her, or so it is said, apparently without believing that there was an urgent need for this understanding (but what do we really know about this?), he who applied himself with such care and concern to his wife Estelle's first children, did he not suffer greatly by not having a son? Whether or not he suffered, in any event, the people of the county share this prejudice on the subject of inheritance.

These affirmations and suggestions are all the more striking since paternity (in his works) appears to be dried up and useless, at least as concerns the founding of a line of descendants. All his life, Faulkner seems to have accepted this impotence rather than submit to the legitimate authority of a possessive mother, who nonetheless was, from the beginning, the only one to believe in his talents.

As in any traditional, colonial environment, we are here far from the pioneer woman energy: mothers are frail, sickly, absent, invariably beautiful, and usually abusive.

From Saint-John Perse's *Eloges:*

> *How beautiful your mother was, how pale,*
> *when so tall and so languid, stooping,*
> *she straightened your heavy hat of straw or of sun,*
> *lined with a double seguine leaf.*

White aunts and grandmothers who had no children, or who had stopped having them, exemplify risk and determination. Beneath a stupid appearance, Mohatala (Ikkemotubbe's mother) is a fascinatingly baroque character, full of energy and secrets.

Why bring up notions of the epic and the tragic when studying Faulkner and his novels? The place (subject and object) where these works are situated is a community. To begin with, all of the personal adventures—the novels—based there will shed light on this place. Not only is the community a setting and framework for adventure and torment; it is also a wager, both possible and impossible, for a humanization where this torment is spread.

Legitimacy, the drama of its depletion, and the path of its restoration are the first principles of traditional tragic theater. This is because, in Western cultures, legitimacy guides the individual's destiny and is the indistinct path linking a community to a Genesis, establishing it in its sovereign right.

On the order of absolutes, the worst of all possible calamities would be for this legitimacy (when embodied in a family line) to fracture, either through a corruption of the line of descent or by an intruder's appropriation of it as a son or inheritor. Loss of legitimacy leads to the most fundamental catastrophes: the devastation of a city or rot in a kingdom. On the other hand, the definitive punishment for those who possess legitimacy, once they have failed, is an assault upon their descendants (that is, their male children, especially the firstborn).

Dissolution and the resolution of dissolution, as well as the loss and recovery of legitimacy, are constant elements in Shakespearean tragedy: Hamlet secretly resents not being the legitimate heir to the throne of Denmark; Macbeth is compelled by a crazy dream of legitimacy that leads to his unstoppable downfall, just as Richard III vainly weaves the plot of his impossible claim; Brutus and Cassius are motivated by Julius Caesar's illegitimacy; Othello introduces a dissident element (miscegenation) into the idea of legitimacy; both Capulets and Montagues have taken part in the two legitimate and violently incompatible orders; King Lear's daughters plan to *kill* legitimacy; etc. Just as in Greek tragedy, harmony is most often restored only after the death (the sacrifice) of the hero, usurper or not.

In Sophocles's *Oedipus*—a foundational example of the tragedy of legitimacy—the hero is at once the usurper, through whom dissolution arrives, and the only one to possess legitimacy. But he destroys this legitimacy while corrupting it. This is why Oedipus is an absolute, requiring neither explanation nor commentary. He is self-sufficient: at once criminal, victim, judge, and sacrificer. It is impossible to explain or comment upon the unsayable: the legitimate heir to the kingdom destroys his own legitimacy through parricidal murder and incestuous coupling, leaving behind a trail of pestilence and desolation.

More significantly than any appropriation, incest is the absolute abandonment of legitimacy. From Oedipus's incestuous act, the only one ever to have been realized, one can say that incest is the ultimate crime. The fomenters of legitimacy who later stirred up tragic theater are prey not to incest, but to its temptation. Usurpers, or those placed by destiny in a situation they would rather not maintain, do not go so far as to commit incest themselves. They project the distress they feel for not being in their proper place onto the incestuous temptation.

They fight against the unbearable unease of illegitimacy by trying to defy the fundamental laws of legitimacy.

Legitimacy stands as the absolute opposite of incestuous deeds; incest is the absolute sin that can lay waste to legitimacy. This holds true at least in cultures where a community's solidity, serene or tormented, is measured against a Genesis and the certitudes obtained from this irrefutable source. Since an uninterrupted flow of bloodlines passing from one generation to the next is the sole guarantee of such a union, we can understand that a violent interruption in legitimacy results in (first of all, through incest) a disaffiliation.

A deviation of this sort would not be considered irreparable in the context of other cultures in the world, where legitimacy (and, consequently, this notion of bloodlines as a system and a point of reference) does not have such weight as an absolute. (It is astounding to note, however, the great number of daughters and stepdaughters of the Caribbean countryside, often in preadolescence, who are raped by their fathers or stepfathers, a phenomenon which may be linked to the destructive living conditions of poverty, particularly in the outlying rural areas.) In any event, in composite societies, or in those with very large families, disaffiliation does not directly generate drama and disequilibrium for the community. Perhaps this is what is meant when it is said that Oedipus—the myth and the complex—is not universal.

One Shakespearean hero possesses legitimacy: Prospero, in *The Tempest*. His deposition from the throne of Milan, however, does not lead to catastrophe for the community. From the very beginning, his appropriating brother is presented as a plunderer with a rather agreeable personality, ready to ask for the Duke's forgiveness.

In fact, the purpose of *The Tempest* is to extend Prospero's "Milanese" (Western) legitimacy to the ends of the earth, to the world-totality. It is a prophetic vision of colonial behavior. *The Tempest* is not a tragedy; it does not aim to resolve dissolution, does not require a victimized hero (the savage Caliban is considered merely the ungrateful and rebellious object of Prospero's kindliness), and hardly touches upon the question of descendants (through the presence of Prospero's daughter—he does not have a son).

What is illustrated in the play is the uniqueness of deeds and knowledge: he who masters the science of the four elements can legitimately command the universe he discovers. It is not without relevance that the Globe Theatre building, which Shakespeare designed and where his company performed, reproduced the circular shape of the world in such a symbolic manner.

In Faulkner, the epic and the tragic confront their own impossibilities; that is the source of their greatness and novelty. They signify that resolving dissolution is inconceivable, here where birthright is no guarantee against usurpation or perversion. Despite the frenzied misfortune of the Sartorises, Compsons, and Sutpens—all these lineages placidly or furiously damned—legitimacy cannot reform itself. On the contrary, distress spreads through the entire country. The entire South is not only the catastrophic victim of the breakup of legitimacy but also the symbolic place—the very dynasty—where this legitimacy is broken.

The South is the kingdom of Denmark; at the same time, the Fortinbras family is the legitimate family and Hamlet's family the usurpers. Here, Faulkner's *The Hamlet* is truly and completely *the* Hamlet. This is why one victimized hero (Oedipus or Hamlet) would not be enough: an entire, suffering lineage of people is necessary, an entire race. In *Requiem for a Nun*, Nancy Mannigoe is not simply a person; she is the Black enigma. If this is not what she was, this is what she deserved to be. Given the enormity of her efforts, it is not surprising that she tries to attack Temple Stevens, through her children (descendants), in or-

der to reclaim herself. In the Deep South, disaffiliation strikes everywhere, anathema does not breathe only on the family of the prince.

There is no more virtue in bloodlines; tragedy does not resolve dissolution.

These works do not speak in the manner of *The Tempest*; for Faulkner, legitimacy, knowledge, and power cannot be reconciled or even
conceived together in the "postage stamp" that is Yoknapatawpha or
in the world as a whole, the world-totality. Both on the Plantation
and in the world developed around it, something's rotten in the act of
appropriation and colonization, as long as one persists in slavery and
its unpardonable derivative, miscegenation (founded on rape). Faulkner never says this (he shouts it out indistinctly every so often) because
he suffers in his flesh (his South) from truly thinking in this way.

Faulkner takes the infinite openness of the epic and the tragic (and
their ultimate failure, but a failure that completely renews them) and
makes the fullest effort since Nietzsche to "rethink" them: these ideas
of Being, identity, and belonging upon which Western ontology had
been based for centuries. Here we find them not exposed, but hidden
behind and within a throng of people who strike our attention, each
in his or her individuality, before convincing us of their community.
From the throng, I would like to return to the borderline case of Colonel Sutpen, and to incest.

The temptation of sibling incest (feverish and contained between Caddy
and Quentin Compson, tragic and glaring between Henry and Judith
Sutpen, or friendly and diffuse between Narcissa and Horace Benbow, although, in *Sartoris*, Benbow is said to observe his sister, "darting from beneath his hidden face covert, ceaseless glances, quick and darting,
all-embracing as those of an animal") accompanies and sanctions disaffiliation in the same way that twins because of their problematic affec-

tion for each other represent the weakening of the bloodline. To be convinced of this argument, we need only try to clear up the muddle of the history of the Bayard and John Sartorises. That would be as complicated as reconstructing the genealogy of the McCaslin family tree—the Blacks and the Whites, and the Carothers and Edmonds McCaslins. Incest between brother and sister wears the bloodline thin, just as the inextricability of the extended family kills off the family line. Charles Bon (Sutpen's first son) may understand this: perhaps he tries to marry his half sister Judith precisely to get revenge for the repudiation he has suffered, and to smother Sutpen's dynastic dream through incest. Once again, this is an example of what Faulkner is capable of hiding, or of what he reveals only at the last possible moment.

Twins have a different meaning here than they do in African belief.

(Another of Faulkner's tendencies is his almost instinctive association and use of African customs and models: the extended family, the difficult-to-measure network of "family relations," the mystique of twins, the supposedly magical knowledge of animals—especially dogs and horses—and the important roles of uncles.

Compare, for example, this passage from Saint-John Perse's *Eloges*:

> ". . . So the Uncles were speaking to my mother in a low voice. They had tied their horses up at the door. And the House remained alive under the feathered trees."

The uncles, the mother, the house: rudiments of endurance in the colonial world. [We cannot forget the horse.] African tradition asserts its inextricability, as well as its troubling and passive fertility, in the rigid patriclan. The "exchange" is there; and the trace of Africa has been extended.)

·   ·   ·

In Faulkner, contrary to African belief, the father of twins is not a superman. Real or symbolic twins demonstrate destiny's hesitation before the future of a family line. On the very day of their father's death, Uncle Buck and Uncle Buddy leave the family home, where they keep their slaves, to go live in seclusion in a log cabin. In Faulkner's world, it is as though fate decides that the loser wins, in order to designate which of the two was "responsible" for their downfall. John or Bayard? One of the Sartoris twins will always go the way of darkness. Through twins, legitimacy wanders into damnation and dares show its impossibility. Bloodlines are lost in the shifting sands; the temptation of incest brings this impossibility full circle, back to the place where it will settle. In this case, every fraternal relation is troubled; and twins of any kind are cursed.

Is there no instance of "consummated" incest in the Faulknerian universe? I was struck by some information on Milly in the "Chronology" and "Genealogy" following the text of *Absalom, Absalom!* Milly's daughter so disappointed old Sutpen, the sire, that he would not even let mother and daughter into his stable. The same day, Wash Jones killed Colonel Sutpen with a single stroke of his scythe, then slit the throats of his own granddaughter and just-born great-granddaughter, before being killed by the neighbors and the sheriff (the Spanish major), who had come to see what was going on. Here are Faulkner's words:

In the Chronology:

1850 Wash Jones moves into abandoned fishing camp on Sutpen's plantation, with his daughter.
1853 Milly Jones born to Wash Jones' daughter.
. . .
1867 Sutpen takes up with Milly Jones.
1869 Milly's child is born. Wash Jones kills Sutpen.

And in the Genealogy:

MELICENT JONES.
Daughter of Wash Jones. Date of birth unknown. Rumored to have died in
a Memphis brothel.
MILLY JONES.
Daughter of Melicent Jones. Born 1853. Died, Sutpen's Hundred, 1869.
UNNAMED INFANT.
Daughter of Thomas Sutpen and Milly Jones. Born, died, Sutpen's Hundred,
same day, 1869.

This information names Milly as the daughter of the daughter of
Wash Jones. Then, in the Genealogy, she is named as Melicent Jones's
daughter. This information is too impartial not to catch our attention.
There is no reference to Milly's father, whoever he was. Nor does the
novel say anything about this father, or about Melicent, for that matter.
Are Milly and Melicent characters too insignificant for the text to
focus on them? Nonetheless, they are mentioned in the Chronology
and Genealogy. And Milly, the last chance for a male descendant for
the aging Sutpen, is not just anybody.

What if Faulkner, who hides as much as he dares to reveal, had
hidden the fact—as Sutpen would have been able to hide it from the
whole country, from everyone, including Wash Jones—that Sutpen
was Milly's father, who, in his madness, decided to trust only his own
bloodline to get the male heir he longed for? From his beginnings in
Haiti as a victim of corrupted "mixed blood," Sutpen ended up in
incest, both executioner and victim, a man who stumbles first upon
the incessant presence of Blacks, then upon the inherent curse in his
family bloodline. As Oedipus consumed and depleted his legitimacy
by conceiving a child with his own mother, Sutpen consummated his
inability to beget an heir by seducing his very own daughter. This is
an amazing assumption (one of the extremes to which reading Faulkner
will lead you) but one that sits well with Sutpen's crazy stubbornness,
the probable consequence of which—even if it is never known, if it is

hidden from everyone including Milly herself but not from Melicent nor, on the final day, from old Wash Jones (we therefore understand why his fury is unleashed merely by overhearing Sutpen refuse to let Milly use the rude shelter of the stable)—is no less a final, exorbitant commentary upon the county's abandon.

(Already knowing that Clytie is Sutpen's daughter by a Black slave woman, I suddenly discover in one of the "strokes of consciousness" in *Absalom, Absalom!* that Quentin Compson's grandfather—Quentin, who tells this to his son, who tells it to his son, Quentin—had believed for some time that Bon's child, brought to Sutpen's Hundred by his octoroon mother, "might be Clytie's, got by its father on the body of his own daughter"! It was not unreasonable to find Sutpen capable of this incestuous act, but perhaps Faulkner alludes to it only to hide and yet point to the true act, if it can be called that. The difference is that Clytie, despite appearances, is Black and Milly is White. Like Jason Compson, Sutpen has had his fill with niggers, even if he had begotten them; this is how they differ.)

Ferociously possessed, he does not know, nor does he want to know, that incest is an absolute, irrevocable denial of legitimacy; thus, once incest has been "consummated," although it is different from Oedipus's, it must lead to the same cataclysmic consequences, both immediate (death of all the protagonists) and deferred (the final incineration of the Mansion).

It is worth returning to the original splendor of the Big Woods. Every year, hunters ritually gather in buggy and surrey, with the most important men on horseback. All of them are utterly devoted to old Ben, the fundamental Bear. They all understand it will never be a question of killing him (none of them dares harbor the thought when the dead bear is lying at their feet), the way they kill deer, opossum, and other small game. At most, they hope to follow his tracks, by locating his usually indistinguishable path in the Big Woods, by picking up the noises he makes as he goes through the Woods, or the scent he leaves behind.

Old Ben represents the original situation's resistance to aggression (when time and place were possible and the absolute still conceivable). It is as though the time and space of the hunt are a suspension of human history, a refusal of the inevitable cascade of time over the generations.

In "The Bear," the hunters have no races. McCaslin Edmonds and General Compson do not give up their prerogatives during the hunt for the primordial beast whose trace is about all they can hope to find; but they do not feel superior to Sam Fathers, or even different from him. Once a year the racial divide crumbles; just as it does throughout the southern parts of the Americas, especially in the Caribbean and Brazil, where the Plantation fences and other racial barriers are flung open during carnival season. Hunting season is the wilderness's carnival, its primordial truth.

By vocation, hunters have no wives, or simply exclude them from their lives during the hunt. We recall their willingness to tell misogynist stories. This is a strange a priori for Faulkner: in such a situation, blood ties carry absolutely no virtues for preservation, no saving pardons, nor any power of instruction unless it be that of codifying social relations. Or unless—and most often due to the efforts of Black mammies—these blood ties are used to instill the values of the strict, quasi-Puritan ideal, in which compassion plays such a great role. Neither ancestors nor descendants matter to a life that is an essential search for truth, or at least an attempt to get closer to its secrets. The hunter is alone on the trail. This is the price of initiation. Individuality accepts no weaknesses. Unlike the American dream, it doesn't help one's social standing. It is not the "You can do it!" or the "Just do it!" of this success. One could say it is a bitter contentment with defeat. Individuality is absolute.

These hunters live outside reality. When they enter the wilderness, they leave behind the world of the miserable people who desperately chase after profits, devastate forests, and are greedy to inherit. What are they looking for when they go hunting? Hunting all his life, what was Ike McCaslin looking for, giving up his property, his family, and his whole, rather appealing social life? What are they looking for except (albeit in vain) to get back to an undifferentiated time when Nature, fauna and flora, and all of humanity were free from the contagions that have since corrupted them: slashing and burning, ownership, inheritance, and dealing in race. Yes, it is all in vain because the primal innocence the hunter seeks could never give him a definitive answer to the torments he endures but only vaguely senses. He knows he will never have the answer, just as he knows his bullet will never hit old Ben, the immemorial Bear. His greatness will be to try anyway; his pride comes from steadfast endurance, despite failure.

We can situate Faulkner in this doubled place. On the one hand, there is the apparent (what surrounds and threatens the wilderness), a daily routine regulating lives, where all one needs is to suffer patiently, endure without lamentation, and accept with humility; this is the absolute real, marked by the inevitable degradation of "progress." On the other hand, there is the marginal (which you enter only through initiation into the wilderness of the unnamed), where there is a secret logic of an inaccessible life, a truly unshakable truth, and a diversion from things. What is unveiled is a question that is not a question, ordering every life yet postponing it indefinitely.

Essentially, it comes down to this. To explore this double field—the flat reality that flaunts and exhibits its monsters, and the realm of primal truth that, if its mysteries can be fathomed, should finally allow a weighing of reality's monstrosity—Faulkner invented very naturally a language that does both *at the same time*. It describes and *at the same time* seeks to say what cannot be said through description yet fully signifies (establishes through disclosed reason) what is described. The pitch and fluctuations in Faulkner's writing come from the fact that also, *at the same time*, it constantly reminds you that this full disclosure is impossible.

Faulkner's writing originates from these three elements: a hidden truth (prior and primordial, such as the impossibility of the county being well rooted, its illegitimacy) that regulates the description of the real; a visionary description (determined by intuition and premonitions of primal truth); and the disturbed assurance that the secret of this truth will never be revealed.

These three elements, or three modes—the hidden, the described, and the inexpressible—are interwoven throughout a book (*Absalom, Absalom!*, for example), just as they are within a chapter and sometimes in a single sentence, carrying the reader to a vertiginous unknown, which is the most precise manner of approaching what can be known. This vertigo is that much more reeling because Faulkner's writing is, *at the same time*, wandering and dense, swinging and transported, straight to the point and suspended. This is what I call deferred writing. Others have called it oblique writing. Referring to the expository technique and the dialogues in *Requiem for a Nun*, Albert Camus called it breathless writing.

Through successive waves of a single current, the deferral of this writing (its obliqueness, its breathlessness) stems from a presupposition, which we never really reach. There are other, famous examples of presupposition. For Joyce's *Ulysses*, for example, there was Homer's *Odyssey*; Bloom's wandering in Dublin repeats that of Odysseus through the Mediterranean (Dublin whorehouses and Circe's cave, etc.). But Joyce's writing tends neither to "reveal" nor to reproduce Ulysses's itinerary; Bloom is not Ulysses. Here the use of presupposition is an attempt to uncover the disturbed, uncertain, unconscious, or hidden element of a particular human fate.

In Faulkner's works, the narration's presupposition—the illegitimate foundation of the South—is never formally expressed. The writer's task is to reveal this presupposition while revealing its painful parallels in the present and also making it clear that the true revelation will be put off indefinitely.

.   .   .

(When he talks about *Absalom, Absalom!*, for example, it is not the Old Testament story but rather the calamity of bloodlines that is the presupposition, a reference surely accentuated by the biblical reference and tone; this is noted but is never openly recognized in the text.)

The incomparable suspense in Faulkner's writing denies the foundational power of the Story. By this very denial, it establishes another dimension, a poetics that is not narrative but creates a relationship between what is narrated and what is unsayable. When Faulkner says he is "a failed poet," we understand he is aware of having already explored the other dimension where writing—hesitant, swelling, and unfurling over itself—raises, in turn, impossible poetic encounters: between the ambiguous and the obvious; between the unknown and cursed knowledge; between memory and doubt; between the times when everything goes smoothly and the times that shatter you into chaos; between the death that grants mercy and the death that we savagely defy.

It has been suggested that *The Sound and the Fury* and *Absalom, Absalom!* are not only chronicles of Yoknapatawpha County (and consequently of the entire South) but metafictions, reflecting upon their own form, their techniques of construction, and so forth. Faulkner undoubtedly contributed to this idea when he claimed, as he liked to do, that he had "dared," that he had created something new, etc. He clearly liked to present himself as a technician-magician of literature.

Such a view, even in a minor way, separates form from the principal subject or intention of his books. In fact, these novels—we can add *As I Lay Dying*—are not more technically revolutionary than *Light in August* or *Intruder in the Dust* or any of Faulkner's other books. The works as a whole are revolutionary; that is, they fulfill their own organic needs not derived from any literary precedent, even though we know that Faulkner was versed in the canon of Western literature. He was proud of being an autodidact, and a farmer. Perhaps he felt he had escaped his inheritance as a "gentleman."

If these three novels are striking in their form, it is because they appeared at a moment in his career when he felt he had to return to his presupposition, but could not do so in a linear narrative. So he had to break through this obstruction. Faulkner exulted in the feeling that he had done so, speaking of "ecstasy" and "anticipated surprise."

Indeed, these three novels in particular attract our attention because they mark the point where Faulkner goes to the crux of the question, knowing he must return to the realm of the uncertain, spread the contamination, and fling the floodgates wide open.

Intruder in the Dust, for example, can only move forward through a simple and confused obscurity stemming from a single force (the already mentioned Lucas Beauchamp: "a damned highnosed impudent Negro who even if he wasn't a murderer had been about to get if not about what he deserved at least exactly what he had spent the sixty-odd years of his life asking for"—that is, his lynching). This obscurity seems rudimentary only if this novel is separated from the others, which would be like trying to separate *Swann's Way* (and Odette's banality) from the architectural whole of Proust's *In Search of Lost Time*.

Critics seem to bend over backward in their desperate efforts to classify Faulkner's short stories as "successful," "imperfect," or "failures." But Faulkner did not give a damn about his short stories; they served him as tools for tilling, weeding, and scavenging ideas. (But the short stories were also his bread and butter; he had no choice about that.) In the sense that they are sketches or studies for later work, the short stories are just as "revolutionary" as *The Sound and the Fury* and lead to as much vertigo as *Absalom, Absalom!*

Because the presupposition of the county will always be percolating beneath the real that is apparent, Faulkner's writing takes on the risk of revelation rather than simply being an exposé, a presentation, an analysis, a description, or a story.

Because this presupposition will never be known, the writing juggles a series of technical approaches, none of which reaches a conclusion and all of which spin into vertigo.

Because this unknown but endured presupposition is ardently desir-able as a known (like a state of ecumenical, but unattainable, equilib-rium), each of these approaches implies its opposite. What is seen and described infers the underlying and invisible.

What is hidden makes us feel what is disclosed or revealed all the more strongly. In Faulkner's work, it is what "we don't understand" that helps us approach the dark and luminous mass of what we think we have understood.

One precaution that Faulkner does take (whether by intuition or mas-tery, it is hard to tell) is never to present cause with effect. He disperses. When he stigmatizes greed, as in *Go Down, Moses*, he will not say, "You see, greed has caused us to upset the order of things and this is why we have been defeated." Rather, he cites the destruction of the Big Woods, the perversion of the lands and nature, and the loss of the immemorial, and through a character like Old Ike McCaslin, in abusive language that is far from "progressive" or even pleasant.

When he develops what we can assume are his own views about slavery and racism (in *Light in August*), they seem to be the causes of the curse placed upon Joanna Burden and Joe Christmas. Never will he say, in one breath, "You see, we lived off the suffering of an entire race of people, we reduced it to slavery and have ignominiously profited from its labors; that's why we lost the war and were defeated, much more by ourselves than by the Yankees."

He disperses the different elements of the presupposition, taking care never to link them directly to even a trace of ideology or moralizing. He makes hints, not acts of faith. As the critic René-Noël Raimbaut explains: "He makes no effort to draw out the causes; he records the effects. Once his characters have been invented (that is, re-created after a real-life model), severed from him and let loose into the scene, they become free and independent." I would add that Faulkner does "draw out the causes," but he does so by hiding them (and first of all from himself). This is what determines the structure of deferral in his writing. I repeat: if his works had explicitly linked cause (the presupposition of the county's damnation) with effect (the damnation of particular residents of the county), they would have been didactic—and so not nearly as powerful.

Whether or not they are independent and free to believe in this damnation, the people in the county follow their only true obsession: never to adhere to any kind of norm. They will fight to the death for their beliefs, but they refuse to accept dogmas. Ultimately, this is the wellspring of their community: they reject unicity.

The writing is inseparable from this freedom. It dissociates cause and effect, delays revelation, diffracts the perception of the real. When Faulkner does occasionally "speak" of the presupposition, he does not indicate its path but merely its trail. Revelation and contamination follow the circuit of these uncertain but adamant traces. We have seen how, each time he spreads the tragic curse to the entire county (the madness of individuals, the dauntless countryside, and the unpredictability of both wild and domesticated animals), he takes care never to state the reason why.

Writing techniques that allow for this sort of gradual revelation are found especially in the books where the presupposition floats imposingly on the horizon. Faulkner's style is much more "direct" in his short stories and clearly "flat" in the Snopes trilogy; it is as though, in these tales of the triumph of mediocrity, it was no longer important to question damned suffering—as though everything was settling into a peaceful dullness that was a kind of liberation.

In this sense, the Snopeses could paradoxically appear as the "solution," the resolution of the dissolute circumstances of the county; we see Jason Compson join in their venture, and, in a sour, mediocre way, become one of them. Contrary to what I said earlier, the Snopeses have no need of revelation or techniques of deferred writing. Their crooked bookkeeping is good enough for them. We must agree with this. Great literature devises and orders its own limits.

In one very violent instance, Faulkner lets the presupposition explode. One of the McCaslins asks an Arkansas Black, " 'Dont you see?' he cried. 'Dont you see? This whole land, the whole South, is cursed, and all of us who derive from it, whom it ever suckled, white and black both, lie under the curse? Granted that my people brought the curse onto the land . . .' " But right away this same McCaslin begins to quarrel, asking for time. He thinks the Northern nigger blabbers on about freedom, "measured and sonorous imbecility of the boundless folly and the baseless hope."

"Delta Autumn," the second-to-last story in Go Down, Moses, has the same function in the collection as "An Odor of Verbena," the last story in The Unvanquished. Each mixes two stories: in the one, the initiation of young Ike, and his old age; in the other, the initiation into violence of young Bayard Sartoris. We can sense a tragic impossibility here, the seemingly irremediable languor of solitude. The Sartorises will live to see their own descendants (the parade of indestructible grandfathers and crazy young men that cannot be struck down), and Carothers McCaslin's children will be multiplied through the Edmonds branch; but in both stories, you can feel a certain consensual decline, as at the end of a bloodline.

What accompanies this end? The two impossibilities: incest and the mixing of blood. For Bayard, the end is a matter of giving up his family's violence and perhaps love or happiness as well, by giving up incest. For Ike McCaslin, the end is the violent and disgusted rejection of miscegenation.

•   •   •

A pretty young woman comes to visit Ike McCaslin, who is practically bedridden in the old shack he refuses to consider his own property. She turns out to be the great-grandniece of their common ancestor, Carothers McCaslin. She had loved young Edmonds, her third or fourth cousin, and is pregnant by him. Knowing the purpose of the visit, Edmonds came to see Uncle Ike and left for him (or rather had a Black servant give him) an envelope stuffed with banknotes, asking him to give them to the young woman, emphasizing the single message, "No." What he perhaps already knows is that Ike, during his impassioned conversation with his young visitor, will discover, with shock and repulsion ("You did the laundry?. . . . This means that . . ."), that she is a Black woman and, if she descends from the Carothers branch, it is through the Black branch of the family. Here we find an echo of the main argument in *Absalom, Absalom!*: while an incestuous relationship is conceivable (besides, in this instance the cousin kinship is rather distant), racial mixing is absolutely not.

Bayard Sartoris, having suffered the most absolute forms of violence during and after the Civil War, renounces violence in an even more violent manner, confronting alone and unarmed his father's murderer, Colonel John Sartoris, thus ending a long series of assassinations that were the basis of family tradition. The day before these events transpire, he also lets himself be kissed by Drusilla, the Colonel's bold, young, new wife, who had fought by his side "like a man" during the war. Incestuous temptation is there. Bayard will confess his behavior to his father, who doesn't care since death is pressing down on him. Drusilla (at once repentant, distressed by this death, and outraged that Bayard has renounced his chance to avenge his father) leaves the Sartorises' home. All that is left for Bayard is the odor of the verbena sprigs she used to decorate her hair and scatter in her bed, filling the house with their fragrance. The odor of verbena sweetens the temptation of incest (when they kiss), as well as the renunciation of incest (and violence). When Bayard finds himself alone with Aunt Jenny and Louvinia in the house, he sees, through the half-open door to Drusilla's room ("that unmistakable way in which an open door stands open when nobody lives in the room any more"), a single sprig of verbena on the pillow, its odor "filling the room, the dusk, the evening."

In the dusk of this story of violence and swiftly repressed love, the odor of verbena predominates over that of magnolia, like a secret persuasion. A plant that gives off its scent so powerfully, verbena is nonetheless a very intimate, household herb. You can drink in its fragrance. It also operates on the unconscious level. The magnolia embodies the outward splendor of the Plantation: it hangs over balconies and decorates the grove of all the great gardens.

Verbena and magnolias were not the only flowers on the Plantation. Inadmissible secrets take root in these mansions. Retarded or crazy children whom one would never dare expose to public view were sometimes hidden away in storerooms. This is what Jason allowed to happen with his brother Benjy Compson.

Narcissa, widow of the last Bayard Sartoris, confesses to old Miss Jenny (Virginia) that she went to Memphis to become a federal agent's prostitute (it is hardly innocuous that the novel notes he is a Jew) in order to get back the scandalous letters sent to her anonymously. She could not bear the thought that someday someone else might read them. Sitting before her open window, Miss Jenny cuts her off twice, asking haughtily, "Can you smell? . . . the jasmine."

Long ago Miss Jenny brought seeds from Carolina to Mississippi and, like a pagan priestess, spent frigid nights protecting her young seedlings from freezing with little fires of paper and candles.

Jasmine can rival magnolias in splendor. Its decorative flowers give off a persistent and presumptuous fragrance. "Some bush or shrub starred with white bloom—jasmine, spiraea, honeysuckle, perhaps myriad scentless unpickable Cherokee roses." In the Caribbean, there are many well-formed flowers that bloom in out-of-the-way places. In Martinique, on both sides of the Route de la Tracée (the Trace the runaways made), there are flowers that last a long time but give off no odor: arums, cannas, *rois-des-rois*, and porcelain roses.

Magnolia and jasmine are not bound to the troubled resignation of the big House residents, nor do they share (or reveal) its secret, or lessen its torments with their fragrance.

At the end of *Sartoris*, Narcissa Benbow Sartoris seems utterly nonchalant about those anonymous letters—besides, she had succeeded in guessing the identity of their author. Whereas in the short story "There Was a Queen" she is greatly affected by them. Such variations, such "contradictions," indicate disturbances in the county.

Plants and flowers—petunias, lilacs, zinnias, begonias, daturas—are like useless goddesses, solemn and shapely. Even flowers that, unlike these, do not have feminine names in French—*un delphinium*, for example—can be intimidating.

Every one of these flowers is unaware of the disturbance, the disequilibrium of this place.

None of them give rise to an obsession—as do wisteria, honeysuckle, or verbena—only to appease it afterward.

They live outside the system, on the other side of the double condition (the Great Mansions and outlying shacks). They are like the Caribbean *à-tout-maux*, a plant that heals everything, like the leafy, low-growing vine that spreads out in great beds like a calm sea, and like the *bois-campêche*, the logwood that leaves its scratch marks on children's legs. They are wild or domesticated, sacred or common, planted next to little houses or wildly growing throughout the West Indian savannas. I have taken the garden flower, the jasmine or magnolia, to symbolize everything, privileging appearance over reality and external blossom over internal truth.

·   ·   ·

But beauty is not splendiferous truth; truth is reticent, hidden, and deferred. If Cherokee roses cannot be picked, there are others that make great tea. House plants (like favorite servants, slaves that are far too faithful) are neither hardy "hoe" plants (like Blacks who toil for their lives in cotton or sugarcane) nor proud garden plants (like goddess-flowers that indulge the imagination). They are plants of personal torment and hidden deprivations.

Other plants like honeysuckle (identified with Quentin), wisteria (which so charmed his father, Mr. Compson), and verbena (for Bayard Sartoris) leave a vague aroma of everything that could have happened and everything that was renounced.

In the receiving rooms of the great homes, decorated in eclectic simulated European splendor, or under the torpid shade of the verandas, the odor of verbena allays curses and prolongs melancholy. Outside, "in the heat of the night," magnolias (or jasmine) smolder in secret.

5

THE REAL—THE DEFERRED

"They were Protestants and Democrats and prolific; there was not one Negro landowner in the entire section." Whether good or bad, farmers or seekers, crazy or sane, sheriffs or killers, these "ordinary" White folk of the county are all cut from the same cloth. They all show the same fundamental stubbornness, implacable and unmoving. They do not care about money, even when they kill to get it; they are indifferent to etiquette or respect. They live in the country in rude, run-down shacks that they defend with their rifles against all comers. In town, they do their best socializing in front of the prison or court-house where those who take an interest in public affairs go to see an accused man condemned, "to look quietly at the cold embers of a lynching," to hear a business dispute, or to watch a Snopes cast his spell on a victim. They gather on the grocery steps or near the horse dealer's stalls or within earshot of the barber (for the idle thrive on gossip). Except when redemption or damnation is involved, meetings at the bordello don't count.

Each one seeks a hidden, fierce, and inexhaustible goal; the point of the story is to find it. They are not complex and troubled people like the great Compsons and Sartorises, whose fixed ideas they share nevertheless. Yes, it is as though the land itself had molded them all out of the same mud, before differentiating them—the tribunes fallen from aristocracy and the weary commoners.

In Faulkner, "psychological" variety does not derive from his knack for plumbing the hearts and minds of the characters or from his eyes for finding diversity but from his own genius and his determination simply "to see" these people as no one else sees them, and to describe them in a ceaselessly fresh way as the representatives of one and the same species: the relentless.

This is the source of the continuity between the novels with character "types" (great families gone to seed, poor White eccentrics, immutable Blacks) and the short stories, in particular those in *Knight's Gambit*, that multiply these "ordinary" people through the space and time of the county. There are no stereotypes here. The future or rather the destiny of the land itself, hostage to fate and site of the impossible, mobilizes all the inhabitants in the same attitude. I have already mentioned "the storyteller's mission, communicating the sense and passion of the impossible."

This is the place where Faulkner encounters those about whom he speaks.

He is fascinated by this aspect of existence and the life of the mind. Not to tempt the impossible would be his most serious and easily prompted complaint against a writer. Without fanfare, he levels this accusation at Hemingway, fomenting their secret and tormented rivalry. He charges Hemingway with not daring enough as a writer and of being a "literary technician," for while Faulkner takes great pleasure in technique he also believes that behind or outside or throughout every literary project there is an unattainable that the writer should look squarely in the face. He finds no such concern in Hemingway's work. (Especially at the beginning of his career, when he still was not sure of his own project, Faulkner had time to spend in a provocative appreciation of other writers. Thus we read this unusual remark in

Soldier's Pay: "Jones grew up in a Catholic orphanage, but like Henry James, he attained verisimilitude by means of tediousness.")

There are the things that are possible, that must be done if we are to continue to live, to please those we love, to earn the approval of our peers, to help those in need. And there is the impossible, when we are left to stand alone—already knowing that we can encompass nothing, or so little, of what pulsates all around us, but knowing too that we must at least try.

What would it mean for Faulkner to do the impossible in literature? Let us hazard that it would be this: to speak the impossible of the South without having to say it, to create a literature that patiently confronts everything inexpressible in this impossible, and perhaps to effect change through the sheer force of this literature. That, in my opinion, is what he achieved—except on the last point, for if he undoubtedly brought about change, it was far away from his country.

This country stands for him as the embodiment of suffering, as Russia did for Dostoevsky and the land of the Zulus for Thomas Mofolo, who chronicled the epic of the emperor Chaka. Its anguish does not arise from the oppressed but from the usurpers, the illegitimate people who claim legitimacy. The misfortune of appropriation does not diminish the anguish in any way or redeem the illegitimacy. He has to elucidate this mysterious damnation that originates in self and arises out of one's own fault. Knowledge of it must ever be deferred, while returning to its path without respite, to try to understand, no, to live in suffering, to see how damnation operates and how it might be forgiven. There is only one way to do this: to push into the obscurity of the country, into the place where no one goes.

A country that is a river, a river lived on like a country. Just like the Nile, the Ganges, the Congo, the Yangtze, or the Amazon, the Mississippi mixes myth in its water. The many people who traveled it and

changed its face received the atavistic myth of Amerindian civilizations as a composite heritage. This is easy to say; but it is enough to
take a simple ferry, near St. Francisville, Louisiana, for example, passing prosaically from one bank to the other, surrounded by the pickup
trucks of farmers or the rental cars of tourists, and feel the wind from
who-knows-what past times of suffering, hate and adventure mixing
together on your face with the exhaust from the engine—inexplicable,
certainly conventional, but unstoppable.

Is this kind of convention to be despised? No, because the river tells
you at the same time that everything is different and yet nothing has
changed. As if on its banks and in its midst, there seethed the same
hard and indiscernible substance, patiently persistent, resistant to evolution. Allusive image of a chaos-time when even the idea of a future,
of a logic of transformation, of an energy to move farther ahead, seems
to have been whirling forever.

The river does not follow the rules of linear thought; here, one can
step in the same water twice.

We also admire it when, in a plane, we fly over the landscapes it
crosses, watching as it proceeds not in long loops but in a circularity
that seeks and rediscovers itself, endlessly. It comes and goes in time,
deviating and turning time around, in a stationary drift. An impression
confirmed by the ghostly character of the gas refineries near Baton
Rouge, for example, that do not give any hint of modernity, but, like
a mirror, reflect refurbished relics and illuminated apparitions in the
humid radiance of a Louisiana noon.

Like the Rhine or the Rio Grande, the Mississippi forms a frontier.

That is, it gathers the real from two sides of a fracture that is not
named, and precipitates it into an unknown. A paradox rises all around
this disturbed life of a time in chaos, where yesterday pushes tomorrow,
like an insensate barge in a current stunned by a whirlwind. Chateaubriand imagined and passed through this Meschacébé and saw it with
his emigrant eyes that were already prey to romantic chimera.

The lands that touch (that establish) the Mississippi are not romantic. This mythic wind blows harsh on your face. Too many bales of
cotton, too many screeching wagons, and those crosses burning in a
triangle in front of corpses strung up by the throat. And not only that.
Not only because of crime. It is also because this ponderous weight
seems to cut deeply into something—into the land, into the hills, and
back into the land again. Being part of it, they are uncertain of their
future, always ready to tip over, always on the point of spilling over
into the improbable or the unexpected. Yes, this is a frontier river.

As far as I can tell, Faulkner never devoted any decisive pages to the
river.* Not a single grandiose setting, worthy of this majestic current,
with its desired reflections. Not even in *The Wild Palms*, where one of
the two stories told in counterpoint is called "Old Man River." The
river is not described here as an object, as an artery or a breathtaking
spectacle; it is a character, a living body. It is brimming over, whirling,
breaking the dams; it enters into the torment of the other people in
this story, as if it were part of those who fight against it.

Music, at least the music that is indistinguishable from the river
(gospel, blues, New Orleans jazz), is strongly absent from the Faulknerian place. The novelist did not think of Negroes as musicians. Not
for an instant do we believe that he thought theirs was the music of
savages. (Let us continue the citation from *Intruder in the Dust* that we
interrupted earlier: "And as for Lucas Beauchamp, Sambo, he's a homogeneous man too, except that part of him which is trying to escape
not even into the best of the white race but into the second best—the
cheap shoddy dishonest music, the cheap flash baseless overvalued
money," and so on.) Indeed, on the last page of *Soldier's Pay*, Blacks
saturate the air with their hymns: ". . . the darkness and the heat
thicker, making thicker the imminence of sex after harsh labor along

---

* I am not referring here to the quasi-autobiographical "Mississippi," published in April
1954 in *Holiday* magazine.

the mooned land; and from it welled the crooning submerged passion of the dark race. It was nothing, it was everything." This is a mechanical explanation, didactic, pretentious, and beside the point.

Faulkner, like so many surrealists, simply had no ear for melody, except the symphonies of his own creation.

In the hall at the Schomburg Center for Research in Black Culture in Harlem, the rivers of the world decorate the floor in a network both scholarly and flourishing. The Congo, the Mississippi, the Euphrates, and the Nile occupy the central portion. Around them flow the Ganges, Amazon, Volga, Seine, Latibonit, Coatzacoalcos, Yangtze, and Murrumbidgee rivers. Words from Langston Hughes's poem "I've Known Rivers" are engraved along the sinuous currents: "I bathed in the Euphrates when dawns were young" (in the dawn of all dawns). And the one that interests us here: "I heard the singing of the Mississippi." Hughes's phrasing is similar to the Creole way of saying, *"J'ai entendu le chanter du Mississippi."**

* At the Schomburg Center, respected by everyone in Harlem—a neighborhood that has the reputation of being dangerous—you can look at many priceless documents: for example, a handwritten proclamation by Toussaint L'Ouverture, the original edition of a rare work by Abbé Grégoire entitled *La Littérature des nègres*, and a statistical chart by the Tuskegee Institute on lynchings in the United States from 1900 to 1931, at least those that were officially reported.

You notice, in the roster of the states, that Georgia tops the list (302 lynchings, with a minimum of a dozen reported every year). Mississippi follows with 285. Texas, Louisiana, Florida, Alabama, and Arkansas are next, in descending order. During the same period, there were only eight states and the District of Columbia where no lynchings occurred. Perhaps it is worth pointing them out, relative to that period at least: Connecticut, Maine, Massachusetts, New Hampshire, New Jersey, New York, Rhode Island, and Vermont. It is difficult to say whether this means a lot or not much. New York State was generally thought of as being "free" of slaves, but we know that before the War of Independence, the colony of New York was second only to South Carolina in the number of slaves owned. Slavery was the norm in New York until it was outlawed in 1827. In a short article in the May 22, 1995, issue of *The New York Times*, which some considerate students brought me, along with some other press clippings they thought would interest me, Brent Staples writes in his report that in Manhattan some famous buildings and places, such as Madison Square Gar-

The landscape is never detailed in Faulkner; at most, it is developed in the consciousness of a person, as in that of the young White hero in *Intruder in the Dust*, who walks along "the motionless uprush of the main ridge and the strong constant resinous downflow of the pines where the dogwood looked indeed like nuns now in the long green corridors" and who is literally conscious of the countryside "unfolding beneath him like a map in one slow soundless explosion: to the east ridge on green ridge tumbling away toward Alabama and to the west and south the checkered fields and the woods flowing on into the blue and gauzed horizon beyond which lay at last like a cloud the long wall of the levee and the great River itself flowing not merely from the north but out of the North circumscribing and outland—the umbilicus of America . . ."—and then it is the very layout as well as the signification, not just of the land and the country, but also of its inhabitants and again of its future, however unpredictable, that are briefly scanned and given meaning, from Canada to the farthest South: the being-in-the-world that is the county.

We find this same extension of space and meaning in the landscapes described by Saint-John Perse and Aimé Césaire. Thus we find the following in Césaire's *Notebook of a Return to My Native Land*, regarding Martinique:

"And my unfenced island, its bold flesh upright at the stern of this Polynesia; and right before it, Guadeloupe slit in two at the dorsal line, and quite as miserable as ourselves; Haiti, where Négritude stood up for the first time and swore by its humanity; and the droll little tail of Florida where a Negro is being lynched, and Africa caterpillaring gigantically up to the Spanish foot of Europe, its nakedness where death cuts a wide swath."

---

den, Washington Square Park, the New York Public Library, the Waldorf-Astoria, City Hall Park, and the new General Services Administration building have been built on the cemeteries of Africans and the poor. One was just recently discovered.

"To dig up two thousand graves to build a hotel? To plant trees in a cemetery and call it a park? . . . We didn't hesitate to do that in the eighteenth and nineteenth centuries."

American landscapes are appropriate for such extended riffs. Even when cultivated, they lose nothing of their exorbitance, which has nothing to do with their reach. The swells of the plains; the submerged churnings of the Atlantic into which so many Africans fettered with ball and chain were dumped; the gardens of the Caribbean, terraced on the heights, far from the Plantations, where the foot of one species supports the next; the ups and downs of the ravines; and the perfectly diamond-like little island set as though on the edge of an imminent eruption: everything opens, calling out to the faraway, stirring up winds and cyclones. The inextricable spreads like lava.

The descriptions of such places are never enough in themselves, because the places convey more than their appearance indicates. They reach far out into the distance. Faulkner does not describe, but diffuses the landscape everywhere. I am not certain that there is a single sequence longer than twenty lines that solely depicts the landscape and can be pulled from the whole like a decoration.*

"A great primitive, faithful servant of old myths." So Maurice-Edgar Coindreau refers to him in his preface to the French edition of *The Wild Palms*. Much more than on the landscape, he concentrates on life tormented by the elements: the air and wind and furious cyclones, the water and rain and uprooting floods, the earth and shifting sands and chasms that swallow, fire and flame, and their disturbing effects upon human beings: through these primordial bonds of which one can speak only with the language of the obscure. The primitive element can meet the human only in exasperation. One does not connect to the ancient blazes, to the most abyssal communications, in calm and placidity.

---

* A careful reader somewhere may catch me up on this statement, confronting me with my errors and blind spots. Perhaps he or she will show me whole pages of description that I will read with pleasure. Faulkner can never be read in entirety; it is a pleasure to discover some new fragment of his text, because we know that even a fragment is a cutting taking its root from the rest.

•   •   •

The Mississippi is ubiquitous in the work, in the backcountry, in a blurred and fading view of a wagon, in a rain that you can see but that does not fall; there is an imperceptible humidity under every skin— just as the minor music of misfortune is present everywhere.

This is how Faulkner reaches the most obscure, the "most essential," really the place where no one goes. He does not describe or create generic tableaux.

The landscape is diffused in the text, connected to the people who speak. The rich foliage in the Big Woods is manifest more in the density and profusion of prose in "The Bear" than as a painterly technique. You remember that the Woods, leaning toward Sam Fathers and the young Ike McCaslin, took on the aura of a primordial Mother. The whole book is a wilderness. This way of treating the subject ensures that the landscape truly becomes one—a landscape—a subject and a person, rather than just an acquiescent decor.

Similarly, Faulkner does not dawdle with descriptions of the county's activity as a whole. We might say he surprises people on their holidays, almost free of their daily routines, in the exasperated moments when they literally step out of their lives in order to crazily devote themselves to their survival.

Lucas Beauchamp serves as a serene example when, in "The Fire and the Hearth," he haggles with Roth Edmonds over the nights he will spend seeking buried treasure: " 'You aint got any complaints about the way I farm my land and make my crop, have you? . . . Long as I do that, I'm the one to say about my private business. . . . Besides, I will have to quit hunting every night soon now, to get my cotton picked. Then I'll just hunt Saturday and Sunday night.' Up to now he had been speaking to the ceiling apparently. Now he looked at Edmonds. 'But them two nights is mine. On them two nights I dont farm nobody's land, I dont care who he is that claims to own it.' "

The fury, the quest, the exasperation are present in the day-to-day, outside the realm of work, during quiet moments in the daily bustle. Faulkner does not ignore or underestimate everyday life; his peasants are really peasants, and not conventional characters. His grocers really count every penny, his con artists know how to make a lame horse look like a spirited charger, his Negroes slave away like animals. At the same time, however, they are something else, just like the country, which, under its provincial appearance and restricted by the endless round and regulation of days and nights, is really something else altogether.

This something else is the enigmatic curse, unknown and all-powerful: "[S]ince He had created them, upon this land this South for which He had done so much with woods for game and streams for fish and deep rich soil for seed and lush springs to sprout it and long summers to mature it and serene falls to harvest it and short mild winters for men and animals and saw no hope anywhere."

The file of days and nights is not enough to circumscribe such a reality or the description of the work and the sorrows signifying it. Everyday objects are not absent; on the contrary, as tools and ornaments, they acquire a density of presence that takes them out of the ordinary. In particular, there are the gins, one machine that separates and another that hulls the cotton; they cover the country, rented and dragged from one place to another, establishing the link.

But these objects are eclipsed by the array of desires and obsessions. It is the capacity to be possessed by fixed ideas that preserves the people in the county, keeps them alive and moving. The absolute certainty that one day she'll cross paths with her ex-fiancé again fuels the energy and optimism of Lena Grove, who seems rather passive by nature. Her prospective husband (we know he doesn't exist, at least not as husband material) is like a pole of tranquil desire—

like all the other objects, miraculous or fetishized, useful or fanta-sized, that give a hidden sense to the Faulknerian universe. Some of them are worth citing.

—The quasi-totemic padlock of the small community that would be-come Jefferson (*Requiem for a Nun*). Brought by an intrepid courier from the big city over there in faraway Carolina to these first settle-ments, it becomes a cult object, which, to tell the truth, no one uses. It is monstrously large and heavy. Only the pressure to create a prison and make it look official will convince the inhabitants to hang this object from the latches or bolts on the main prison gate, more as an ornament or an emblematic figure than a guarantee of enclosure.

—The elegant red slippers Issetibbeha brought back from Europe, almost women's shoes ("Red Leaves"). On no occasion could his suc-cessor Moketubbe go without them; hypnotized, he kept them close at hand on the palanquin on which his slaves paraded him. At Issetib-beha's funeral, Moketubbe's feet were forced into these slippers. It was his habit not to talk much, and so he wore them, suffering in silence, until he fainted.

—The set of false teeth that Anse Bundren ceaselessly dreams of having fitted during the pilgrimage that his family desperately takes to escort his wife's coffin across country (*As I Lay Dying*). He puts them on at last when he takes the new wife he has found.

—The outlandish red car (a Jaguar?) that Gavin Stevens receives as a wedding present (*The Town*). He trades it for national defense bonds with his enemy, the banker Flem Snopes. For years, the car remains idle, parked in the garage at the bank, without any batteries or tires, a symbol of both wealth and ineptitude.

—The steamboat that went aground on a riverbank, and that Doom makes his people drag across the wilderness for so many hellish months to serve as his palace (*Go Down, Moses*). It is a boat of time, a ludicrous sign of permanence in the great dwelling of the Big Woods. It calls to mind the beached ship in the middle of the jungle in García Márquez's *One Hundred Years of Solitude*.

Miraculous objects, signs of the obscure, things that double the Jeffersonian real. They are ordinary items, diverted from their everyday use or at any rate "loaded" with the supernatural weight of obsession.

Animals are even more plentiful in Faulkner's world, and only these fabulous animals can be placed in apposition to the objects. Their legion is so large one hesitates before enumerating it.

—Old Ben, the primordial Bear, whose role in the Woods we have figured out. The old cripple with the legendary limp, without hatred and without any interest at all in the men tracking him.

—Lion, the mongrel dog, more frightening than a lion, more deaf than a bull, that the hunters will finally choose as the only one capable of confronting the Bear.

So many dogs in the Faulknerian world. (I can still see the packs of dogs that used to run the streets in the small towns in Martinique and throng the traces or paths of the countryside. Nightly, the dogs would congregate, spelled from their daytime bedlam. Antilleans do not remember them with fondness. The hairless dogs that we called *chiens-fer* have now disappeared from the landscape. At street corners, town criers used to announce what day the city officials would hand out poisoned sausages on the public square in an effort to stamp out and control these gangs of runaway dogs. You remember the stiff carcasses with extended claws and yellow fire exploding in their wide-open eyes.)

—The mules (which, in this world, trail rats in intelligence, but come before cats, dogs, and horses, for mules serve man only when they want to). Especially the mule belonging to Ned, the stableboy in *The Reivers*, that could run like a racehorse. " 'Them convicts. A mule's got twice as much sense.' " " 'A mule's got twice as much sense as anything except a rat,' the emissary said in his pleasant voice."

—Mr. Faulkner's cow.

—The wild little ponies, coming from faraway Texas—were they accomplices of Flem Snopes?—that introduced chaos into the region.

—And then the horses: the one belonging to the first Compson, unbeatable for six hundred yards but dying a half yard later; the one in *The Reivers* that loved rotten sardines so much; and then the proud horses, like Colonel John Sartoris's Jupiter or Colonel Sutpen's black stallion, that so greatly resemble those untamable steeds (with such extravagant names) that Faulkner himself tried in vain to tame toward the end of his life.

—The snake—the timeless beast young Ike McCaslin meets in the Woods after Sam, Lion, and old Ben have died. (In Martinique, we are warned not to say that name, and must use all kinds of paraphrases, images, or symbols instead: the enemy, *la bête longue*, the necktie, etc.) "[I]t crawled and lurked: the old one, the ancient and accursed about the earth, fatal and solitary and he could smell it now: the thin sick smell of rotting cucumbers and something else which had no name, evocative of all knowledge and an old weariness and of pariah-hood and of death."

Young Ike salutes the beast as it crawls away from him: "Chief," he said, "Grandfather."

We could say these unapproachable animals or objects that are too desirable or too symbolic are "loaded." By nature or in the urges they excite, they inhabit this other world where one must go to find answers to "the question." Animals and objects are the markers and verifiers of this undisclosable and disturbing presupposition that the White population of the county suffers not knowing, but is subjected to nevertheless. Most often it is the all-powerful Negroes, miraculous artists, who take care of the animals. One of them (Ned) helped Pat Stamper cheat old Ab Snopes on some mule harnesses (*The Hamlet*), and it may be Ned who helps Boon and young Lucius Priest win the fantastic race in *The Reivers*.

Could we not find comparable antecedents, for example, in the lives of Indian and Black populations? Are not the genealogical roots and fountainheads of mystery for the other inhabitants just as indispensable to the arrangement of the ensemble? Would we not need to rediscover them, to envision them, and to bring them in line with the adventures of the Scottish ancestors of the Compsons, with the delirium of Sutpen's bloodline, and with the curse of the young Sartorises? How can we think that a totality as complex as that of the county could be approached from the point of view of White decadence, even if what was at work there was so obviously a slave society?

For the Blacks, there was the drawn-out damnation of the loss of family heritage, the erasure of collective memory, the initial trauma of the Middle Passage, the belly of the slave ship, the agonizing obliteration of old and familiar objects, and the need to master a plethora of new and frustrating tools (even more fantastic for these poor travelers than the objects that filled the White unconscious in Faulkner's universe). And then there were all the forbidden tools: guns and other weapons, books, pencils, and notebooks. For a slave, a book was an even more fabulous object than the red slippers were for Moketubbe or dentures for Anse Bundren. Without factoring in the burden of having to tame so many dangerous beasts (even more terrifying than Lion, for example: the trained dogs—as in the Caribbean—trained to track runaway slaves, *who could smell the scent of the Negroes*). All this compounding a progressive disappearance of antecedents from Africa, where one could find a presupposition as terrible as the one that tormented the Sartorises and the Sutpens.

Should we not have linked all this to the lost gods of the Indian rivers—to the forgotten language of the elements that still spoke to shamans, to the dreams of destiny where the white Buffalo appeared, to the mirages carried by the Spirits, who no doubt tormented Ikke-motubbe himself, as indifferent as he had become? And could we also reimagine the lineage that Doom had so irreparably disturbed? Or could we not at least try to fathom why neither lineage nor legitimacy no longer mattered here?

Faulkner would not have been able to assume these tasks and no one would have demanded it of him. As for Blacks, after the arguments of Richard Wright's generation, we had to await the genealogical recom-positions of Alex Haley, the explorations of mystery and malediction in Toni Morrison, and the plumbing of the real in Alice Walker, before these tasks could even begin to be accomplished. One cannot write or reveal for others; it is fitting, simply, that they enter their own history, and that all these histories ultimately connect. Each person must go to the end of his or her legitimacy (even illusory), or pursue his or her genealogy (even if mechanical and forced), so that later on he or she may participate fully in the transcendence that will be required of all.

One can deplore that Faulkner's work has tended to treat Blacks as things. Nonetheless, through suspense, fragmentation, uncertainty, and deferral, the writing of these works has made it likely—and has even authorized a time to exist, a time near our own, when these stories will meet; when these diversified poetics will be united in networks and rhizomes; when these lineages will lose some of the exclusivity that has been the basis of their demands; when legitimacy will fade in the compass of Creolization; when the givens will be clarified without being reduced to a priori certainties; and when curses, simply by being revealed and without any denial of their dazzling force, will wane.

Faulkner's work—and the holes it rips open in the traditional fabric of narrative—will be decisive, because it is an effort to give account to the real, going from the deferred to the given inscribed in it. And this given (the original sin of the county), in turn, quietly opens gaps in the act of writing, again and again.

The result is a fluid construction. This is work that has entered into conversation with many other works, in many different languages, yet allied in their versions of the "scream of the world."

Some people in the county fight the curse without realizing what it is. For them, it wears the face of injustice. Most of these people are women. We can try to understand why.

Of all the personalities that Faulkner gathers in Yoknapatawpha, Lena Grove is without a doubt the only one who is absolutely happy. We see, however, that she constructs this happiness by refusing to accept or assume that she will never again lay eyes on her prospective husband, who promised her an honest wedding but whom we know to be a cheat. The expectant Lena Grove presents one of the few examples of a happy pregnancy in the county. She is not one to be tormented by curses against the bloodline. Though she comes from afar, she has in common with the people in this place an extraordinary resolve to remain optimistic, an ineradicable stubborn clinging to the hope that tomorrow will be *the* day. She uses this stubbornness passively to shore up her illusions the way the other people use it actively to reinforce their damnation. Joanna Burden *is* damnation. Narcissa Sartoris is unperturbed, serene, and unreachable. But can we believe that she is happy? Happiness is not possible for women in the Faulknerian universe. The aunts and the grandmothers—Miss Rosa Millard, Miss Jenny, Miss Rosa Coldfield—are the designated victims of the agitation and madness of men. When a woman (in *The Hamlet*) attains what we believe to be utter happiness, as the new wife of farmer Houston does, it does not last three days: she is kicked by a horse and dies, even though she had been warned to be careful of the animal. The mothers are so self-effacing that they are barely present. And the women who aspire to love always end up tragically: Miss Emily, who lives for two years with the corpse of the man she loved and killed; Elly, who drives her grandmother and her lover, two "impossibles," off a cliff in a car; and Drusilla, about whom we never know if she would have tolerated a daily routine and grown weary of young Bayard—the avenger of Granny Millard—Sartoris. Or else they are marked by fatality: Caddy Compson, who looks her curse in the eye and defies it; Eula Varner, built for laziness, languor, and love; her daughter Linda, thin and dry and voluntarily despairing; Addie Bundren, veritable visionary of the adultery she committed in times past and of the death she sees approaching; the "special" women, Belle and her daughter, Little Belle, ever tempted by the frivolity of pleasure; and Temple Drake, always haunted by her tragic aura. And there are so many others.

It goes without saying that happiness is out of the question for the Black women. Dilsey is calmly diligent, responsible for the Compson household; her conversation is composed (except with Jason in his moments of crisis) and she demonstrates a surprising common sense and authority in the chaotic universe of the Compson children. Elnora, the domestic for the Sartorises, does not have Dilsey's firm immutability. She delivers furious soliloquies, always ready to strike her son Isom (companion to one of the Bayards), who became adept in the art of staying clear of his mother's outbursts. The story "There Was a Queen" suggests that she is the half sister of old Sartoris, the one who came from Carolina to live in Mississippi, but neither one nor the other seems to know this or care. It has no importance whatsoever: the Black and White threads in the weave of lineages are inextricably intertwined and the right of the master over his slave wife was unquestioned. Who would bother to claim such bloodlines? Elnora is sure of the unique characteristics of the Sartorises (" 'Nome,' [she] said. 'Aint no Sartoris man never missed nobody' "), even if she cannot go as far as Aunt Jenny ("this band of imbeciles and proud ghosts"), and even if she is no less aware of the importance of the lineage (" 'She won't never be a Sartoris woman,' Elnora said").

These Black women—Louvinia, Elnora, Molly, Dilsey, domestic ser-

vants and hostages to this misfortune—have no personal histories of
their own. The only one who truly acts is Clytie, almost white of skin
and almost black with despair (as the saying goes); she sets fire to
Sutpen's Hundred, but she does so to sanction the end of everything,
like the visionary Nancy Mannigoe. The history of these women is
that of their masters, and no tenderness nor even any deference on the
part of the latter could ever make up for that. But not one of them
complains.

Not a single one of the women in the county, Black or White, ever
protests, even at the extremes of grievance and despair. In this generalized misfortune, misfortune is their lot in particular. But some of
them balk in unexpected ways.

We remember that in 1943, an old maid, Miss Melissa Meck, the li-
brarian in Jefferson, finds a photograph in a magazine that shows Caddy
Compson posing beside a Nazi general. And she tries in vain to involve
first Jason, Caddy's adversarial brother, then old Dilsey, yelling at them
to do something, no matter what, but do something! " 'You have to
save her, Jason! You have to save her!' " . . . But it is too late for Candace Compson . . . Jason is already a Snopes, and Dilsey is too old,
blind and powerless in her ramshackle home (*Compson Appendix*).

We remember an old maid, Miss Worsham, who forces a man of the
law (Gavin Stevens certainly) to spend two days of his time arranging
for the body of Samuel Worsham Beauchamp (Molly's grandson and
a descendant of slaves once belonging to her family) to be brought
back to Jefferson, after Beauchamp, who had turned out badly, was put
to death in another state (*Go Down, Moses*).

We remember Miss Habersham, that fearless old maid (probably a
descendant of the founders of the city), who helped the young hero of
Intruder in the Dust to get Lucas Beauchamp off the wrong track.

Timid, but invincibly obstinate, they are just like the aunts, Miss
Jenny and Miss Rosa, as well as their opposites. These two groups of

old White ladies, unmarried or widowed very early and generally child-less, share between them the energy of the place. These imperious aunts or grandmothers are the keepers of memory and tradition, but they can be quite fragile under their straitlaced hauteur. The old maids without wealth or hope are just as frail, but are committed to a very singular sense of justice, honor, and charity.

To a greater or lesser extent, these women I have just named make up the conscience of the county.

Unlike Gavin Stevens (and probably Faulkner), these women would not express a preference for truth over justice. The same alarmed stubbornness that Lena Grove applies in pursuit of her elusive husband, they employ in service of a cause, and they are usually successful. Men of the law are their favorite targets, and we have to admit that the men leave them alone. How could they do otherwise? Rules of polite society command courtesy toward old ladies, especially those in need.

Gavin Stevens is a prime example. He is perhaps the person who appears most often in the stories told here. When you think of Faulkner's work as a whole, however, Stevens is not the one who first comes to mind. You think of the Compsons, the McCaslins, and the Sartorises, certainly; Sutpen surely (and Caddy and Benjy and Popeye and Lena Grove and Joe Christmas)—but not Stevens, even though he, too, comes from one of the oldest families in Jefferson. It is as though he is invisible or transparent. As the district attorney or county lawyer (which amount to the same thing), he is familiar with the workings of the curse without ever appearing implicated in it. He is a kind of secular agent in this religion of misfortune, charged with disentangling its rituals. I don't need to stress how ubiquitous lawyers are in American society. Gavin Stevens is more than a lawyer; he is the measure of the county—a role for which he must be imbued with transparency, for how else can we envision the quotidian and everyday if not through a clear lens? Stevens rises to the challenge of being invisible; installed in front of the scene, engaged in special pleading, he merges with the commonplace.

Stevens also hides behind his good nature and sympathetic understanding—vital traits if you are going to be approached by little old ladies in search of equity or by young nephews disturbed by life. Prominent in *Intruder in the Dust* and *Requiem for a Nun*, in the "detective stories" in *Knight's Gambit* and in a number of others ("Smoke," for example, and the title story in *Go Down, Moses*), for more than twenty-five years, Stevens delivers his willfully pedantic perorations, whether he is in the courtroom before juries composed of farmers and grocers he knows, or settling some quarrel in his office, or giving counsel to a nephew who is trying to escape the fate of the place. His preferred method is the Socratic, and he'd rather persuade than elucidate like a "detective." Oh so gently he leads the people to accept a state of rights in which the law can prevail over the savagery of origins. When in his company, people tend to forget what is really going on, not only in the county but in Mississippi and all over the South.

What is forgotten is the genuine savagery that tortured, hanged, and set the match to thousands of Blacks, most often in the presence of prejudiced, smiling White children; the parades of the Ku Klux Klan all through the countryside; the obsessional pretexts of the rape of White women officially used to authorize these atrocities; and the White supremacist cries of poor Whites on the verge of intellectual and moral extinction and of wellborn folk, delighted to reassure themselves for a moment against the uncertainties of their future.

Men like Gavin Stevens and the fragile and stubborn old ladies represent the future, just as the Snopeses, through their business speculations and profiteering. Having no direct heirs, and living most often with brothers, sisters, or cousins who welcome them without hesitation, are they not all (but the Snopeses are different, unruffled as they are before the tricks of destiny) signs that the patriarchal curse is being erased?

Stevens, however, usually braves the realities that seem so diminished in the atmosphere of Yoknapatawpha compared to what they really were in the mortified South—the horror of lynching, for example.

A television documentary, filmed in the United States in 1995, claims that lynching is an American invention. Lynching becomes so commonplace that we forget how extraordinary it actually is, and that it is analogous to a ritualized pogrom. The lynching scenes (in *Intruder in the Dust* and *Light in August*) are too ritualistic to account for the barbarism they signify. They are, in the dry concision of their narrative, like sacrificial rites. As for the lynching in the short story "Dry September," it captures our emotions because of everything that surrounds it—the preparations, the growing rumor, the arguments of the White men, the hesitations of some of them, and the terror of the lynching victim—but we hear nothing of the act itself, except that the leader of the lynch mob, when he returns home to his pretty house, abuses his wife, who had been waiting up for him all night long.

Consistently, acts of collective violence in Faulkner—murders, sudden deaths, lynchings, and rapes—are treated sketchily rather than described in detail (except for the castration and assassination of Joe Christmas, and Flem Snopes's murder—which can be considered collective, with Linda waiting in the next room—two deaths practically consented to by the victims; and, of course, the garish death—a moment of metaphysical splendor—of farmer Houston, killed by a shot from Mink Snopes's rifle). The relationship of the text to the subject generally stops the moment the act begins, leaving open gaps at these sites of exasperation, suggested more by their locale than through clinical description.

In a work of such total and tempestuous violence, there hovers a modesty that keeps the actual violence at bay, as if it were useless or redundant to include violence while disclosing the real. The approach of violence, meaning the moment when it is being prepared or contemplated (afterward), is much more crucial. Both Temple Drake, when she is being raped by Popeye, and Joe Christmas, before being beaten and then castrated, acknowledge the same flashes of consciousness or insight in their bodies: "Something's going to happen to me. I feel that something's going to happen to me." In the unpredictability of existence, only misfortune was predetermined. Perceived, but not pointed out in advance.

The ritualization of violence corresponds to an intention to probe deeper. In this violence, for example, we discover not only social, historical, and other causes on which it is perhaps not important to dwell, but also a decisive function in the universe of the county, if not in the South as a whole: the victimization of Blacks is therefore one of the detours through which Faulkner passes, in order to propose redemption for the sins of the Whites.

African-Americans (as we say today) would not consent to such a vocation. And Faulkner would not willingly see them bound into History, into the brutal changes stirring their masses into action in the United States. He would ask for more time.

Did he think of the *reality* of such scenes as the one we see in a photograph in the Pléiade *Album* on Faulkner: a young couple obviously in love(!), an old lady, a little grumpy but doubtlessly honorable, and other ordinary people—these people are *rejoicing* beneath the bodies of two ragged blacks hanging from the branches of a tree? Such people still live in the United States today, and while they have adjusted to the changes in society, they still bear within an indestructible germ of horror.

This is the only temporality that matters. How long will it really take before we can erase all this? Against this endless stretch of time, every rupture is of great value.

In the same *Album* there is a photograph of a young woman with a sign, "Race mixing is Communism!" and a boy holding a placard that proclaims: GOVERNOR FAUBUS, SAVE OUR CHRISTIAN AMERICA. They are two in a crowd protesting integration of the public schools. More than likely they are still alive. Even if they now understand that "The Mix Is the Message," do this young woman and this young man still rant inside?

Here in Yoknapatawpha, Blacks had to *tolerate* a great deal so that Whites could think: in fits and starts, in bursts, in amazement.

The time that Faulkner was asking them to have the patience to wait for, this same time he had already traced backward into the past of the Compsons and the McCaslins. He does not, however, go back as far as the trauma of the slave trade, which, for Blacks, is the source of everything. It is as though, suffering object of the South's neglect, the Blacks had no need for ancestors, ancestry being deemed unsuitable for them. It certainly was not up to Faulkner to do this work—but the work he did do would not have reached its fullness if it had not asked that one day others would take up this task from their own point of view.

We still have to look at the workings of chance—its rough spots and stunning interconnections—which covers the ideas in the work with a grainy texture as innocent as breath on the first day of Nature, as stubborn as prickly grass on the savanna. We still have to travel all through this county where (thanks to reader's privilege) we do not run the risk of being stopped by an overly complacent sheriff or facing an angry, overwrought crowd at the end of an August day that has been much too hot in a town that is much too isolated.

Let us run the risk of the unpredictable in these works. We can do this by a thousand different routes, choosing one on a whim. Let us go down the length of this trace, at least as far as we can travel at one time, weighing and discerning, without fear of having to affix names to this or that, which would not be appropriate.

Sam Fathers, who acknowledges in a murmur the passage of old Ben, on the path, the trace the Bear had opened in the wilderness: "Chief . . . Grandfather" ("The Bear").

Issetibbeha's slave, who has been bitten in the arm by a poisonous snake, and who, in the swamp where the runaway has hidden, caresses the head of the animal as he is being bitten over and over again, saluting it in a murmur: "Olé, grandfather" ("Red Leaves").

("For twenty years . . . while others of his race sweat in the fields, he served the Man in the shade. Why should he not wish to die, since he did not wish to sweat?")

Boon Hogganbeck, the giant who was born nowhere (he is part Chickasaw), can hardly ever shoot straight. Yet he is no less than one of the immemorial bear hunters in Go Down, Moses. After the trip the Reivers took with young Lucius Priest and Ned, the miraculous stableboy, Hogganbeck brings back a woman he has abducted from a "special" house (in Memphis) and whom he will marry. Boon Hogganbeck, the plebeian, is there at the beginning and end of everything, in the Big Woods (Go Down, Moses), in the hamlet, and soon thereafter in the city (The Reivers).

"The smell of the Blacks" (the Negro smell, "rancid," heavy, ubiquitous) that maddens, revulses and subjugates Joe Christmas, the alleged mulatto in Light in August who is always fighting against his Black blood and against his White blood, and who lets himself be gunned down (he is Joanna Burden's killer) without trying to defend himself.

The interminable and convoluted speech of Ike McCaslin and Gavin Stevens, and the delirious ramblings of Hightower: they all give reasons why we should think that this war was never really lost, why they believed for a time that it would never be lost.

Dawn, always foggy but sparkling cold, the only true haven for fugitives, the solitary, the damned, treasure seekers, and bootleggers.

(And this: "Maybe you will, since you don't seem to want to know as much as you want something new to be uncertain about.")

The calm anathemas and revulsions of the ladies and gentlemen faced with the threat of mixed blood. Elly's grandmother, Ailanthia ("'Mr. de Montigny! From Louisiana!' she screamed, and saw the grandmother, without moving below the hips, start violently backward as a snake does to strike"): "'Not contented with deceiving your parents and your friends, you must bring a Negro into my son's house as a guest'" ("Elly").

Old Ike McCaslin: "He sprang, still seated even, flinging himself backward onto one arm, awry-haired, glaring. Now he understood what it was she had brought into the tent with her, what old Isham had already told him by sending the youth to bring her in to him—the pale lips, the skin pallid and deadlooking yet not ill, the dark and tragic and foreknowing eyes. *Maybe in a thousand or two thousand years in America,* he thought. *But not now! Not now!* He cried, not loud, in a voice of amazement, pity and outrage: 'You're a nigger!'" ("Delta Autumn").

And Aunt Jenny: "[S]he knew at once that he was a Jew, and when he spoke to her her outrage became fury and she jerked back in the chair like a striking snake, the motion strong enough to thrust the chair back from the table. 'Narcissa,' she said, 'what is this Yankee doing here?'" ("There Was a Queen").

They rear up and coil backward just like snakes ready to bite.

Percy Grimm, "too young to take part in the Great War," who took some time before he figured out that he could never forgive his parents: "Percy . . . was suffering the terrible tragedy of having been born not alone too late, but not late enough to have escaped firsthand knowledge of the lost time"—and who castrated what was not yet the corpse of Joe Christmas.

(And Sutpen: "He went to the West Indies.")

The violence of their childhoods: wild and hard for Sutpen, unsettled for Christmas, cold for Popeye, barren and blind for Mink Snopes. In those times, the Blacks had no childhood of their own, at least according to the official record.

The violence of foundations: impossible for Sutpen, cursed for the Compsons, waning for the Sartorises. Even Flem Snopes's patient schemes and advancement (which do not establish a foundation) would prove useless in the end.

Joe Christmas: "the . . . blood . . . seemed to rush out of his pale body like the rush of sparks from a rising rocket; upon that black blast the man seemed to rise soaring into their memories forever and ever."

Reverend Hightower: "Yet, leaning forward in the window, his bandaged head huge and without depth upon the twin blobs of his hands upon the ledge, it seems to him that he still hears them: the wild bugles and the clashing sabres and the dying thunder of hooves."

Someone must bear witness to all this.

The witnesses testify less to the real than to what it means beneath the surface: women and children, as in any shipwreck worthy of its name. We have already spoken about them; I take them up again here, exhaustively.

They are preserved and protected from every disruption, held prey to an innocence nothing can reduce, but, when it comes to what concerns the White Aunts and old Black Mammies, they are uncompromisingly clear. Miss Rosa, Dilsey, young Ike McCaslin, young Charles in *Intruder in the Dust*, and young Lucius in *The Reivers*. These are the ones who contaminate the others and who never cease to question, even if they do nothing but finalize their initiation or lament the ruins. They reconstruct what others would have the tendency to misunderstand or overlook and what they "stare at fixedly." They are hallucinated memory, where what is reinforced is their innocence, their stubbornness, and their ability to "endure."

The contaminated. Those belonging to the race and ilk of Quentin Compson, who, for the benefit of his university roommate, Shreve the Canadian, forges the link between his father's stories and Rosa Cold-field's (regarding Sutpen); thus, he sings the damned geste. There is what he saw firsthand, what he saw when he was with Rosa Coldfield, what she told him, what his grandfather the general saw and told his father, who then told him, and so on, in the great contamination of *Absalom, Absalom!* We know that he will kill himself immediately afterward, but we do not really know whether he does so because he cannot stand the idea of the South anymore or because he cannot resign himself to his sister Caddy's recent marriage. For these witnesses, the stories they tell are a history that effectively contaminates them, even though they play no special part in it and bear no special knowledge. It is not the knowing that touches and transforms them, but the anguish of having to choose between knowing and not knowing. They are, so to speak, suffering itself—suffering that questions. Therein lies the source of their wound: their terror, the extremity of their feelings, and their irrefutable taste for the void.

To conclude with the impartial witnesses, we find: Horace Benbow, a man of the law who has vague literary aspirations (especially when he writes to his sister, Narcissa); Gavin Stevens, the ubiquitous lawyer who presides over the County Review Board during the Second World War; some members of the Edmonds family; and Ratliff, the sewing machine salesman. Theirs are lives apparently spared by the curse. When they become tangled up in their impulses, it is often in a smug and detached way, almost joyful, as when Benbow is tempted to commit incest with his sister. These witnesses form the hinges in Faulkner's work—in the county, that is. One cannot always burn with the passion of the Quentins, Bayards, Darls, Ellys, and Lindas. These others need humor, irony, and detachment; they cultivate distance and ease.

But the unquestionable witness is surely the "continuous stream of consciousness," composed of outbursts and fractured thoughts, anxious, stammering, aching, stubborn. Like a tumultuous Mississippi, it runs all through the county.

The meetings of all these sensibilities are confirmed in the text by an astounding blur of pronouns, almost all of them are indefinite, regardless of the referent ("he," "one," or "we"), and by first names that are often androgynous (Quentin, for example). There are definite "strokes of consciousness" (which I adapt from "stream of consciousness"), just as there are meetings between the bodies of lovers. Here is one example: in *Intruder in the Dust* (a much more important book than is generally believed), Young Charles thinks about the relation between people in the South in a very broad sense, "whereupon once more his uncle spoke at complete one with him and again without surprise he saw his thinking not be interrupted but merely swap one saddle for another." Thought rides from one person to another, the way the loas (the divinities in the voodoo religion) ride those they have chosen to possess. But here, in the county, possession is contagious. The individual is singular in his or her stubbornness and multiple in relation to others.

The truth is distant, inaccessible, deferred. No one person or even a group of people can gain access to it through established facts, reasoning, or deduction. That is why the "stream of consciousness" is the best witness and vector of truth's nearness; it is formed through contamination and interplay of shared suffering.

She tells me frankly as I was thinking out loud that I am speaking nonsense. Oh! no, she says—she does not want to appear in this book

I am writing. Her words have nothing to do with what I was saying. Yes, there are indefinite pronouns, she says, such as *one, we, he, she*. I tell her that a pronoun has power even when you do not know who is hidden behind it. Some argue that "she" is Mycea, "the one with whom the poet is enchanted." Others deduce an imaginary identity, if this interests them, perhaps a synthesis of several elements at their command. She tells me she does not want to hide. She laughs. She tells me not to work like that, needlessly, and not to construct my Faulkner out of this pronoun, which, after all, is hers.

You could say that there are no contradictions in Faulkner's work because the various ways of telling one single fact add up to progress, no, to evolution—to the ride, to the stream of consciousness that summarizes (or at least tries to) the circumstances of the country.

It is true that these contradictions are more striking when the "riding" of thought is no longer at work, in the trilogy of the Snopes family, for example. In *The Mansion*, the concluding volume of the trilogy, Faulkner raised the question of contradictions in a prefatory note: "the purpose of this note is simply to notify the reader that the author has already found more discrepancies and contradictions [in this chronicle] than he hopes the reader will." He goes on to attribute them to the progress he has made in his knowledge "of the human heart and its problems" after having lived with them for thirty-four years; "he knows the people of his novel better than he knew them then."

Faulkner's amused refusal to "correct the contradictions" suggests that he considers his characters people whose "strokes of consciousness" affected him greatly. His words about "knowledge of the human heart" (solemnly reiterated in Stockholm) have been taken as breadfruit from heaven. Often, we hide behind this search for knowledge so as not to see what truly animates his works.

The smallest detail counts once told in the chronicle by the most ephemeral person, even if something else, another witness, another view, contradicts it later on. Faulkner writes in rhizomes.

.   .   .

Tragic disclosure is never intended to build up an incontrovertible truth. Truth is deemed more precious than justice, while it is always deferred and conjectural. What forces disclosure is, first of all, a passion, a suffering. Contradictions form different kinds of stigmata of suffering, indifferent one to the other, yet indisputable, shared, and communicated. Stream of consciousness is suffering that perpetuates itself, constant yet always changing.

The Sound and the Fury differentiates this stream, from Benjy's inane but perfectly consistent perceptions to Jason's angry impotence, the unpredictable and shameless impudence of Caddy, and so on. As different as they are from one another, the Compson children of the last generation resemble one another to a surprising degree, given their pernicious parents. So much mania: Benjy, Jason, Caddy, and Quentin, not to mention the other Quentin, Caddy's daughter. The lineage has come smack up against an impasse. Together, they diffract what brings them together.

Absalom, Absalom!, on the other hand, confuses the current, transforming it into a singular rush of lava that soon overwhelms Quentin Compson.

As hunters trace the faint trail of old Ben in the Big Woods, the witnesses follow the history of the South. In Faulkner, the idea of the trace sends established truths back to contradiction. The story traces a path that one must have the patience and passion (not to mention the art) to detect.

Absalom, Absalom! is the most successful example of Faulkner's technique of deferral. It is the book that has transcended the ordinary structures of narrative more than any other in this century.

We can reread this story tirelessly, letting it cast its evil spell again and again. As in *Sartoris* (for the family of that name) and in *The Sound and the Fury* (for the Compson family), it is a matter of fierce obligation for Thomas Sutpen to establish a family seat, a lineage, a dynasty— and tragic failure ensues. But if the Sartorises and the Compsons have been able to endure at least, Sutpen exemplifies the "immediate" mal- ediction. Not only is it true that he is not of aristocratic descent or a traditional Planter, but he has also suffered (in Haiti) the disturbing, denaturing onslaught of *métissage*.

To broach this (for he could not simply *tell* it), Faulkner developed "the continuous stream of modified consciousness" that runs through these tormented narratives—passionate interior monologues, the alarmed responses to these monologues, and the questioning of pro- tagonists and spectator witnesses, all contaminated by deferred reve- lations, which brings them nearer and nearer to an impossible truth: like a river of perceptions and sensations, full of flashes and shadows.

The first "stage" of the deferred explains an unknown: Why can't Judith, Sutpen's legitimate daughter, marry Charles Bon, whom she met in New Orleans and who has become the boon companion of her brother Henry? It is because Bon is Sutpen's son, from his first marriage in Haiti. We discover this, or suspect it, almost immediately.

The deferred is thus at play, and it doubles in force when one un- derstands that the insurmountable cause of such an impossibility is not really incest, to which old Sutpen might have consented in his mad desire to have a male heir, as would Henry, even offering the precedent of a prince from Lorraine or Burgundy who married his own sister. Rather, the problem is misalliance, an unspeakable *métissage*. Despite appearances, Bon actually has Black blood from his mother. Toward the end of the novel, in a rare scene in which they speak face to face, Sutpen convinces Henry ("He cannot marry her," "I tell you that he can't marry her") that the family relationship between Judith and Charles Bon is nothing; but the tiny, invisible drop of African blood blots out everything else.

.   .   .

What we have here is the antithesis of an episode in one of the "dramas in the family of David" recounted in the Second Book of Samuel in the Old Testament. There, as everyone knows from the beginning, Amnon is the half brother of both Absalom and Tamar, his sister, whom he will rape. What we do not know, and what Amnon himself may not know, is that he may well plan this rape as revenge for the favoritism that David, father to both of them, has always shown Absalom. Through Tamar he aims at Absalom, and through Absalom at David. Pretending to be passionately in love with Tamar, he entraps her *with the unconscious help of the king.* Amnon is disgusted as soon as he commits his crime. We can understand this psychological about-face (the rapist disgusted by his victim) much better if we suppose that Amnon dimly understands at that moment that Tamar has been only a pretext. In reality, is he not fighting mainly against the bloodline? Amnon is certainly King David's child and is loved as "his eldest son," but he senses that David's attachment to Absalom is greater. And it is Absalom who defiles his own legitimacy (consecrated by David's affection) by killing his half brother and rebelling against his father. We could say that this whole story—in which Jonadab, son of David's brother Shimeah, plays a key role as instigator and organizer of the incestuous rape, the murder of Amnon by Absalom's henchmen, the flight of the latter, and his death, which David never wanted; he even recommends to his captains to take care of his son—has as its goal to prepare the accession and reign of Solomon, who then gets rid of his rivals, including this Joab, the all-powerful general who had Absalom put to death. Joab, as well as Amnon, is the expiatory victim in this tragedy of legitimacy, and one feels that the motive force behind all this excess is the question of who will be David's successor.

A work interpreting this biblical text, which Jeffrey Wert, a next-door neighbor, lent me (like the honeybee in the Vert-Pré hills, I go everywhere propagating my subject), neglects to point out that Amnon was the "firstborn," but it does note Jonadab's role. Perhaps he had been nourishing dynastic ambitions all along.

In Faulkner's novel, Henry-Absalom has none of the heroism or severity of David's son, who once contemplated his father's death. In direct contrast to Absalom, Henry counts for almost nothing except the single pistol shot he fires at the entrance to the House. It suffices to know that Sutpen never really seems to care about the destiny of this son, whereas David lamented Absalom's death (much more, in truth, than Amnon's death), and that Henry survives (until 1909) inside Sutpen's aborted projects but as a perfect zombie (buried in the empty carcass of the big House), as though he had never lived.

We can compare Sutpen's indifference with the precautions the Old Testament text undertakes to make Absalom's death known to David. Two messengers are sent, and the second, who deeply craves the honor of being a bearer of (bad or good) tidings, overtakes the first messenger on his way, but at the last moment he renounces the chance to announce the news of this death to King David.

The king was not waiting, as he usually did, "in front of the gate," but *between the two gates* of the city, the interior and exterior ones, equidistant from two truths: that of the guilty son (the exterior truth) and that of the beloved son (the interior truth). The second messenger (who was now first since he had overtaken the other one on the road) approaches David, and probably very much out of breath, describes the crowd of soldiers around Absalom. Then he pretends to have left the scene at that moment and not to know what happened next. Thus he accedes to the dignity of the royal messenger without incurring any curse as the bearer of bad tidings, nor even the wrath of the monarch. The king asks him to stay while he calls in the second messenger (once the first). This messenger demonstrates his personality, ambition, and initiative; furthermore, we learn his name, Ahimaaz, son of Zadok. The second, who was designated the first by Joab, has no desires and no fear (all we know of him is that he is a Cushite, *that is, an Ethiopian,* "whose black skin marks him as the rightful bringer of bad news," according to the commentary in the Pléiade edition). He finally comes in and plainly announces the death of David's son. Knowing nothing of the king's pain, he praises David for having vanquished his enemies.

"O Absalom, my son, my son!" *Absalom! Absalom!*

This is not a case of deferral, since the reader already knows that Absalom is dead. Rather, it is a very measured disclosure intended to spare King David as much as possible. The presupposition that could have positioned this Old Testament story in relation to the novel is not really a presupposition, unless we suppose that Amnon's mother was one of the foreigners (Libyan or Ethiopian, or, analogously, Haitian) that David, and especially his son and heir Solomon, so liked to spend time with. We have already noted that Charles Bon, the legitimate and oldest son (although repudiated on account of racial pollution), was much more aware of this situation than Amnon could have been.

"You are my brother," Henry tells Charles Bon (which is exactly what Tamar cried out to Amnon as she tried to push him away). Henry is seeking to distance Charles from Judith, their sister and half sister, but Charles answers, "No, I'm not. I'm the nigger that's going to sleep with your sister. Unless you stop me, Henry." Amnon actually committed the act. For Charles, incest was only a temptation because Henry's bullet stopped him.

No announcement is made of his death (he survived his father by forty years), nor is one necessary. But we can make a comparison between the sophisticated and significant way the news of Absalom's death was brought to David—placed in the symbolic framework of a disclosure stressing the temporary rupture of descent (of legitimacy), which Absalom's death outlined—and the brutal and common announcement of the death of Charles Bon-Amnon which was made to Rosa Coldfield: ". . . and then Wash Jones sitting that saddleless mule before Miss Rosa's gate, shouting her name into the sunny and peaceful quiet of the street, saying, 'Air you Rosie Coldfield? Then you better come on out yon. Henry has done shot that durn French feller. Kilt him dead as a beef.' "

The "error" (in this case, incest and then the murder of the brother) made ready the line of descent for the kings of Jerusalem, clearing the way for Solomon: the same flaw (the threat of incest and actual murder), complicated by the stain of racial mixing, liquidated the Sutpen line forever.

Why should we draw so heavily on Absalom and Amnon as precursors in order to emphasize the tragedy of Charles and Henry? Because what the two stories share derives from damnation, inheritance, and the fortunes of legitimacy. By adhering so closely to the biblical passage, Faulkner makes us realize that his hypothesis concerns the whole county, not just Sutpen. He is dealing with the tragic splendor of a community, and not the memoirs of an individual or a family.

In the novel, other instances of the deferred affect the relations between Judith and Henry, and Bon and Henry. The seeds of fraternal incest, the temptation of homosexuality: these are not really "deferred," they do not enter into the "stream of consciousness," and we only intuit their presence. Incest and homosexuality are disturbances in the bloodline; they point out an impossibility. The real failure of filiation becomes apparent little by little when we discover that the bloodline is menaced and corrupted by black blood. It is impossible to establish a line of descent and guarantee its legitimacy. Disaffiliation prevails. Everything collapses in the nebulous black bloodline, useless and uncertain, diffuse and without object, already lost in the beyond, in the world, in the evanescent.

The power of the novel derives from the contamination, which spreads from Rosa Coldfield to Mr. Compson, to his son Quentin, to Shreve the foreigner, passing through the derelictions of the players

(Sutpen, Bon and Judith and Henry, Clytemnestra, Wash and Melicent and Milly, and Miss Rosa herself). The contamination is not
spread through a sudden awareness of what the reader can have learned
and what many critics have analyzed: latent incest and aborted lineage,
the openly expressed horror of miscegenation, the failure to establish
a foundation. No. For the people of the county, contamination is not
a sudden understanding, but an acceptance of suffering. The cause is
not given with the effect. What is disclosed is not a detective-story
truth but a color of damnation.

Will they be done with fatality, once the cycle of these tribal catastrophes is complete? Is it true that the reign of the Snopeses puts an end
to the great tragedy as it does to the tragedy of the families of the
Atridae, the failed descendants of Oedipus—which is what the Sartorises, Compsons, and Sutpens really are? Has Yoknapatawpha entered once and for all into the world called modern, and do telephones,
Jaguars, malls, et cetera, make life in the South *normal*, somehow?

Is the pettiness of the Snopeses really the key to ordinary happiness,
the most secure kind there is? To put it differently, does the deferred—
which has played the part of the damned in this story and which, again,
does not apply to the flat reality of the Snopeses—allow no place at
all for any ambiguity, any suffering, or any disturbance?

Let us look at Flem Snopes. Ruthlessly pulling himself up by his boot-
straps, he tramples everything and everyone around him, starting with
the members of his own clan. He wants to be the only one who dom-
inates. It is not his intention to become a Planter but, times having
changed, to become the most important financier and banker in the
county, the image of the self-contained individual, a machine of sorts.
And he succeeds, albeit at the price of the death of his wife, Eula, and
the destruction of the majority of the people in his family: he is a
Sutpen of trade.

Yet when all is said and done he feels the tribulations of the curse.

Through his children. His daughter Linda is clearly not his; she never refers to him except as her "so-called father." She ends up by acknowledging a relationship (in *The Town*), and rejects the idea (in *The Mansion*). Just as Clytie, Sutpen's Black daughter, burns down Sutpen's Hundred, Linda will coldly plan the murder of her so-called father, and then do no less than auction off for a pittance the Snopes estate, the immense house, the land, and the bank; actually, she gives them back to the descendants of the men Flem Snopes once dispossessed. It is a liquidation as total as a fire.

That is not all. From one end of this chronicle to the other, Flem Snopes changes considerably. He does nothing to avoid death; he accepts it as a deliverance, or as his due. He faces Mink, who fumbles ridiculously with an ersatz revolver. Meanwhile, Flem Snopes doesn't even stop chewing his gum. In this, he is not like Sutpen so much as Colonel John Sartoris, who virtually planned his own death by confronting a mortal enemy without a weapon. As Sartoris grew tired of killing, Flem Snopes discovered that he was tired of swindling.

Sartoris and Snopes die the same kind of death; they belong to the same race, finally. We have long believed (as did Faulkner, during the thirty-four years of the saga's gestation) that Flem Snopes was a limit, only a limit. And certainly this Snopes knows nothing of the ardent ride, of epic excess. But then we discover that he is also an abyss, a void which Faulkner himself did not suspect when he began the Snopes chronicle. He learned this at the very end. Perhaps this is what he called "the [acquired] knowledge of the depths of the human heart." We would venture to say that Flem Snopes is the tragic dimension of the impossible, in the same way that Nancy Mannigoe was. He and she have survived the death of the former epic—the savage ride of Sutpen, the elegant and disguised suicides of the Bayard Sartorises, and the defiance of Candace Compson; he and she have survived times of disaster, only to enter into the unfathomable.

.   .   .

Gavin Stevens. I have suggested that he seems to have been protected from the curses in Yoknapatawpha. But when I consider the part of his story that has to do with the Snopeses, I am led to qualify this assertion. Gavin Stevens is present all through the Snopesian chronicle, and for a time he is completely caught up in it. The man is romantically in love with Eula, Varner's daughter, who marries Flem Snopes and finishes her life miserably. ("Her eyes . . . were darkest hyacinth, what I have always imagined that Homer's hyacinthine sea must have had to look like.") Twenty years later he finds himself in love with Eula's daughter, Linda: at least that is what he tells her. This young woman had lived *elsewhere* and had fought in the Spanish Civil War on the side of the Republicans. She had lost her husband there and was a card-carrying member of the Communist Party. And she was totally deaf as a consequence of a bombing. She is a perfect replica of Drusilla, the woman who was first the companion in war and then the wife of Colonel John Sartoris. As Drusilla pretended to love Bayard, Linda says (in her deaf woman's shrill voice) that she loves Stevens. He is dominated by fatality, caught under the shadow of incest (the mother, then her daughter), which he escapes only through impeccable abstinence on each occasion, although we cannot tell whether this is a sign of virtue or of necessity, lucidity or fear.

Stevens knows that he is changing, we believe what he says at the time. He writes in Linda's notebook: "*I am happy I was given the privilege of meddling with impunity in other peoples affairs without really doing any harm by belonging to that avocation whose acolytes have been absolved in advance for holding justice above truth I have been denied the chance to destroy what I loved by touching it.*" Speaking to Ratliff, he tries to justify his actions in the matter of Snopes's murder: "It was because I not only believe in and am an advocate of fate and destiny, I admire them; I want to be one of the instruments too, no matter how modest."

He becomes an unwilling and then a determined accomplice to the machinations through which Linda leads Mink Snopes to kill his cousin Flem Snopes, her "so-called father," out of vengeance. Romantic but cautious, he ends up marrying a rich widow in an honest-to-goodness union that will be childless nonetheless. His bride, Melisandre Harriss (formerly Backus), already has two children of her own: a violent and ineffectual boy whom Stevens forces to join the army and move out, and a daughter who marries an innocent Argentinian polo player and disappears into oblivion.

Melisandre Harriss is (or rather was) the same young woman who was mixed up in the adventure of the Sartoris family silver that Granny Rosa Millard undertook to save from the "rapacity" of the Federal troops. It is told in a picaresque manner in the short story "Granny Millard and General Bedford Forrest and the Battle of Harrykin Creek." At the end of that story, she marries a handsome Confederate soldier, her savior, Philip St. Just Backhouse, whose name is most aptly changed to Backus. When she meets Stevens, she is the widow of this pseudo-Bacchus. Gavin Stevens, already connected to the Snopeses, is finally linked with the Sartorises and Rosa Millard and the tragic story of the county circles back to the beginning.

Implicated in incest and murder, as well as in a bourgeois marriage and in a lack of direct and legitimate descendants, Gavin Stevens is a fitting image of the county: evolving in vulgar progression, but always quietly haunted by the former curses that he has eluded for so long.

In the days of old Issetibbeha, the Chickasaw king and Ikkemotubbe's uncle (not to be confused with Issetibbebha of *Requiem for a Nun* who was Doom's successor and brought the famous red slippers back from Europe), we find members of the great families among the colonizers (Holston and Grenier, Sartoris and Stevens, Compson and McCaslin, Coldfield and Sutpen—yes, Sutpen, even though we learned elsewhere that Colonel Sutpen was the son of a humble farmer, a poor White who was violent and always drunk)—as well as Peabodies, Pettigrews, Tuls, and one named Ratliff, the bootlegger who miraculously resolves the matter of the compensation due to old Alec Holston for the loss of the huge padlock from the prison door. We like to think of him as the ancestor of Ratliff, the businessman and Gavin

Stevens's favorite financier, whose biography is sketched out in *The Town*.

"To be unschooled, untraveled, and to an extent unread, Ratliff had a terrifying capacity for knowledge or local information or acquaintanceship to match the need of any local crisis." Everywhere in Plantation country, we see this kind of person who, with a lot of brouhaha, makes the liaison between every rumor and temptation. He is the newcomer in town, neither Sartoris nor Snopes, who has maintained something of the Ratliffs' finesse, cleverness, and resolve, and something of the rustic's common sense and the cunning of bootleggers and businessmen in general.

Ratliff is not Stevens's bosom buddy or his factotum; he is Stevens's equal, and may even be superior to him in intuition. Although he has no talent for the "stream of continuous consciousness," he is the public teller of tales in the county, the *storyteller*, the one who makes the link—like an itinerant peddler—between the dramas, comedies, and novels. He has such acuity and speed of thought that his conversations with Stevens—full of double meanings, innuendo, quick and brutal conclusions, and stunning conjectures—strongly resemble the "stream of consciousness" process. What is at play here is truth, not contamination. Sometimes embellished, exchanged by people who are complicit and love to have figured it out beforehand, truth is no longer remote and inaccessible; it is caught up in the web of the everyday.

Stevens and Ratliff seem to still be walking on the crest of the abyss into which, by the end, Eula, Linda, Mink, and even Flem Snopes have plunged. I have suggested that the writing in the trilogy is flat. Certainly, relative to what is revealed of the county's lofty damnations, it is. But even if this Snopesian writing does not fall into the abyss, it is composed with a dense complexity in which the real must be disentangled from people's motivations and the minutiae of their actions. It becomes a Socratic dialogue of sorts, with Ratliff, the sewing machine salesman, as a "rural bucolic grass-roots philosopher and Cincinnatus," and each person who enters into dialogue with him, whether wily peasant, naïve day laborer, or sly merchant, as a seer who talks beyond himself.

They have not finished with fate; it has simply adapted to the grayish filter of this endless toil: *"[T]he majesty of Fate become contemptuous through ubiquity and sheer repetition."* Contemptuous, or rather deserving of contempt?

At this moment, the country in question carries the mark of the tale: those stories of yesteryear ritually declaimed and sung, and those stories of daily life (horse trades, shady deals, obvious adulteries, loaned creamers and cotton gins, contests for mules and all known kinds of animals, promises of marriage, and all of life's outrageous dirty tricks) stitched together with the greatest possible inventiveness and verbal embroidering.

The tale makes the orality of all things flourish and leads to the art of conversation. There is no longer anything to discover through deferral, nothing to put in perspective through a progressive strategy of disclosure, nothing to spread through the pain of contamination. The finesse and cleverness of the speakers suffice to reveal the amusing schemes and usual tragedies in these dialogues which are surprisingly wise, as they comprise all that is human in a country that tries to evolve and so survive.

From the hamlet to the town and back again to the mansion, we see this evolution become clear in Yoknapatawpha, or at least in Jefferson, which emerges more and more as its center, vital and proud. Garages replace horse rental shops. Elections become democratized (that is to say, people become more and more subtle in the fine art of stuffing the ballot box). Streetlights are installed at intersections, and the boards of directors peddle influence as they run the banks, the hospitals, and city halls. Newspaper editorials take over from the country tale. Bars and beauty salons open up, and the new citizens of the new city gather there. The art of telling a tale has disappeared from this landscape, but it has been replaced by a conversational art no less incisive, in which Ratliff and Gavin Stevens excel to such a great degree. With them, the cycle ends.

We follow the trace of this path from the language of the tale (a ritual, popular language that first inspired the writer) to the splitting of the deferred word (a tragic language of poetic quest) to conversation and dialogue (the civil language of the society being constituted). What emerges is a renunciation of imperious alternatives (whether damnation, legitimacy, pessimism, or genealogical absolutism).

In fact, we would not lend any credence to any of these stories of Blacks, Indians, and Whites—which seem so minor compared to all the eruptive changes in today's world—and we would not be convinced by any of these moonstruck farmers, Negroes with fixed stares, demented aristocrats, or stubborn old ladies, if we did not feel that what has been played out here is a game whose goal is the unlimited opening up of every identity to every other identity without anyone having to give up his or her truth.

First of all, structures damned in the foundation have to come crashing down, just as dreams of intolerant unicity are collapsing into blood and crime everywhere else. Faulkner's lesson extends well beyond Yoknapatawpha, in the same way that the landscape of the county stretches toward the horizon of space and meaning. We will explore its frontier and imagine its outer reaches.

In the end, there are the "ordinary" people.

All this savage agitation has been slowly extinguished in glum, withdrawn civility. The "South" has fallen asleep and awaits other transformations. No one can say what they will be.

In that sense it is like so many other areas in the world, unsettled or sleepy, chaotic or tropic, Polynesian or Swiss, continent or archipelago, that are groping their way into the enormous Relation of the world-totality. But such is the epic endeavor, forgoing traditional epic (foreshadowing and encapsulating an open epic word, proposing another kind of identity politics, difficult to sustain, unpredictable yet unavoidable), that remains and is of help to us beyond the county.

Has the land of the South fallen asleep or, finally conceiving of itself as frontier, is it merely open in turn to the subterranean quakings of everyday life in upheaval that Flannery O'Connor, Eudora Welty, and Toni Morrison have patiently explored? Faulkner has shown the passage from mansion to hamlet, from Plantation to City. But this South is itself transience and passage, never ceasing to be Plantation, ever hesitating to become City. It exists at the limits, on the margin, of what is "happening" in the world: a changeover that leads from the stubborn single root to the spreading of the diaspora.

Faulkner's work is a trembling preface to the shocks and complexities of our world-circularity, our infinitely catalogued real, and our store of points in common that no one can predict. Lists of characteristics spewing out the real—accumulations, circularities, monotonous regurgitations of banalities—where our thought, which we considered original and unique, is suddenly taken up, taken over, and taken on by so many other echoes in the world, which we echo in turn. We finally realize that these are the new modes of knowledge, the leaves indicating the trace, the voice trembling on the surface of the water.

All this work is in suspension—as supremely as is our thought of the world.

Perhaps I should have also traced through the ingenious reduction to banality that we have seen deployed at the end in the ultimately regulated county, through this clever and brilliant gift of conversation and exchange, in order to arrive with sadness at our final destination, in order to feel that death is the great earthly rallying point—just as Faulkner evoked it for Sam Fathers and the dog Lion buried in the Big

Woods. "[N]ot held fast in earth but free in earth and not in earth but of earth, myriad yet undiffused of every myriad part, leaf and twig and particle, air and sun and rain and dew and night, acorn oak and leaf and acorn again, dark and dawn and dark and dawn again in their immutable progression and, being myriad, one." And, from the moment we are born, the earth (as Mink Snopes—the dim-witted but visionary peasant, the instrument of fate for Flem Snopes and the murderer of farmer Houston—thinks and feels at the end of *The Mansion*, and the work) never stops pulling us imperceptibly down to where all who have suffered hell on this same earth are assembled with neither rank nor interference nor discrimination. And yet what a miserable compensation this is for the failure of the great enterprise of making a foundation—especially for Mink, who never had any reason to make a foundation, who was not a dynast, but who had shown as much resolve as the others he will rejoin in death: "[H]imself among them, equal to any, good as any, brave as any, being inextricable from, anonymous with all of them: the beautiful, the splendid, the proud and the brave, right on up to the very top itself among the shining phantoms and dreams which are the milestones of the long human recording— Helen and the bishops, the kings and the unhorned angels, the scornful and graceless seraphim."

6

THE DEFERRED—THE WORD

The word in the Story is not dictated by a God, or derived from a Law.

It is the composite word, which contests, even if not openly, any idea of a Genesis, a creation of the world, a legitimate genealogy guaranteed and passed down through generations. I am speaking of the Creole tales of the Americas.

Amerindian stories undoubtedly are not like this; at times they explain how the world was created and how everything came into being. It would be interesting to know what Faulkner heard in his childhood and what he chose to listen to in his adolescence and later, and if he preferred one kind of story or another. What we do know is that he became part of the circle of regular listeners to the *storytellers*, and from these White farmers and old Chickasaws and Black dayworkers he began to gather not only life stories but also ways of telling them. Atavistic Indian tales, legends passed down or adapted from their Scottish or Welsh origins (or really from all of Europe, journeying West), African tales (or the recuperated traces thereof, spared from the disaster of the slave ship), Creole tales spun on the Plantation. No matter what appealed to him most, he certainly took lessons from these atavistic Western, African, and Amerindian cultures. His world is rife with a claim that is forever frustrated, aborted: the urgency of a Genesis, and its tragic denial.

Thomas Sutpen, in his madness, could have been compared to the God of Genesis. Or perhaps (a hardly less grandiose comparison) to the king of kings. Sutpen forces a world to be created, not a world inherited from anyone but rather a world that originates from his will alone, from his own deeds. Through his blood (by having an heir, a role his son, Henry, failed to fulfill, at least in Sutpen's eyes) he intends to guarantee the legitimacy and permanence of his dynasty. Herein lies his damnation. Perhaps we can say that Henry's damnation was to have realized that his father had not rested the full charge of any such hopes on his shoulders. This fervor is no less strong for the Sartorises than the Compsons, at least for those in earlier generations. The later generations do not have the slightest understanding of such preoccupations, except perhaps Quentin Compson, who kills himself.

Faulkner knew full well that the word in the story, except for atavistic Indian tales, was not inherited from an idea of Genesis but, on the contrary, was organized based on an opposite paradigm (which he set against the consuming dream of establishing a Foundation): one of listing and accumulating, repeating and going in circles—methods that work on a theoretical level, so contrary to a prophetic, decisive, and resolute act of creation.

The Creole stories of the Antilles, for example, question the Creation myth or throw it into turmoil. There we see a god trying to create the West Indian again and again. The result depends on how long this god leaves the clay of being in his cosmic oven. Sometimes the result is charred; sometimes it is insufficiently browned, even undercooked. The idea of the tale is to challenge the sacred and absolute nature of any

Genesis. At the very least, the sacred and the absolute are not linked to a mythic beginning.

The word in the tale cannot pretend not to know that at the birth of the Antillean or Caribbean people there was no Genesis, but a historical fact established over and over again and erased over and over again from public memory: Slavery. The holocaust of the slave trade and the belly of the slave ship (millions and millions of people displaced, killed, mutilated, raped, belittled, and made degenerate) confer a much more imperative Genesis, even if the origin proceeds from a point that is hybrid.

This new type of "origin," which is not about the creation of a world, I will call a "digenesis."

Every composite culture originates from a digenesis (which is not, in every case, a catastrophe such as slavery) whose component parts are multiplied ad infinitum. The god of Creole tales is a Plantation owner, the boss and arbitrator. He is wise and shrewd as a manager-in-chief. Already, he is a composite god.

Some of the Amerindian foundational myths also tell how the gods had to make several attempts before establishing the equilibrium of Creation. Creation occurs only after a series of tries, not as the product of a single decisive stroke. Further, these myths leave a sort of black hole, a gap of the unknown, between Creation itself and the beginning of human history.

So this is a Genesis, founding the sacred, but doing so outside the absolute legitimacy of possessing a community when it feels chosen by an unhesitating creator-god and when it has preserved this legitimacy by means of a family line, passed down from generation to generation. Children of such a Genesis conceive of themselves as the legitimate owners of the territory where they live. By contrast, Indians in the

Americas usually think of themselves as guardians, not owners, of the earth.

New York, December 1995. She gives me a playbill for a ballet by a Native American company: *Harvest Ceremony. Beyond the Thanksgiving Myth,* written by Marty de Mortaño and directed by two *storytellers.*

"We Are All Related"

Mita kuye oyasin is a Sioux word that means "we are all related" or "all my relations." It is widely used by many Native American people today and is used at the beginning and at the end of the day. It refers to the concept that not only are all people related, but that we are all related to the animals, plants, and to the earth. *Mita kuye oyasin* is often used at the closing of a prayer instead of "amen."

As I think of these words in French, *mita kuye oyasin* becomes "*nous sommes tous en Relation*" or "*tout m'est relation.*" First of all, it is an example of what I have called *la Poétique de la Relation,* the poetics of Relation. Second, this validates my intuition that atavistic cultures, when they have been oppressed, are best able to demonstrate and defend the selflessness of Relation, the interdependence of every sovereign and independent part of the world-totality. This is the lesson of *mita kuye oyasin.*

Ikkemotubbe-Doom neither marked nor consecrated the end of the Chickasaw people.

The word in Faulkner is constantly caught up in concrete realities, in everyday speech, in animal or human forms, in the harshness or sweetness of plant life, in a sort of common pleasure in brute existence, if not also in a jovial or angered vulgarity of people and things (that ironic and incisive way, perhaps endemic to whiskey drinkers, to tie the real with the unseen, making it dense, a quality he shares with Raymond Chandler, for instance), all of which mask the intentions of their words. He does this in such a way that to try to trace back to the deferred he uses and to the methods he pursues would necessarily mean turning these words into the abstract. Citing the texts themselves does nothing more than offend the whirlwind. Nevertheless:

Even if we believe that the tales and stories Faulkner heard in his youth never challenged the foundational authority of a Genesis, the way Creole tales do, we can at least believe that he sensed in these tales a denial of a challenge to the absolute legitimacy of a dynastic bloodline. The oral techniques of accumulation, repetition, and circularity combine to undo the vision of reality and truth as singular, introducing the multiple, the uncertain, and the relative instead.

Using oral techniques in a written text does not guarantee its beauty. If all we had to do was follow a writing formula, we would be quite valiant, those of us who write little but wander much and take our excess from the thousand imaginations comprising the World-Totality (that's what the crafty participants in the Faux Faulkner competition do with delight every year or so in Oxford, Mississippi). With that formula, we would construct beauties beyond numbering. Still, would these formulas ever give an accurate accounting of writing (Faulkner's) whose true object is the inextricable?

But the intuitions that we can have concerning this new organization of the word makes us feel that if these methods are not "sufficient," one can make lists in an insignificant way, use repetition foolishly, or employ circular or spiral methods and be inept. These procedures seem, just as validly, to be indispensable in this menagerie of oral and written forms combined and from which new associations of expression and divination are drawn.

·   ·   ·

For any storyteller, the most familiar way to describe something is through *accumulation*, by piling up the component parts of this so-called reality, or at least the elements whose presence he can detect.

To describe or present what exists by multiplying details of its constituent parts means challenging the pretension of penetrating the sense of things in a single shot. The list is one of the vectors of baroque thought, in opposition to the "search" for depth.

Making lists is a method to inventory, assemble, and reveal the component and often hidden parts of a digenesis (hidden when the digenesis tries to pass as a Genesis). This method is nonetheless not absent from the great, foundational books of communities. We know that it is because these books (contrary to the sectarian and exclusive use that has been made of them afterward) draw nuances and divert the "depth" of established roots to the variances of the expanded area, and to the accumulations achieved through wandering.

Even when the process of accumulation is not systematic, it permeates the fact of writing. Such is the case with Faulkner.

It would be wrong to require organization in these lists, or else dismiss them as a hodgepodge. The more the list pulls together distinct, heterogeneous elements, the more it does its job. According to Pierre Reverdy, this is the function of the poetic image and is exemplified in Apollinaire's repetition of "*Il y a*" ("There is").

There are all kinds of lists. Some can be differentiated not by what they accumulate but by the rhythm they give to the accumulation. Some lists blur our vision, dispersing us into multiplicity, into a flood of energies. Others aim to make a ritual of our worldview. Still others try to make connections between one reality and another.

Saint-John Perse's solemn lists are well known: lists of professions, places, and historical moments as in the melodic repeated figure "He who . . ." of *Anabase* and *Exile*, for example ("he who finds his calling in the contemplation of a green stone," etc.). These lists string out their material in a procession of individuals that seem terribly inevitable yet complement each other so well. Inventory of the magnified universal. Ritual rhythm. Human breath measuring the world's immeasurability.

And there are the breathless lists of Aimé Césaire's poetry that always begin: "Those who invented neither gunpowder nor electricity," etc. These lists group their material together into an open community, like enormous flames that try to scorch all reality, like emanations from a fabulous and black sun.

Faulkner's lists meticulously multiply the little wounds of daily life, encrusting everything into our field of vision. Faulkner uses lists to blow up to its infinite possibility a reality he wishes to survey; to defer the time when this reality is brought into true focus; or to expedite— there is no other word for it—its description of a reality that has meaning because of its dispersion.

". . . circular mail matter and mail order catalogues and government bulletins of all kinds. In one corner, on an up-ended packing-box, sat a water cooler of stained oxidized glass, in another corner leaned a clump of cane fishing-poles warping slowly of their own weight; and on every horizontal surface rested a collection of objects not to be found outside of a second-hand store—old garments, bottles, a kerosene lamp, a wooden box of tins of axle grease, lacking one; a clock in the shape of a bland china morning-glory supported by four garlanded maidens who had suffered sundry astonishing anatomical mishaps."

This sordid accumulation that subtly distinguishes itself from realist norms (*"lacking one"* and *"bland* morning-glory" and *"astonishing* mishaps")—this resembles Jacques Prévert's disorderly, disembodying lists. By the very act of extending its accumulations, the list adds to its object.

The poetics of the list (of objects, persons, or attributes) is derived directly from the orality of the tale, which cannot describe through striking and omniscient revelation. When a storyteller wants to stress the importance or the beauty of a house, he accumulates a list of the elements that compose it, exaggerating quantity over quality. This innocent practice has its virtues. Classical thought, devoted to harmony and depth, rarely utilizes this method of listing.

To disperse the knowable in space, or gather it into a focal point whose angles of approach are multiplied, is to renounce revelation and visitation by the Spirit. Since the universe is composed of a finite quantity of atoms (as Democritus and contemporary physics alike claim), the world-totality rallies around a finite number of places, and yet this list will never be exhausted because these places are constantly transforming themselves into one another. The accumulation is finite (in the mass it animates) and infinite (in the relation it proposes).

Repetition is a contrasting method whereby an element isolated from the real—or an aspect of thought—insistently reenters the discourse. This return bears a characteristic rhythm. Repetition marks the rhythm of the tale or narrative, stressing its important ideas. Most of the great, uplifting discourses of the contemporary world can be scanned in this way, such as Martin Luther King, Jr.'s "I have a dream" speech. This speech was uttered in the homiletic style of Black American preachers, men who imperceptibly enter into the chanted word as well as choral music. In the same way, assonance very often intervenes in the methods of repetition. When the written text adopts the economies of orality, it frequently tries to suggest or imitate this music.

Let us listen in on the buzz and hubbub of the Compson family and on the confusion of Benjy's expanded conscience:

> We could hear the roof and the fire, and a snuffling outside the door.
> "Where was he going to get a frog in November," Father said.
> "I dont know, sir," Quentin said.
> We could hear them.
> "Jason," Father said. We could hear Jason.
> "Jason," Father said. "Come in here and stop that."
> We could hear the roof and the fire and Jason.
> "Stop that now," Father said. "Do you want me to whip you again." Father lifted Jason up into the chair by him. Jason snuffled. We could hear the fire and the roof.

Jason snuffled a little louder.

"One more time," Father said. We could hear the fire and the roof.

Through repetition a secret contentment is born, a kind of innocent and provocative pleasure in infinitely multiplying expressions of the real, varying or elegantly giving them new nuances through what is said, slightly altered, and said again. The reader does not notice, at least at first, whether these repetitions are intentional or not, pertinent or not. Elocutionary wandering sends the certainties of the edict into divagation.

In the novels where there is a return to a hidden knowledge, a tearing through the veil to an unsuspected real, it's an expression of pain, or a screaming out of the forbidden—that is, in the traditional county novels, from *Sartoris* to *The Unvanquished*—list and repetition intervene as elements multiplying the real, from which uncertainty and indeterminacy arise. In fact, the more an object becomes known through the accumulation of its qualities or circumstances, the less one agrees with—the more one renounces—its "essence."

In the Snopes novels and the short stories, these methodologies appear in attenuated form. The Snopeses favor the art of the spoken word, of dialogue and conversation. As for the short stories, their objectives are too urgent for the prose to be slowed down with such tactics of diversion or unrestricted remultiplication.

All through the beginning of *Go Down, Moses*, especially in "The Old People" and "The Bear," Faulkner insistently returns to the makeup of the convoy that the hunters organize to get to their camp: "and now the boy made one—himself and his cousin McCaslin and Tennie's Jim and Major de Spain and General Compson and Walter Ewell and Boon and old Uncle Ash to do the cooking, waiting for them in Jefferson with the other wagon, and the surrey." At least five or six times, we see this same wagon and surrey leaving ("the boy and Sam and Uncle Ash in the wagon with the dogs, his cousin and Major de Spain and General Compson and Boon and Walter and Tennie's

Jim riding double on the horses"). We end up believing that old Ben is already there waiting for them, knowing they will come in procession on this same date every year. Here, this throbbing repetition confirms the solemnity of the time when the hunters reestablish their contact with the primordial life, and it heightens the importance of the episode in the initiation of young Ike McCaslin.

Another obsessional list is that of the aviation aces of the First World War (in *A Fable*): "the ringing heroic catalogue: Ball: Mc-Cudden: Mannock: Bishop: Barker: Rhys Davies: and above all, simply: England." "Victors or vanquished," all are grouped together in the same pantheon; you have the impression that Faulkner turns them into the heroes of his personal epic. Every time the list reappears, the order of presentation is slightly changed, as if he wants to mark the lack of distinction in the same glory.

Repetition enhances the list and its accumulation.

The *circularity* in the text proceeds directly from these techniques. One detail or one aspect augments its rhythmic momentum during development, returning the thought (of the person in question, of the author, or the reader) back to the beginning, but something is added each time, a variant that permits a certain spiral progression (unlike the variants in repetition which are purely playful).

Challenging the certitudes of linear narrative, this spiral expansion introduces improbability. Here again, it is fitting to cite whole sections of text to offer some examples. The reader has already found them, or will soon discover them, with satisfaction.

Circularity is reactivated by the semiritualistic use of "And" at the beginning of paragraphs:

"And at two o'clock that afternoon . . ."

"And it was noon." Etc.

Vertigo is revived and maintained by a sort of continuum just as the tone of a poem is maintained by this very same method at the beginning of each stanza or verse. This feeling of suspense is rein-forced by a formula of a different kind—but equally quasi-ritualistic—that Faulkner very often uses (after an exchange of dialogue that re-solves nothing): "And that was all." Then "It was all." Then "And that was just about everything," and so on, in a whirling textual rhythm as, for example, in the throbbing rhythm beating in the heart of "The Bear."

This formula effects no closure, but opens with a repetition, a reprise, a new development of a thought or an action.

Circularity heightens tension, allows a return to the deferred, and especially links the component parts of the "stream of consciousness." It is one path in the work of revelation. The more the motifs of the real add up or repeat themselves, the wider is the field that circularity enters, and the greater the vertigo of knowledge.

The dialogues in *Sanctuary* in particular—as well as that of Dewey Dell with her father, Anse, about the money she is going to get out of him in *As I Lay Dying*—work in repetition: each person who speaks stays stuck on his own idea, never breaking through the shell of the other, and the dialogue reaches no conclusion, but leads rather to a complete vertigo. The same uncertainty principle troubles the dia-logues in which a response—usually known by the reader, or at least assumed by him—never comes. The people in dialogue stubbornly spin around both question and answer. Vertigo.

A masterly example of this spinning is given in what we could call scenes of the incestuous game between Caddy and Quentin Compson, set in the scent of honeysuckle, where dialogue flows like a river but with a haunting circularity, like the Mississippi with its turns and bends, returning to the same daily (and what we could call pitiful) obsessions: Caddy's breasts, Dalton Ames's name (her suitor, her husband-to-be?), what Benjy does, etc.

Caddy
Dont touch me just promise

If you're sick you cant
Yes I can after that it'll be all right it wont matter dont let them send him to Jackson
   promise
I promise Caddy Caddy
Dont touch me dont touch me
What does it look like Caddy
What
That that grins at you that thing through them

Without any measures taken to distinguish them from one another, these dialogues are embedded within the masses of other dialogues with other people, all of which spin into the consciousness or suffering of Quentin (*The Sound and the Fury*).

An analysis of these methods can also allow us to grasp—and understand?—how the people in the county speak their own specific language without Faulkner needing an excess of systematic mechanics (like "peasant" speech, for example, in a play, or "slang" in a detective novel) and, *at the same time*, they speak a literary language (but without the ornamental affectations of "style"): the mysteries of language lie elsewhere—in stubbornness and fixity, repetition and circularity—which is why the language chosen for the protagonists of *As I lay Dying* works: they express themselves as poor White farmers *and* as literary characters. And in *Absalom, Absalom!*, language passes through the deferral, revelation, and contamination on which the writing functions. This is at once a sacred text and a vulgar proclamation, very down-to-earth and concrete.

All the same, when the young and already feverish Quentin Compson "tells" his friend Shreve ("with the conscientious corpulence") about Colonel Sutpen's childhood ("he could nonetheless smell whisky, hear in his father's voice this same fierce exaltation, this same revenge: 'tonight we really beat up one of Pettibone's niggers' "), we understand that the father's revenge is not directed against the Negro—who is but an object—but against Pettibone, who is rich; and we do not know if, in this "subjective narrative," we are perceiving things through the consciousness of Sutpen as a child, or through Quentin (or perhaps even Shreve, questioning what he is hearing), or through the narrator, who, we assume, was following this story as feverishly as young Compson.

This is not indecision or a confusion of "styles" on Faulkner's part. It is the spreading of a stream (of consciousness but, even more, of suffering) throughout the county, carrying different accents, which blend together in such a way that they inspire awe and alarm.

An important principle of Faulkner's writing appears in the *not only . . . but* construction, which appears quite often. Not only what you see but what you want not to see—are afraid to see. Not only the plowed earth, worn out by man's relentlessness, but the image of the earth, formerly still, untouched, and covered with its unspoiled Big Woods.

Not only the implacable rectitude of dynastic Foundation, the impossibility of which declares anathema and pronounces damnation, but even more so its perpetually deferred plot.

Not only the most miserable reality but the torment that deepens this misery and confers a grandeur upon it.

Jason Compson: "so that he had been robbed not only of his thievings but his savings too, and by his own victim; he had been robbed not only of the four thousand dollars which he had risked jail to acquire but of the three thousand which he had hoarded at the price of sacrifice and denial, almost a nickel and a dime at a time, over a period of almost twenty years: and this not only by his own victim but by a child who did it at one blow, without premeditation" (*The Sound and the Fury*).

This *not only . . . but* broadens the perception and vision of the real until it becomes a sort of whirlwind, relativizing our first idea of reality

with a second that spins it into vertigo. For one of the great battles of
the First World War, for instance, we read: "what would be known
afterward as the First Battle of the Somme—a matter which would
give even those who had survived to remember Loos and the Canal
not only something to blench for, but the discovery that something
even remained to blench with" (A *Fable*).

This principle of writing "problematizes" the real, allowing Faulkner
to sketch its underside (not its "depths") and expand its suggestive
possibilities, connecting up "the real" with other people's perceptions
of the real.

It is not through imperative description but rather through this *not
only . . . but* that the "strokes of consciousness" operate. Straight description would have exhausted the perception of the real and made
it rigid, making these floating, burning contacts with the "continuous
stream of consciousness" impossible.

In the Faulknerian text, *not only . . . but* and *perhaps . . . but* are the
most common devices of Faulknerian suspense which divides the real
and sometimes reverses its logic. Consider this example: "Then Ratliff
. . . found the solution, such a simple, limitless solution retroactively,
that they were not even surprised that no one had already thought of
it." To the reader's interjection "Why not?" comes the reply "they
were surprised that no one had yet thought of it." Then follows a
"solution that not only resolved the problem but annihilated it; and
not only this one, but all the problems from this day to perpetuity."
This suspense of writing is delectable in Faulkner yet ridiculous when
imitated.

Perhaps Ratliff had noticed the gulf that the ax had opened in what
had been Sam's throat, hardly any less red than the setting suns a young
boy dreams of when he is tormented. Or perhaps he had been paralyzed
by the immobility of the corpse wedged between the three impervious
rocks. Suddenly he found himself running, exhausted and on the look-

out, as though fleeing not only the spectacle of death but the very idea
or fear of it.

No, it is not wise to imitate this effect, even when you discover that
it is a caricature of itself in a speech by Ratliff, for example, or someone
like him, one of these experts in popular rhetoric who, like Shakespeare, purposely either exaggerate their language methods or accumulate them in parody: "Or maybe he just didn't know he had a reason
for Jefferson. Or maybe married men dont even need reasons, being as
they already got wives. Or maybe it's women that don't need reasons,
for the simple reason that they never heard of a reason and wouldn't
recognize it face to face, since they don't function from reasons" (*The
Mansion*).

These methods tell us nothing absolute about how Genesis takes
place. They are the endless detours by which a *digenesis* weaves its traces
and Faulkner enters into the realm of the worldly conjectural.

Writers operating in this bifurcated cultural sphere meet on common
ground outside the givens implied by their different languages.
Whether Faulkner erects a *damned Taboo* against any foreseeable Creolization, or if Saint-John Perse ultimately places his trust in the mag-
nitude of a *Universal* of language and knowledge, or if Aimé Césaire
goes through the ferments of the African diaspora in his search for a
painful Black *Essence*, in every instance what emerges from all these
totally different styles is the prescience of the tale and the memory of
myth, mixing the lesson forthcoming from any digenesis with the already decreed rules of a sovereign Genesis, until recently assumed to
be inescapable.

The sacred is what is woven in the Diverse and in the Relation.

Finally, we must look at the "function" or purpose of the narratives
and short stories separately. It should be repeated that Faulkner is not
a short-story writer, not a writer of novellas and short fiction. Nor is
he Pushkin, Chekhov, or Maupassant. That is not his concern. He

does not sculpt or polish. None of his short stories can be taken alone; they are not autonomous. But it is worth looking at them in their totality, for they all serve his complete works. What they share between them is not a unity of structure or intention. Chance certainly had its part in the writing, but so did an underlying continuity and Faulkner's need to put these ideas out into the open.

They clear the field (of the county, the South, the United States, the other places linked thereto—the locatable, knowable, inhabitable?) and mark it as a surveyor does, not as properties but as possibilities that need to be explored further. They introduce people who reappear later in his novels, or they return to others to submit them to a more intense interrogation. They let us wander through the county in every direction and, as in the case of the "European" short stories, they extend these characteristics abroad: this is what damns the population.

Many of them come together as novels—such as those that make up *Go Down, Moses* (the early editions were called *Go Down, Moses and Other Stories*)—or those that form *The Unvanquished*. It seems likely that at the time they were written Faulkner considered the prospect of bringing them together as one volume or novel and so shaped them with this end in mind rather than in line with the specifics of the short-story genre.

In many instances, adding a particular story to a finished novel or larger saga changes its very nature and our view of it: it can be sparse, off-center, endlessly multiplied. The structure of *The Unvanquished* or *Go Down, Moses* is as innovative as that of *The Sound and the Fury*.

Sometimes the stories operate as works distinct from one another and yet all refer to the same project. The lengthy short story "Evangeline," for example, which has been reworked in the novel *Absalom, Absalom!* and in the "true novel" *Flags in the Dust* is little by little transformed into *Sartoris* (ultimately projecting into *Intruder in the Dust*), without our really being able to say that any of these is the definitive version.

In the same way, *The Mansion* reuses many scenes and features of *The Hamlet*, approaching them in another way and leading them toward something different. This has long since been established, particularly by French commentators. In his preface to the French edition of *These Thirteen*, René-Noël Raimbaut writes, "But what more can be said about these short stories except that, outside of the novels, they make you think of surplus materials temporarily placed on reserve during the completion of the edifice? Within the totality, they take and assume their rightful place at the proper time." They certainly do. These forty-odd short stories and other texts serve as points of reference in a geological upheaval. This is ignored whenever these short stories are grouped and judged in terms of their relationship to one another.

Sometimes these short pieces "fill the gaps" between novels. This may reflect Faulkner's attempt to complete the portrait of a character neglected until that point, represent one landscape over another, give further precision about parts of the county history not broached until then, establish delicate and unsuspected bridges between diverse places or episodes, confirm or praise features of nature or characters, or further illustrate their predilections, whether for malediction or failure or solitude. They are the stitches in the narrative fabric. In every story, the details vary considerably from one version to the next.

We know from Faulkner himself the dates of composition of almost all his works; who knows, however, whether he left many of them lying in drawers for a long time, exposing them to "the gnawing criticism of worms" before digging them out and christening, renaming, and dating them anew. In any event, "Wash" prefigures, or takes up again, or re-creates from the beginning the story of Sutpen's factotum, and tells of the birth of Milly's girl, Sutpen's visit, and the death of all of these people, Milly, her daughter, Sutpen, and Wash himself, somewhat as all this is told in the stories of *Absalom, Absalom!* (transmitted "like a contagion"). Sometimes the story repeats the text of the novel word for word. But the variants (the "contradictions") are no less fascinating to identify. Not for a moment does the reader think the repetition is without purpose.

Three or four of these short stories provide complementary information about family genealogies: for the Sartorises in "There Was a Queen," for the founding families in "Hand upon the Waters." Yet no dates are given except when necessary for the story itself. Time has become astounded by impossibilities. If these short stories are the threads that tighten the county's narrative fabric, they also serve to stretch it, filling it with unknown and unyielding times and spaces.

Nonetheless, you sometimes wonder which "uncle" is the subject of the story you are reading, or if the Spanish major who is a hunter in "The Bear" is the same one who is the sheriff in *Absalom, Absalom!* and the same one who is the mayor of Jefferson in *The Town*. The three majors are the same man, but you have to struggle to figure this out. All these people are contemporaries even if dozens of years separate them. It is befitting to find one's bearings in this whirlwind.

When I was finishing this book, Americans finalized their campaign against all demon smokers. To be accepted in the United States, the French comic cowboy Lucky Luke had his rolled cigarette replaced with a sprig of grass. In science-fiction films the outlaw gang was called the Smokers. From that point, "Smokers!" took on the connotation of "Pirates!" On television only the bad guys would drag on tobacco spliffs.

My friend Muriel Placet was kind enough to make me a photocopy of an essay by Faulkner that I had not remembered reading. This Faulkner essay seems most fitting for the subject at hand, for it is called "Mississippi." It was published in the April 1954 issue of *Holiday*, and I am tempted to compare it to the *Compson Appendix* or to the beginning of *Requiem for a Nun*. As always, Faulkner returns to the Chickasaw and the Choctaw, the Natchez and the Yazoo; to the families that produced colonels for the war, and then to the war itself; to the Blacks, who were one of its pretexts, and almost immediately to the Snopeses. It is a summary of what he scrutinized throughout his works and felt in his life.

"Mississippi" is a personal recollection (particularly the long homage to Caroline, i.e., Mammy Barr) with a historical fresco, the latter marked by destiny and—what would seem impossible, destiny being inflexible—by the improbability and uncertainty of the South.

This essay does not have the metaphorical and almost legendary aspect of the *Compson Appendix*, or its dazzling coincidences; nor does it have the epic tremors of the beginning of *Requiem*. But echoes of these two works can be found in "Mississippi," which is about, or all around, each of his works.

In the essay, you can feel an aggressiveness, a certain disguised plea, and an interrogating irony. There are also some strange deviations in it, such as Faulkner's reflection upon two incarnations of the Ku Klux Klan: the first desperate and, to a certain extent, honest, born at the end of the Civil War (as a justified reaction to Yankee oppression), and the second completely repulsive, dating from the 1920s!

Developments in the history of the "Negro"—slave, small farmer, railroad laborer, etc.—as well as reflections on the evolution of Jefferson always initiate short yet complete, incisive novels (where people appear for an extended dialogue or two). These novellas inform us about Faulkner's vision and about the real.

No longer than forty or fifty pages, they are punctuated by dates corresponding with the narrator's life that are clear and easy to follow. The descriptions in these stories concentrate on the landscape of the county and its outer reaches.

Time and space once again become ordinary, everyday, and verifiable.

The Snopeses are ever-present, and a "pre-Snopesian" time is talked about in the same way that one speaks of an "antebellum" house or as Faulkner himself evokes a pre-Culloden mode (speaking of the place that witnessed the defeat of the Scottish poet-warriors and where one of the Compson ancestors was lost in 1745)—Scotland before defeat, the South before defeat, the county before the Snopeses—the golden age that can be felt or dreamed of at every turn.

This essay flows in "relation" to the work as an ensemble; Faulkner the child is "staged" for the same reasons as the county inhabitants or the author's own family; the imagined Jefferson is described, as are the real, great plains of the North that lead toward Alabama; in the same way, the river, the Old Man, is narrated by everything that travels on it or surrounds it: boats, plantations, cotton trading (cotton bolls and "baled" cotton), Memphis, the bayous, Pontchartrain Bay, fish and crayfish (whose flesh, rather faint in taste because of the vast river's freshwater, calls for red pepper and highly seasoned sauces), New Orleans, the splitting up of this great waterway, the works themselves indivisible from reality and, once again, the distant places, the Caribbean ("a place called the West Indies to which poor men went in ships and became rich, it didn't matter how, so long as that man was clever and courageous"), the inseparability of the world from the county.

Why touch on an autobiography of this kind—mixing history, critical analysis, and an indirect presentation of his works with an uncontrolled temper—at a time when I am trying to get closer to the Faulknerian word, his disguises and systematic evasions? Because this is what the whole text means, and Faulkner sums it up in the last, single-sentence paragraph:

Faulkner (the child, the adolescent, the mature man): "Loving all of it even while he had to hate some of it because he knows now that you dont love because: you love despite; not for the virtues, but despite the faults."

It seems to me (if we accept another insolent simplification) that

•   •   •

Let us return to what is evident and what is deferred in the writing.

It is amusing, or amazing, to note how Faulkner, on the occasions when he speaks of one of his books, immediately represents himself as a meticulous and modest commentator, reducing the work to a pretext and to the literal coherence of its "story." On *The Sound and the Fury*: "I thought it would be interesting to imagine the thoughts of a group of children on the day of their grandmother's burial," or about Sutpen in *Absalom, Absalom!*: "he violated all the rules of decency and honor and pity and compassion, and the fates took revenge on him. That's what the story is," etc. Faulkner coolly plays at being simple. It is as though, faithful to a T to his project and to the very method of its creation, he hides while revealing. Giliane Morell, in her introduction to the French translation of *Mosquitoes*, interprets it this way: "It is as though the words in which the subject is unknowingly alienated, captured in a discourse that unconsciously determines them, were manipulated by Faulkner like a double-edged weapon"—he was content to clarify merely the possibility of the work in question and, in his commentary about it, to choose to conceal the deferred, the already buried intentions, and the impossibility of writing. This is something he never admits.

"Go see for yourself, because it's written there."

I would say that if Faulkner is manipulating a weapon, he has not chosen to brandish it (we could say that it is the work that has little by little molded him) or that he has not whetted his double-edged sword, having found it fully formed in the savannas where warriors died or, perhaps at the same time, in the cotton fields where Blacks labored to death.

The conversations between Linda (Eula Varner Snopes's daughter) and Gavin Stevens are among the few true endings in the entire work—consequences of the evident and the deferred.

Let us recall the circumstances. Linda has come back from the

Spanish Civil War, where she lost her husband and her hearing as consequences of a bombing raid. She is odd; she is possibly being followed by the FBI and is barely tolerated by the ordinary residents of Jefferson, who call her a "nigger-lover" because of her reasoned and moderate defense of Blacks. Stevens protects her. He thinks he is in love with her, and she with him. But we suspect them of being as careful to avoid each other as they are eager to meet. When they see each other, they speak through a conversation notebook in which Stevens jots down his answers to Linda, while she speaks to him directly. She is the voice; he is writing. The voice is female; writing is male. At least, that is what a first reading of this convention of a new genre suggests.

This is not a way to flood the writing with the methods of orality—such as repetition, lists and accumulation, circularity, music and assonance; nor is it a way of mixing together two or more insights of the real, and their insinuations, as is done in the exchange between Stevens and Ratliff, or in the chitchat in the county; rather, it is a way of resolutely appending the spoken to the written, watching to see what will ensue.

These verbal joustings, whose separate elements can be isolated only with difficulty since the game is played so cautiously, are a hymn, a praise-song to the relationship between the writing and orality. I will try to illustrate with a single, brief citation, where the *written*, and its regrets or enticement, is italicized.

> He could have written *I have everything. You trusted me. You chose to let me find you murdered your so-called father rather than tell me a lie.* He could, perhaps, should have written *I have everything. Haven't I just finished being accessory before a murder.* Instead, he wrote *We have had everything.*
> "No," she said.
> He wrote *Yes.*
> "No," she said.
> He printed *YES* this time in letters large enough to cover the rest of the face of the tablet and erased it clean with the heel of his palm and wrote . . .

Here there is every possible fracture and craving between silence and shouting, sudden insight and hesitation, expression and dissimulation, reserve and excitement, concise sentences and jerky explanations, exclamations and intuition, drafts and corrections, regret for the spoken and textual deviations, immobile bodies and gesture—Faulkner uses the whole gamut of the written and the spoken in their apposition and opposition. Genesis is a memory here, and digenesis is in perspective. The depths, arisen from days of yore, and an expanse into the infinity of the world. Feminine and masculine perhaps mixed anew, attaining another transcendence or questioning.

The hypothetical element of such writing, hesitant at the edge of a powerful orality, and yet composing with it (we are far from "spoken language"), is ultimately akin to what has marked the language of revelation in the novels of malediction with such distinction. Here, in an absolute sense, the language of revelation is returned to a truth, albeit deferred, distant, and uncertain; the new form of writing defers as well, but defers to what is perhaps another kind of truth: relative and open, neither damnable nor contemptuous.

However, to what reality of the county does this latter form of writing introduce us? What comes at the end of this prolonged wandering, this divagation of the word? On what—or on whom—can we then rely for the development of the story?

On the slow and ordinary misfortune of Linda, locked up in her deafness. On this most conventional "installation" of Gavin Stevens, whom we suspect will see less and less of his friend Ratliff, the last herald of the word in the land. On the wandering or vagrancy of Ratliff, who is incapable of settling in any particular place in the county long enough to benefit from it. He tried to establish a business in the heart of Jefferson, but was swindled by one of the Snopeses. From then on, his wandering was dull and fruitless. As if the renunciation of tragic grandeur could engender only limitation and banality, or lead only to uncertainty, which does not possess the grandeur and stature of the Uncertain.

So we remember Boon Hogganbeck, a commoner and descendant of the Chickasaws. Just as the slave Sam Fathers was a descendant from a princely lineage, Boon was a descendant of the people who had arrived in wagons, one of the guardians of the memory of the Big Woods, the only one of the officiants of the ritual hunt who was never able to kill any sort of animal. After the deaths of the three others (Ben, Sam, Lion) he smashed his rifle, married a bighearted prostitute, and knew a transparent paternity, perhaps the first in the county: the birth of a son, whom he and his wife named Lucius Priest Hogganbeck, in honor of the young runaway in *The Reivers*—linking the wilderness to the city, the great families to the new people, the natives to the immigrants, and the totality to the totality (even though the wilderness had dried up and the town was already threatened).

This "final" literature, as we were saying, yielded no ethic or moral. It simply consented to the real on the condition that it could derive a hidden meaning from it. But we discover that what is bastard, mixed, ordinary, or even reprehensible in Boon is the very thing which, in the long run, endures and enlightens.

And this real in the county is a frontier-real—that is, it negotiates a path of reconciliation through a number of unforeseeables.

So then, yes, we feel intuitively that damnation has exhausted itself, and the world is becoming more open. Writing has conquered fatality. But Faulkner will never say this explicitly, he will never draw such an overt conclusion. That would amount to giving away the cause with the effect.

Is this, the ordinariness of things, once again unspoken, a definitive renunciation of epic language?

We sense that the word, which from now on cannot be questioned in the traditional way, through these identities that are closed back on themselves and which we stubbornly perpetuate everywhere in our world—the word from now on is useless in the county that believes it has lost everything in losing damnation, and the word has reserved itself for another purpose.

The way in which the epic voice has put itself into question, and how it has immediately responded to this questioning, bringing the entire real of the Mississippi into the movement of virtue and blame, has opened up another movement, another word, one that is exploded. And in being exploded, this word has created Relation, which in its circularity has engendered Totality and, finally, from having always been diffracted, forms an archipelago—or at least points to one—in many places of the world.

What have we discovered at the end of the story? If we must give up the wild (innocent) passions of the traditional epic form, be it Moses or Absalom or Priam or the impetuous Achilles, and if we agree that in all this sound and fury of the world, the tragic Sounds and Furies are unappealing and inoperable for us, we can nonetheless "open" up to a different wandering and a different establishment of roots, affecting our conscious and contemplative presence in this world-totality. At this pace and on these traces we can agree that the very idea we have formulated regarding our surroundings and our everyday lives is to dream in a different way. And that our countries—our country—open precipices for us that we have carefully avoided. That our daily lives, our most conventional foundations, are separated in these depths of our relationship with the world. That we find ourselves to be an open frontier.

And that we should, we could, begin again—completely, totally—a new type of humanity.

·   ·   ·

All of this can be found in the work of Faulkner. Yes. But we will not easily see it, impressed as we are by the author's artistry. We are dazed by what we call his "depth," his knowledge "of the human heart," and by the phenomenal staging in which he "captures" all these people he conceptualizes. We are lost in the inextricable, in the tangle of everything that he conceals and reveals simultaneously with the trace, the path down which he takes us.

Would it be better not to delve into his works and simply to enjoy them without asking any questions? But this is where we live, here, there, over there, everywhere ("darkness and darkness"), prey to happiness, subject to our damnations or giving voice to our revolt. We cannot abstract ourselves from the notion: "To keep our place in the world in order to signify the world in its entirety."

Furthermore, what do we feel about the disorder in this world, especially when we believe we are sheltered from its fits of anger? Savage poverty wildly ragged in enormous cities, solitude but no haven in the old countries where madness hibernates, overly flat landscapes smoothly covering over their boils, convulsive assassinations and the impassive suicides with which they conclude, successive murders ("serial killers" in action), and the genocides, if not newly legitimated at least met with universal indifference. There are millions of deaths that we no longer ask any television station to tally up for us. The invisibility of the international structure of power and finance, whose center is everywhere and boundaries nowhere; and the multinational force of mute terror that, with such regularity, has killed off Gandhi and Martin Luther King and Malcolm X and Yitzhak Rabin and those whose names we have forgotten. Where are they, these anonymous and immeasurable obituaries? What cold mechanism makes yesterday's slaughtered today's butchers? There is the everyday: the waste of our rivers, the air, the mountains, the damned and distressed oceans and dying forests, the unstoppable stupidity of the great convulsions of planetary consumerism with its crude tastes, simple interests at eye or ear level—hold on! What gives you the right to deem things crude or simple, what gives you title to these pretensions of delicate senses and tastes, huh? And all of this is heating up, it is the inextricable banality of the world chaos of which no single description, no accumulation of information on any Internet, and no narration will ever exhaust the rhythm or point out the finite quantity. Time races so quickly over all this that we find ourselves confined inside this deathly pale multitude even before we can witness the collective putrefaction of the dead bodies that we already are. We predict, however, that it is this struggle in the distended, naked world that clashes, kneads, and mixes—while we obstinately feel (think) as though we have always been able to go to our churches, our communal huts, our temples, our synagogues or our mosques, or sit under the shade of our totems near our fires, cooking our rice or yams or bread, living the exclusionary lives of those who assemble in groups only to be able to separate themselves from others—which leads us into lives of contradiction.

And there we would find not only what could be called hope but also what we could conceive of as the only opening: a detour through the imaginary and impermanent, in our own sensibilities, the contradiction between this expansion and this confinement. To be at one and the same time the insane tree from here and the bird of multiplicity from over there. To enter into a new emotion and an unprecedented feeling of the world collectivity, where we neither lose nor dilute ourselves, and where the frontier of the inside-outside would no longer give rise to, or maintain, an impossibility.

This is difficult.

In an essay entitled "Poetry and Knowledge" (published in the January 1945 issue of the journal *Tropiques*), referring to Rimbaud and the "modern idea of the energizing forces in matter that lie in wait for our peacefulness," Aimé Césaire remarked: "And you know the result: strange cities, extraordinary countryside, worlds that are twisted, crushed, and tattered, the cosmos given unto chaos, order made into disorder, being made into becoming, the absurd everywhere and everywhere the incoherent and demented. At the end of all of this, what do we find? Failure? No. The dazzling vision of our own destiny, and the most authentic vision of the world."

Most of the communities in our world (those that have been formed traditionally, around the fireside) are physically threatened in their very existence, even beyond what is comfortable for us to consider. But no longer are any of them threatened in their right to assemble. That right is no longer debatable. For such a great number of peoples in Africa, Asia, in the Americas and in Oceania. Extinction, yes; famine, yes; genocide, yes; epidemic disease, yes; "yes" to terror and disappearance—but even in the parade of living skeletons or in the endless line of unburied corpses, no one is any longer denied the human and very tacit right to be recognized as self, as a non-other, as outside of others.

Daring to offer up a hymn, repetitive and pulsating but revitalized, to the notion as well as to the word: "community"!

1. The only community today that is struck down in its right to constitute a community is the world-community.

2. In so many of these traditional communities threatened by physical disappearance tragedy remains, but the new epic word emerges from out of this community, the only one that does not conceive of itself or feel itself as a community: the world-totality, the whole world.

3. The epic has the responsibility for the word in every community:
   —the excluding epic, of yesterday or of days long past, from the time

when human communities conceived of themselves in ethnic and almost genetic terms, as much by the "universality" of their individual cultures;

—the concluding and participatory epic that could lead to the appearance of the world community of today, in which the "universal" would be the finite and infinite quantity for all cultures and all humanities.

4. Let us strike up this epic song, and take care not to sacrifice ourselves to it uniquely, because it takes care not to be univocal.

5. The literatures of the world are present and presented all together in such a prodigiously diversified way in this epic—as though appearing before the stunned face that, once again, all together, looks at us.

In the extreme situations he uses to represent what is extreme in the world, Faulkner has shown that the tension of the traditional epic, defining each community through exclusivity, is no longer a factor for us.

The grandiose epic that excludes the other is nothing but frippery for us, even if we may still savor and admire its immense nobility in *The Iliad* or in d'Aubigné's *Tragiques* or in so many other foundational works of the communities of yesteryear, from the Old Testament to the *Kalevala*.

We are closest to these great, inspiring books of the civilizations of yesterday. To these, we can add the epics of the African emperors. Legends of the gods of India. Songs of the Berber and Arab heroines. Cosmographies of all these cultures. Trips to the lands of the Dead. Tens of thousands of lines of poetry, verses, and stanzas declaimed throughout the world and in every language by singers with their incandescent memory.

The lesson in these books, in these compendia, is inexhaustible. Their wandering and their establishment of roots. Through them, we get a sense of how the epic word functioned.

Faulkner's works have taken their vertiginous turn.

The tragedy of the Sutpens, the Sartorises, and the Compsons (the denial of Foundation); what is inextricable in the fierce relations between races, families, and people, and the damned rejection of everything that verges on the mix—these are the very signs that we can begin something else: the unpredictable, the uncertain, the ambiguous—world chaos.

Each one of us sensed it, every time one of these books appeared that take us along the trace. We have sensed the colors, that certain mauve that is more melancholy than mournful; the smells, stubborn and obsessive, like tangible objects; and the feeling of the inevitable. We have sniffed the flowers that cannot be picked, and felt the suspension of the word, the word of the tale which is that of our digeneses, and which still bears traces of memory from the former geneses. There is nothing greater than this.

The world-community calls forth this other epic which was prefigured by Faulkner: that of the difficult Relation.

7

THE FRONTIER—THE BEYOND— BACK ON THE TRACE

The fascination that frontier worlds exercised on the imagination seems to have been universal. Thirty or forty years ago, the cowboy and pioneer in the Far West were the heroes of film, lionized by everyone, everywhere in the world, even in colonized countries, and little children in Africa or the Caribbean screamed to let frontiersmen know when a stealthy Indian was sliding up behind them. Tarzan ruled the sensibilities of the young, wherever they happened to be. The wars of decolonization, those waged most recently in Vietnam, for example, have undoubtedly led to a turnaround, and the film industry has decided to make films exposing the dispossession of Indian nations: commercial successes such as *Cheyenne*, *The Blue Soldier*, or *Little Big Man*, with all the ambiguities commercialism commands. The very same ambiguities, if not the same paternalism, filled the screen with the first Black heroes in Westerns or films about history, *The Black Sergeant* or *Glory*. Commercial success continues to anoint subjects that are just as sensitive: women's issues, *Boys on the Side*, virtual reality and multimedia, *The Net*, all on a constantly revolving platform of violence. From one style to another, the image impassively glows; film thinks of itself as singularly eternal.

For our subject: courage without fail, a rigorous sense of duty, an inherent respect for the rule that requires everyone—Black, White, Indian—to stay fixed in the situation and place assigned to them. In reconstructing historical truth, there was a need to move forward cautiously, one step at a time, so as not to shock the public, which was unprepared for any revision.

The mirage of new spaces, the thrill of unknown danger. Because of film and other media, these common reactions in sentiment or impulses to go West were felt by everyone, especially those who never ventured far from home, people who never had either the desire or the means to explore or colonize, but who remained fascinated customers, avid consumers of the spectacle of adventure.

What is at work, then, is the formidable enterprise of reduction, from the Diverse to the Same. For participants as well as onlookers, the frontier is the place that includes all that and where, paradoxically, an opening (a transformation, a change) is available at every moment.

All during the time of colonization, there has always been a frontier, endlessly renegotiated. A physical frontier offering new space to colonize, and an intellectual and mental frontier between Western ideals and the threatened realities of colonized peoples. Just as the physical frontier encourages and satisfies a yen for adventure, rape, and murder, the mental frontier generates problems and anguish on both sides of the border.

Because Algeria was a colony which France populated (much more so than Morocco or Tunisia), it was one of these vexed borders for people like Albert Camus, who obviously could not identify fully with the Arabic or Berber cultures or see themselves in relation to the laws of colonial or settler right.

Because it was a land populated under slavery, the American South, more than the Far West (where the expanding frontier allowed the pioneers little leisure or time to contemplate the soul), knew and suffered the troubled condition of those who tried to justify themselves after turning their fellow men into slaves. I cite those who, like William Faulkner, did not accept that the South was utterly condemned because it was a slave society, and yet could not see, in this situation, a violation of the humanism they otherwise claimed to have.

Saint-John Perse, who belonged to the same Plantation world, but in the West Indies, could not help feeling that Blacks were more than just raving witch doctors in service to the big House, bighearted servants, or simple children addicted to noise and drama. Once, when he was famous and outside the fray, he took the trouble to have a young poet say he "was not the colonialist I thought he was."

On the frontier, the relationship with the other is expressed emblematically: the frontiersman withdraws unto himself screaming the usual absurdities: "Let's kill all the Indians" or "Arabs" or "Jews" or "niggers" or "immigrants"—in other words, all the horrible people. Mentally there is conflict between his necessary humanity and a refusal to condemn *what* offends humanity in racism and intolerance. This is the uncomfortable, anguished stance of Faulkner, Perse, and Camus. They sow the seeds for a poetics of becoming, a nexus for diverse cultures.

When the frontier is a national border, it is also prey to such polarities. There is a xenophobic nationalism in the feeder cities in the east and southeast of France (which Brittany, on the coast, and the southwest, where menacing waves of immigrants no longer pass, and Paris, the heart of the country, were to some extent spared). In those places, there was a reticent, alert awareness of the sort you find in big cities such as New York or Los Angeles which thrive on the "mix." You can see how contradictory the world is: in America, the regions least threatened by immediate immigration, the Midwest for example, are the ones where conservative nationalism is most tenacious (accompanied, it is true, with a strong support of states' rights). Finally, there has emerged a new belief in a common identity when the frontier has been able—as in the Caribbean and the Pacific—to destroy its own contradiction, before reformulating it within a national exclusivity.

Of these three writers, it seems to me that, through his work, William Faulkner possessed the strongest sense of these interconnected roots and plantings, of a new poetics. Perhaps that is because he is the only one really to have implicated the setting of his work, the Place, in the vague interrogation of legitimacy.

Saint-John Perse and Camus carried their setting with them like an effervescent and melancholy source. Like a poetics, it can be found in *Eloges* and in *Tipasa Wedding*. And they transformed it into something else, into the clarity of the troubled mind or into the equanimity of Universal thought.

Faulkner locks himself up in the place and confronts it.

Physical frontiers disappear more easily than mental ones, and for a frontier region such as the American South, it is hard to transcend the frontier.

Today, there is a proliferation of frontier worlds, some traditional and others suddenly emergent, suggested to some and imposed on others.

The frontier is like sand that is always shifting, but instead of submerging the conflicts it has provoked or surprised in its environment, it enlarges and exposes them, exploding them to infinity with its disruptiveness.

Faulkner's world is a frontier.

Not only because the Mississippi River is the invigorating torrent, and the Yoknapatawpha and Tallahatchie rivers, rather than tributaries or branches, are its mythic daughters. Not only because the whole South, and by extension the state of Mississippi and consequently its projection, Yoknapatawpha County, are actually frontier sites. But also and especially because the writing Faulkner has used to re-create these places—this Place—has also literally stirred up something: movement, hesitation, transition, uncertain identities, and truths that cannot escape the charm of the possible and the impossible all mixed together.

Certainty—nurtured in the Western tradition by more than two thousand years of word and deed, of literature and customs, of shadows and glories—has maintained that truth is directly attainable, that beauty sweeps us toward it, even across the chasm, and that beauty arises or appears out of the ready or knowing disguise we have developed to fit with the form of what is said. This certainty maintains that there is value in this form, and that this value in turn grounds the law of those who "speak," who are also those who act (who know and conquer the world)—that is, those who claim to be the makers of what they call History.

So this certainty is nothing but the blurred venue of narrative art and the art of governing the so-called future of the humanities: conjoint and indistinguishable.

On the other hand there is the *charm*, the relentless vertigo of feeling that truth is not always revealed this way, that it is deferred infinitely beyond all the expanses that can be envisioned (which explains why the county's limited expanse, pulling all the others together, is enough to indicate it). We approach it only through spurts of disclosure, the way water withdraws in successive waves, each following its own current, leaving behind muddy streaks and silt and spores of life from the deep. And the only certainty, no, the only inspiration that comes out of this is that the unspeakable truth still burns in the county like damnation. Faulkner's writing, undulating the length of this current and riding these waves, making this trajectory visible; and this, in turn, truly establishes his work as a frontier.

Something happens, and then we move on to something else. The writing addresses those who question History, who humbly distrust the proud narrative, who try to amass, reduce, break, and tinker with; who measure and render outside of measure; who do not exercise any systematic thought, but rather follow obstinate and fragile paths. Faulkner's work is one of these paths or traces. An anonymous, various, scattered frontier.

The space of traditional epic is vast, but it is circumscribed.

Either we cannot enter it, except through misfortune, or once we have entered it we find it difficult and dangerous to leave. It is the inviolable Trojan wall, the meandering Mediterranean path of Ulysses, the orbit of earthly Paradise, Land promised and lost and promised again, the arena of Roncevaux ("High are the mountains, and dark and somber") where Roland calls, the circles of Hell surrounding Dante, the sea between Iceland and Scandinavia where the heroes of the sagas hover. Otherwise, epic leads to an enclosed place, but only after wandering forever: the borders of Rome, drawn at its foundation, where Aeneas's course finally ends.

This circularity is not as dispersed as in the Caribbean, in the Pacific or other island chains; it is not digenetic; it does not diffract. It is the all-powerful sphere where Being originates; it is the interior sea. The epic served to distinguish an "inside" from an "outside" and to reassure those on the inside (those in the community), uniting them in the thought that bad times, misfortune, defeat, and tribulations would pass, and that wandering is purifying and has a goal or end.

•   •   •

The South is not just a place of frontier; it is also this enclosed place. Certainly, we find the same characteristics present in the Far West (an obsession with open spaces, cleared vistas, and the relationships with the Indians, which, in Faulkner's work, is more mocking than fatal). But this is not a tailor-made frontier that moves and makes adjustments. It is an absolute frontier, displaced only by the immobile, and carrying within itself its own insoluble contradiction.

Obstinately, Faulkner maintains the enclosed place.

He takes this contradiction all the way to its furthest extreme, sustaining the tension of the earlier epic ("it is up to us to solve the problem") before deciding that it will not work. Then he invents a new epic.

And when he names an elsewhere, he has already transposed this place there—not as if it were a reverberating memory but rather like a burn that cannot be extracted from the skin—that communicates everywhere and all around what stirs and agitates him so frantically.

And when he says that neither the wandering nor the affliction has an end, he already means that the place lives on, nonetheless, in this infinity.

For him, as for us all hereafter and everywhere, place cannot be avoided, in the sense that it reaches far into the distance, not like an expansion of territory, but like a contagion, an infection of the imaginary.

As is true for every country in the world, the South, in this instance, is stronger than its own damnation, more resolute than its "error," more stubborn than any merit or any virtue. The Whites, whether they be farmers or clerks or laborers, come together to dance to the sound of their country music. Today, we see that Native Americans, Cajuns, African-Americans, Black Cajuns, Black Indians, and Hispanic Americans reside there, living together despite prejudice, social inequality, sheriffs, the misery in Black neighborhoods and the isolation of the bayous. Creolization is alive and well there, as it is throughout the United States (where the ethnic mosaic nevertheless still appears impenetrable, noncommunicative, and often hostile to itself) and around the world.

But this is difficult.

There have been contemporary French writers who pointed the place out for us. Amazed, we found that they seemed to position themselves, if one could put it this way, on rather backward and reactionary slopes on their respective mountaintops: Georges Bernanos, Jean Giono, and Paul Claudel. We remember what "the return to the land" darkly suggested for the national revolution. But those whom I have just named also praised the extravagant and extroverted places of the word: *Knowledge of the East* and the *Song of the World*.

We had discovered strange countries.

The monotonous and hypnotic undulations, the temporary rather than permanent residences, the land of the Ardennes running along the horizon, with André Dhôtel.

The urban haunts of Aragon and Breton, the Parisian peasant and Nadja's amazement. We had learned the streets, the strange and worn passages, the dusty public squares (going from Plantation to town—from mansion to hamlet—to the City, which had not yet developed all its tributaries and tentacles), and the pale streetlamps echoed the torches lighting our tales.

For a long time we had pored over Victor Segalen, and learned with him the bitter taste of the Diverse. The variance of place. A variance that would later confirm the fundamental essence that Jean Grosjean had predicted and read in everything.

We had noted the provocative stance of the Beat generation poets in the United States, who constructed in the imaginary, for one of the first times, a nexus of place in this country. Wandering as the site of assembly. And other places, just as concrete and significant, beckoned

in the world: and so did the roads of the Black diaspora in the Americas. The countless, unspeakable places.

There had been this dispossession of the world, which Jacques
Berques would look at one day: this pile of places, stripped of their
meaning, that western expansion has strewn and accumulated everywhere. This meaning had to be regained. From the depths of these
villages in the bush or the savanna, from the sweltering deserts, from
the stalks of cane watching our fear, at high noon. And from so many
other places, trapped in the impossible, at every crossroad and in every
peninsula: in the Middle East, Indochina, Korea, and the Balkans.

And each time a new place was opened and Creolized—in Lebanon,
in Bosnia, or in Rwanda—it found itself splintered by forces that had
reemerged from the singular root. Everyone took part, on one side or
another, with all the good reasons one can proclaim, without ever
attempting or even proposing to uproot this singularity.

In short, a long time ago we realized that the works of an Alejo
Carpentier or an Aimé Césaire were beginning to constitute a new
kind of literature, outside the frontiers of language, one that linked
together churning seas and tremulous earthquakes in a place free of
brush, the enormous and well-detailed accumulations and traces and
etchings of a William Faulkner or a Jorge Luis Borges.

We knew the uncertain deserts of Kateb Yacine and had become
familiar with all the shabby elegance of gray sands and the simple
magnificence in the echoings of Arabic poetry, just as we had known
the beaches of Brittany and *The Horse of Pride* by Pierre Jakez Hélias,
Phantom Africa by Michel Leiris, and *Interior Distance* by Henri Mi-
chaux. Everything that would authorize us to consider place in the
world, to finally approach it, located there in the very place we were.
And it was not just a question only of what reverberated in French,
for we had already heard the pulse of all the languages of the world.

Film allowed us to connect so many different landscapes. We discovered that certain places in Africa exactly foreshadowed a number of

places in the Caribbean. Our imaginary was filled with all the vegetation that Le Douanier Rousseau had predicted.

And so we entered the shared, communal places. Benares and Ja-
karta, Valparaíso and Palenque, Timbuktu and Vernazza, Manaus and
Machu Picchu, the magic names we dreamed about in childhood, have
now taken form in our sometimes reticent vision, totally unlike the
perspective of tourism—visions of the real and of misery, of magnificence and a peace that is primarily banal. Visions of disaster and in-
sufferable fatalities. We feel that Faulkner *was present* in all this, but
in what mysterious stance? And what was the place?

In one of the first books I wrote, like a promise obviously rather
abstract: "This is the place" (which I juxtaposed to what I was already
calling a denaturing "Center"). I remember that, around that time,
Michel Butor published a work called *The Genius of Place*. So what was
this place? The outmoded receptacle for an outdated thought? The
impassioned refuge of all resistance? What one leaves behind in order
to enter into Relation? Where we spend our fantasy time in order to
give a new sense to the real? Where we live? The place we come from?
Where we can linger and seclude ourselves without hope? . . . Here is
the place. Our place.

Let us approach it from the outskirts.

We imagine it, not at all as an extensive domineering expansion,
like any old settler or businessman, but like a poetic contagion pulsing
throughout the world. Yet it does not dissipate. It does not change
because of neglect. It grows strong through a new relation. But this is
difficult.

Let us draw closer in time. The most solitary tree beckons us, there,
here, connecting us to the ancient time when its tender root first bore
into the earth. Even the densest undergrowth lets the light of former
years shine down from on high, and it accumulates, and there we
plunge deeper each day. The most tortured city holds this cemetery in
its depths, and someday it will be found. Place is the seam of Time.

.   .   .

The faraways of Yoknapatawpha repel and repeat place, always.

They loom nearby. When Narcissa Benbow Sartoris (in "There Was a Queen") wants to get her anonymous letters back, she arranges a meeting in Memphis (*somewhere else*, as she puts it—somewhere she can exhaust her momentary shame, far from the spirit of home). She spends two whole days there with the government official who will return her sheaf of letters. Returning to her house afterward, she plunges into the pure water at the edge of the park ("the Jordan," as Aunt Jenny ironically calls it), for a moonlight bath, her child at her side. Memphis, so close, is already far away, a place where the impure becomes menacing.

As for Texas, that is where many of the goods in the district came from, and where those useless and lethal wild ponies were born, the ones that Flem Snopes ended up selling to debt-ridden farmers in *The Hamlet*. Didn't Uncle Gavin, in *The Intruder*, say that in his time Texas was the refuge "bourne . . . for the implicated, the insolvent or the merely hopeful"? For Yoknapatawpha, Texas was a kind of distant outpost.

Was this, then, the ground contrasting Foundation (depth) and Relation (breadth), and was the latter the damned mirror image or crazy replica of the former?

Not because of "reason" or social morals—we cannot refrain from mentioning that, a long time after the time of the Yoknapatawpha saga, John F. Kennedy was shot in Dallas, Texas, and Martin Luther King, Jr., was assassinated in Memphis—but for this continuity of the poetics of fate, people from the county are always lost in faraway places:

through the defeat of a dynasty (in Haiti) for Sutpen, through suicide (at Harvard) for Quentin, through damnation (in Europe) for Caddy, and through the trivialization and disappearance of her daughter Quentin, which takes place who knows where.

At the same time that we consider place as a given in the world, "to reverse the poetic stream" would be to finally conceive the known world as a visionary component of place.

When the county spreads out toward distant shores, its damnation goes with it. As we see in *A Fable*, the huge ship of shadows is built on the run in the glow of bombs and in the terror of the trenches of the First World War. The curse of the European war is complete, continuous, renewed, and perfected in Jeffersonian fatality. The faraway echoes the county.

At different moments in the work there are signs, whether serious or light, that what is distant is approaching. Just as when looking at the horizon, one uses cupped hands like a telescope, bringing near what is far away.

Seriousness, blended with distance and fervent irony, is connected to Scotland, the homeland for the Compsons and Falkners. We find its echo in the *Compson Appendix*, at the beginning of *The Hamlet*, and in the meditative sections of *Intruder in the Dust*. In particular, it is reflected in the county's various patronyms, which are often Scottish in origin. "Gowrie and McCallum and Fraser and Ingrum that used to be Ingraham and Workitt that used to be Urquhart." (Faulkner, who notes this, does not give any further commentary on the symbolism that is so evident in the family names of the people in Yoknapatawpha; in *Light in August*, for example, we find Burden, Hightower, and Christmas. Nor does he say why the heroine of *Sanctuary* has Temple for a first name, to take one of many other undisclosed examples.)

The pleasing tone pertains principally to France (discounting the tragic developments in *A Fable* or in the war and aviation short stories), and it is amusing to note its persistence.

At the beginning of *The Hamlet*, reference is made to the man who founded Frenchman's Bend, and he is described as follows: "He had quite possibly been a foreigner, though not necessarily French, since to the people who had come after him and had almost obliterated all trace of his sojourn, anyone speaking the tongue with a foreign flavor or whose appearance or even occupation was strange, would have been a Frenchman regardless of what nationality he might affirm."

This kind of generalization can be found in most countries. In the Antilles, anyone who comes from the Middle East, whatever his or her race or nationality, is called a Syrian. I remember reading somewhere that this same kind of blanket categorization was also current in second-century Rome! No doubt it is reassuring to generalize and synthesize the characteristics of the Other, so that we can more easily "lump them together" (in order to understand them) and get used to them.

It was natural for Faulkner to mention France in the screenplay he wrote for a film project on De Gaulle; nevertheless, it is surprising to read the words, particularly those given to De Gaulle (the story is set during the German Occupation), for they recall what Faulkner said about Negroes throughout his career: "We have to endure. . . . If France were nothing, she would not have lasted until today. To remain France, she must endure. If she is still France, she will know how to endure."

The expression and idea of "enduring," as they are puritanical, are at odds with the French temperament (if such a temperament can be said to exist). Yet in this film script, which is marginal to his work but participates in it, Faulkner is guided (when he assigns Negroes this specific function of "endurance") by secret or hidden ideals, rather than a reality principle.

In any event, another kind of generalization may account for the irritation, mixed with condescension, that Faulkner (perhaps as much as his fellow countrymen) felt toward France, a country they, in particular residents of deepest Louisiana, otherwise dream of visiting.

An old Cajun farmer asked me, "Do they still travel by horse in Paris? Do the houses still have posts in front of them for tying the reins?" We were deep in a bayou which was fascinating in its silence and isolation, even if very close to a highway that passes over oil wells abandoned by Texaco. The farmer's grandsons are starting to lose the ability to express themselves in Cajun ("a kind of French" is how the people in Yoknapatawpha would have referred to it). And when I told him about the northern highlands of Martinique—Morne Bezaudin, Morne Reculée, and Morne Pérou—he wanted to know everything about the wildlife that could be found there.

In Faulkner's work, the allusions and references are frequent enough for readers to conclude that his deep interest in French subjects is always accompanied by an unshakable and caustic air: the usual and humorous "objectivity" with which he treats what he loves.

In *The Mansion*: "It was 1940 now. The Nibelung maniac had destroyed Poland and turned back west where Paris, the civilized world's eternal and splendid courtesan, had been sold to him like any whore."

Referring to Doom and his friend in the *Compson Appendix*: "Called 'l'Homme' (and sometimes 'de l'homme') by his foster brother, a Chevalier of France, who had he not been born too late could have been among the brightest in that glittering galaxy of knightly blackguards who were Napoleon's marshals."

The enigmatic figure of the knight recalls another kind of Frenchman, the Parisian architect ("[who] had come all the way from Martinique") whom Sutpen isolates and torments (in *Absalom, Absalom!*), requiring him to design and build the huge mansion that is his dream. This architect is as stubborn as he is determined (if he tries to escape, Sutpen will chase him down with the "wild savages"—they do not speak English—he brought back from the West Indies). He will build this palace as an exercise in great art: one of the fabulous "objects" I have spoken about, rich with obsessions and crazy desires. To do so, he has waved aside the megalomaniac fantasies of Sutpen (who wanted a house as grand as Jefferson's): "the little grim harried foreigner had singlehanded given battle to and vanquished Sutpen's fierce and over-weening vanity or desire for magnificence or for vindication or what-ever it was (even General Compson did not know yet) and so created of Sutpen's very defeat the victory which, in conquering, Sutpen him-self would have failed to gain."

After the departure of the architect (we would have preferred to know what happened to him), the imposing house would remain for a long time without windows or fixtures, unpainted and unfurnished. For a time, Sutpen would receive his hunting friends there, and they would sit on the floor feasting on the meals served by his disturbing Negroes.

Notice that in Faulkner what is considered a bit doubtful, scandal-ous, or equivocal—when it comes to racial "mixing," for example—is often reputed to be French, usually coming from Louisiana. So it was with Charles Bon. We remember Wash's cry in the sunny and silent street: "Henry has done shot that durn French feller. Kilt him dead as a beef."

For the county, the real faraway is not another country—be it Scot-land, the land of legend and origins, or France, the land of pleasure and adoption—but the locus of damnation itself. What is faraway and elsewhere echoes the county ad infinitum. There, the individual is madly free in his destiny.

Shreve the Canadian, the student friend of Quentin Compson, sym-

bolizes this faraway more than any country does. In the two books
where he appears, he echoes Quentin, but that is not all he does. He
prolongs the contamination, getting tangled up in its threads, carrying
on his reckless conspiracies *elsewhere*. He has the amazing ability, not
to anticipate any revelations or foreshadow the deferred, but to give a
rhythm to its disclosure, marking its cadence.

"Wait . . . for Christ's sake wait. You mean that he—"

And Quentin reveals what has been made clear in the fluster and
fear, perhaps, of contamination—but that contamination has already
taken place.

Shreve is one of Yoknapatawpha's most intimate strangers, as are
the majority of the people on the other side of the ocean, those who
live, suffer, and die in the disorderly atmosphere of *A Fable*. Being
young, he is particularly cursed, although, after every one of their ses-
sions where the "stream of consciousness" plays out for them, he generally brings Quentin back to the exigencies of the real, back to the
need to eat or sleep.

We also know that he escapes the county's curse. It is not without
interest for us to learn—in the genealogy included in *Absalom, Absalom!*, which is more revealing than we could have imagined—that his
name is Schrevlin Maccannon. So he is probably of Scottish origin.
We also learn that he spent all the war of 1914–18 at the front, as a
surgical captain. Scotland and the Great War: these are two major
references for Faulkner.

A person, as well as a country, is the elsewhere.

"The question" is aimed at this community in the South. Epic
speech, even in its traditional, outdated form, is clearly the most suitable form for posing this question. That is, according to all the conventions by which we have been convinced in the poetics of Western
cultures it is. But any resistance to this fatality that the question raises
is, in the final analysis, assumed by individuals who refuse and persist.
Some of the people do.

The flagrant lack to which failures in epic catharsis and tragic disclosure have led is resolutely assumed only by these people, only these people who, through this failure and refusal, have broken the dam, as strong as the river, as broad as Old Man River, and have opened the floodgates to multiplicity.

The individual: no longer a link in a chain of community, with advantages (a sense of belonging) and inconveniences (restricting customs), both accepted and agreed to, but an escapee from the collective adventure, shipwrecked in the great and futile epic storm. Even when, like Reverend Hightower, he is madly self-congratulatory, he is the end product of a kind of incineration, and the writing, like the irreducible individual, is the residue. All that remains for the individual (but he usually cannot completely resign himself to this fact) is to rely on the manly, Puritan ideal: to endure, to suffer, to sympathize.

He cannot resign himself completely to this fact. His excessive demands push him out of bounds. He is an individual only because of refusal. He endlessly challenges the problematic nature of the frontier, the place where contraries are mutually receptive, even through conflict and extermination.

In at least two instances in his works, in "The Bear" and *Intruder in the Dust*, Faulkner has one of the county people assert that "no man can put up with freedom." This is a most unusual assertion coming from Faulkner, who forcefully celebrates individual virtue whenever he can. The heroes of *The Wild Palms* thrive on this torment. Is this a deliberate call to autocracy or to a form of imperial government that would take care of everything and relieve everyone from the uncertainties and disturbances of their free will?

I read this differently: no human being can put up with freedom insofar as it regards the restriction of customs and the communal imperative needed to support one's status, to express oneself in the apparently inexpressible disorder of the world.

Nonetheless, this is what Faulkner's people do. They give in to this renunciation, they demand it, and demand for themselves this suffering of an unbearable freedom.

These are individuals who withdraw into their tragedy of the impossible and refuse separation. We see what *métissage* means to them: a threat forcing consent. The difference between Joe Christmas on the one hand, revolting against himself in secret horror, and Boon, Lion, or Lucas Beauchamp (each the product of miscegenation), is that the latter have never been held back by their origins or position. Mixing does not corrupt. The common idea of miscegenation becomes bothersome when it saps the energy of the individual who has become trapped within old barriers.

The text of "The Bear" takes special care to declare that only the blood of "Old Ben and the mongrel Lion were taintless and incorruptible."

And poor Roth Edmonds (in "The Fire and the Hearth") cannot stop reflecting on the humiliating difference that lies between him and Lucas Beauchamp: "Now the white man leaned in the window, looking at the impenetrable face with its definite strain of White blood, the same blood which ran in his own veins, which had not only come to the negro through male descent while it had come to him from a woman, but had reached the negro a generation sooner—a face composed, inscrutable, even a little haughty."

No matter what one thinks of Edmonds's Southern prejudices about women or the advantage of having a bit of White blood running through his veins, Lucas remains as an example, as are Lion and Boon, illustrating the fact that being illegitimate or miscegenated does not make one degenerate. And since Faulkner seems especially to have affirmed a continuity for Whites, while ignoring a past for Blacks, it should be repeated that it is Boon who carries and is an incarnation of this continuity: Boon, the rough bastard who married a former prostitute and for whom it was a joy to have children.

the Faulknerian way of writing is made explicit here in this essay. Its virtues or qualities can be seen as a flow of days and nights, wrenched free, saved out of so many possibilities, and presented without digression. And these few old ladies steadfast in obstinacy, and these happy-go-lucky Blacks whose endurance for suffering cannot be explained: they are the description, the evidence, the life that must be lived. What is deferred are the faults that Faulkner calls damnation—where one must unknowingly return, especially without having to say so. The objection is to show—but how to succeed in showing?—that in the close connection to the real (the written form of the tale), we ceaselessly drift with the author, through the written form of the tragic and toward the deferred. These two forms are inextricably mixed, yet mutually ineffable.

Along with the tragic and the deferred there is a third form, which I have already mentioned: the art of conversation, which also partakes of the spirit of storytelling. Ratliff is an accomplished practitioner of it.

We recall that the dialogue in the major books of damnation maintained a vertigo by keeping the replies of the different speakers separate, repeating each other in a progression like hands beating on a drum. Characteristically, the replies were sharp and pulsating, their music muffled and unhurried, and as strong as contagion. The remarks of the speakers are interwoven one into the other; their characteristics are premonition, insinuation, and caustic speed in the expression of thought.

It is the time of the Snopeses, when Jefferson and the county had already begun the change in society that seemed so detestable to Faulkner, becoming a veritable buzzing swarm of mosquitoes (*"ubiquitous as undertakers, cunning as pawnbrokers, confident and unavoidable as politicians. They came cityward lustful as country boys, as passionately integral as a college football squad"*). All these new elements in society are almost as hated, perhaps, as the old errors and the ancient damnation.

It is not fitting to assume that Faulkner (whom I see neither as an aristocrat nor as a commoner but as a man of the world) was brutally shocked by miscegenation or illegitimacy. Both loom as the torment to which individuals are subjected. We find those who do not even have awareness of it (Elnora), those who live it in silent tragedy (Clytie), those who do not care one way or another (Boon, and the dog Lion), those who use it to further their own personal agenda (Lucas, Charles Bon), and those who succumb to it, who are victimized by it and die a sorry death (Joe Christmas). The irreducibility of personal will decides everything. If Faulkner was not offended by racial mixing, he nonetheless may have thought that it was a potential ordeal for those who bear it. He especially feared (the people in the county feared) the *idea* of miscegenation. Hearsay about Blacks and the *idea* of the Black race (as conceptualized either in the North or in the South) was not as inconsequential as would first appear. This is a cliché: the idea we have about people and things bothers us more than their simple or complex reality.

If the proclamation of Charles Bon's death—this imperceptibly miscegenated man rejected by his father and killed by his brother—is crude and blunt, it is nonetheless prepared in the text for quite some time, conveyed by oppressive deferral. If you do not have the impression of hearing two royal messengers (here it is only Wash, almost a refuse of humanity), at least you feel you have heard the message several times. You have been prepared for this pronouncement as though by a prophetic peal of trumpets or of deep conch shells: Wash, "sitting on the saddleless mule in the street before the gate, shouting, 'Hello, Hello,' at intervals until she came to the door, whereupon he lowered his voice somewhat, though not much. 'Air you Rosie Coldfield?' he said."

The individual's stubbornness and irreducibility aggravate the rejection of traditionally epic solidarity, already rendered impossible or unbearable by the county's disturbed "origin." They lie in opposition to any form of Creolization wherein a new epic (one of openness and sharing) could have taken root. Faulkner names this double negativity "damnation."

This naturally brings us back to consideration of the situation set up in the second novel, *Mosquitoes*, the most artificial situation in the world (a cruise on a luxury liner) where the characters speak in turn, just like a thick swarm of mosquitoes, without any one of them standing out from the others by the slightest frenzy: a conversational cocktail party about women and virginity, art and artists, the weather and death, the North and the South, as well as all kinds of other trifles and pretenses of thought about which they speak with delight, these stock characters, one of whom is called "the Semite" from the beginning to the end of the story.

These conversations pretend to be original; each character wishes only to have an effect on the others or contribute to the whole vaunting enterprise. There is no scheming, no surge of enthusiasm, no complicity. This kind of blasé dialogue (with a touch of playful wickedness) is what, later on in Faulkner's career (in the half-shadow of *Sanctuary*), is carried on by Miss Jenny, Horace Benbow and his sister Narcissa, and Gowan Stevens. For better or worse, they engage in this kind of talk while waiting for destiny to knock on the door, destiny soberly personified as a policeman or notary, an enlightened pastor or a too jovial and aged telegram carrier who has already read the message he is supposed to deliver.

Beneath these elegantly spoken banalities or inventive phrases, we already feel the progression toward Faulkner's later work; his exploratory mastery appears here as though he had to rid himself all at once of all of the aphorisms and complex thoughts about every possible thing that had been seething within, and needed to do this before he could enter into Yoknapatawpha, where he could concentrate on the essential, forgetting about character psychology and unusual opinions and pretty words, and fully devote himself to these violent people who dream only of defying their misfortune.

Mosquitoes also reflects another aspect of Faulkner's personality that is difficult to comprehend: a quiet misogyny and at least a restriction of the roles of women in society, in the family, or in the search for truth. Perhaps, on the question of relationships between men and women, he always oscillated between an idea of a gallant and chivalrous love (to be "great" in order to deserve conquering or keeping) and a "realist" cynicism (all of these pain-in-the-ass women, including Mama).

It seems to me that this reactionary tendency is tied more to the attitude of the Southerner (the apprentice Planter, the hunting buff, or horse tamer) than to the Puritan. In this instance, social conventions encroach upon the creative space.

I am even more surprised by the "sexual" reputation that has been associated with some of Faulkner's works. Much as I look for this sexuality, I cannot find it. His situations may be extreme (incest, murder, rape), but his manner of dealing with sex is often so neutral as to discourage further interest. It is treated in a dry, almost perfunctory manner compared to the striking insights shed on malediction. Again, Faulkner does not hold himself back because of Puritanical detachment but because of his code as a gentleman.

In Faulkner's day, a great writer was not supposed to tread upon these scandalous shores. If he did, indifferent to rumors, it was because he was compelled by the cold objectivity that made him see every aspect of the real and what throbs beneath it, and by the same token he called a White a White, a nigger a nigger, and a slave trader—even if he were a general of the Confederate army—a slave trader.

What rises up irresistibly from the turbulence in the writing is violence; this pointless rage is one of the symbols of our times. In violence, the men and women in the county, the "chosen ones" of damnation, see each other as equals before the "exasperated Hand."

Not counting *The Reivers*, which has as its objective to settle Boon in the county's future (a joyful conclusion, of sorts, after the sites of damnation—the bawdy house and the racetrack), it would have seemed normal for the order of the three books in the Snopes saga to have been set up as follows: the mansion, the hamlet, the town. This would have followed a circuitous or evolutionary logic and a geographical or social expansion in harmony with the way things were. In fact, the residents left the universe of the Plantations little by little to try living in town, moving through hamlet or borough. This is doubtless what occurred all through the Plantation world. The spirit of the place must have imposed this "order" on Faulkner.

It is just and proper that the Snopes books were published as follows: hamlet, town, mansion. At the end of the cycle, Faulkner returns to the system's matrix, to sanction not its ruin but its emancipation from Flem Snopes's tyranny. What we find here first of all is evidence of the symbolic permanence of the source (the Plantation) and then the barely disguised rejection of the urban universe. Faulkner did not want to end with the town. He wanted to sanction the apocalyptic (that is, final) passion of these two individuals who were outside the common: Linda and Mink Snopes, both of whom were tied to the fatalistic Flem Snopes, the illegitimate owner of the mansion.

We are not far from a kind of literary hiatus, in the space between a writing of the source (the Plantation), with its slower time and open spaces, and a writing of multiplicity and amazing speed, a crowding together and disconnectedness (the Town). The verdant and the fragmented. That said, we can immediately see that even when writing of the Plantation, Faulkner went as far as possible into multiplicity, accumulation, and speed. There is nothing conventionally bucolic about his view of the verdant.

The writers from the cultural region that is my focus rarely went to the cities, although there were many cities of significance. In the nineteenth century, the fascinating Creole cities bore a resemblance to each other: Havana, Cuba; New Orleans, Louisiana; Port-au-Prince, Haiti; Saint-Pierre, Martinique; Kingston, Jamaica; or the Brazilian towns of this region, Manaus or Belém. We can imagine what Cartagena of the West Indies and the other Creole cities of the Caribbean coast of Colombia were like.

They are characterized by a similar taste for the baroque and for opera, associated with a dissolute and seasonal lifestyle (pursuits equally engaging to a new aristocracy and an old riffraff); Carnival orgies and religious holidays; trade without any industrial activity; a bustling port with fortifications and secluded alleys for duels; throngs of condemned slaves and free persons of color practicing every possible occupation; the rising and intensifying mulatto class working to break down the barriers separating them from the scornful Planters and yet just as insistent to maintain the ones that keep them separate from the Blacks; die-hard clubs and fashionable societies where the art of drinking joined the art of philosophizing or gossiping, newsletters and partisan organizations, and escalating political life that was a distraction without any real consequences except for people to fight and squabble; a mixture of almost every race of the world, Chinese operating big and little shops and Indians from India all over the place. In these cities, the friendliest openness coexisted with the cruelest prejudices, in a system of justice that was often merely expeditious; there were serious stirrings of artistic life (painters and musicians, historians and novelists, not to mention polemicists) mixed with sustained debauchery, touring companies from the Parisian Opera and European theaters—London or Naples or Madrid; opulent carriages everywhere, and extreme poverty, carefully hidden or displayed right out in the open—an endless agitation and restlessness. These cities were extensions of the Plantation system and could not be imagined without them: cotton, tobacco, rum and sugar, spices and indigo (gold and rubber in Brazil) were traded regularly for the refined products of Europe and goods manufactured in the American North.

These glistening cities met with differing fates. Manaus and Belém remained sleepy towns long after the price of rubber plummeted, New Orleans suffered for years after the collapse of the Plantation system, Port-au-Prince fell victim to underdevelopment, the great capital Havana suffers from serious problems of upkeep and urban management, Kingston has become almost synonymous with urban sprawl, and Saint-Pierre was annihilated when Mont Pelée erupted. It took less than two minutes, on May 8, 1902, for a crushing cloud of fire, rocks, and lava to raze the city with its thirty-five thousand trapped residents, all its hedonism, and its brazen creative voluptuousness. In its rage, the volcano united the furies of every hurricane and earthquake ever coiled or knotted in the bottom of the Atlantic Ocean and every fire to come, embedding into the dreams and waking hours of Martinique's residents a vague nostalgia for the Creole vivaciousness that, since then, has slowed to a trickle.

For a long time, all these cities moved to the rhythm of the same fever.

Their baroque frenzy inspired such contemporary Spanish-language writers as Alejo Carpentier and José Lezama Lima. Faulkner was not sensitive to this. His was another kind of baroque. True, it is hard to imagine Oxford (Jefferson) or Memphis in such states of debauchery. The baroque of Spanish- and French-speaking countries in this region of the Americas is much more *métissé* (with its Indian angels, Black Virgins, and native Christs in Latin American churches). In English-speaking countries, the baroque is more "internalized," almost as though this were a Puritanical reaction so extreme it strains the very limits of Puritanism. At least this is how I would interpret Faulkner's efforts. Besides, these grand Creole cities remained for a long time outside the spin and dizzying transformations of northern cities and European capitals. Authors who spoke about the Southern cities did so almost as though they had to debate the Plantations themselves. If Faulkner never partakes of the Creole fruit, it is not because he rejects the fruit itself, returning to the Mansion to finish his works. He rejects New York and Los Angeles, Chicago and Pittsburgh. He rejects the relentlessness of these huge, directionless cities. And, in a manner of speaking, we can say he rejects Dos Passos and not just "citified" literature but, even further, that of the megalopolises, the endless barrios and technology straining against the sky. Was the county passé, or was this the prescience of a threat?

The world invades the land of the pure, ruining everything.

Nothing gives a better picture of this than Faulkner's pretension to master (and to express) the burgeoning, almost innocent technologies of aviation, symbol of progress and evolution and, consequently, the dreamed-of instruments of fate.

"From the V strut out each wing tipped and swayed, and he jockeyed the thing carefully on, gaining height. He realized that there was a certain point beyond which his own speed was likely to rob him of lifting surface. He had about two thousand feet now and he turned, and in doing so he found that aileron pressure utterly negatived the inner plane's dihedral and doubled that of the outer one, and he found himself in the wildest skid he had ever seen since his Hun days."

This passage records the moment of (the last) Bayard's death. Truly, Faulkner was never as ostentatious or didactic. We find the same complacent, technical details in The Fable, in Pylon, and in the short story "With Caution and Dispatch." And, in The Mansion, Linda Varner, who experienced life in a place utterly different from the county (in the Spanish Civil War), is almost an expert in aviation technology. Had her past not made her suspicious, she could have worked in one of the factories making machinery for the air force in 1942. Then there is the young apprentice pilot from the 1917 Canadian training camp, who, like Percy Grimm, perhaps never got over the fact that he was born too late to take part in the sinister orgy of the First World War.

Aviation and the emerging (and not yet menacing) technologies of the new era are full of appeal (primarily the appeal of fate) for those who regret they did not experience firsthand this great moment in world history.

We know, however, that Faulkner also condemned the absurdity of all war, stressing that it gives birth to physical decrepitude, isolation, and malediction (the most common calamities in the county), perhaps worse than death.

The frontier and the faraway. Not only the infinite world in its limitations but already, very near to us, the United States of America, an apparently bifurcated country: North and South, Whites and Blacks, the native and the immigrant, the powerful and the destitute, immense prairies and tangled cities, emigrants and isolationist impulses—all these dualities that official policy resolves by calling upon its people for three things: (family and moral) values, (economic and commercial) investment, and (world) leadership. Yet this country is also so multiple, and so contradictory in nature.

There is an element of distance in Faulkner's works, so close by. Rather than venturing into an endless analysis, I would rather—in the course of (and at the cost of) several days of study—go back to some earlier readings in order to comprehend, in a way that is fluid and cross-pollinating, some of the least spectacular current events, those that come as close as possible to what we could call "daily life," and thereby take notice of the deposits or traces his works have left upon such a life.

To this purpose, I cite two articles from *The New York Times*. I have already mentioned my students, including Susan Barrow, who brought these articles to my attention.

One of them, published on May 22, 1995, and written by Rick Bragg, tells the circumstances and details of the Alston family reunion, held in the manor at Cherry Hill Plantation in Inez, North Carolina. What is unique about this particular family reunion is that it brought all the Alstons together, undoubtedly for the first time, including those whose great-grandparents were slaves and those whose great-grandparents were slave owners.

"It was common, in the antebellum South, for slaves to take the names of their owners. And for years now, many black Americans have rejected those slave names and taken others, to rid descendants of any connection with that time.

"But on the once-enslaved side of the Alston family, a long line of artists, musicians, activists and religious leaders have kept the name and added their own specific luster to it. . . .

"Whites are proud, 'and trace the bloodline back to Adam and Eve Alston,' [Macky Alston] joked. . . .

"Some members of the white side have detected a darkness, from time to time, in the skin of some members.

"They call it the dark streak, and just say, 'Oh, it must be that Italian blood!' . . .

"The white Alstons at the concert [given by a black Alston] did not talk about making amends for slavery. . . .

". . . the late Charles Henry Alston, the son of a slave . . . went on to become a respected artist and a central figure in the Harlem Renaissance. . . .

". . . Robert Alston, a Georgia State Senator, was assassinated in 1879 when he proposed doing away with the convict lease system, a form of slavery that lingered after the Civil War.

". . . Wallace McPherson Alston, a Presbyterian minister, was run out of North Carolina in the 1960s because he preached about racial justice. . . .

"The concert was not intended as a place for white Alstons to apologize for the past, only to give the two colors of people with one name a place to look each other in the eye and make their own decisions about each other. . . ."

. . .

The second article is from May 7, 1995. It is an interview with Dr. Kenneth B. Clark, an eighty-one-year-old African-American social psychologist and author of several works, including *Dark Ghetto*. Clark is presented as "an unreconstructed, if anguished, integrationist," "believing all else has failed." He is interviewed by Sam Roberts, who shows him at home among his "vivid African carvings and walls of books," chain-smoking his Marlboros.

The person described in the interview is a fascinating mix of anti-racist determination and moral rigidity, with a great lucidity about Blacks and Whites, and an immense disappointment relative to the results achieved in the struggles for emancipation and social justice. Dr. Clark goes so far as to make this final remark, which follows:

" 'You've seen the evolution from Negro to black to African-American? What is the best thing for Blacks to call themselves?'

" 'White.' "

I also reread an issue of *The Southern Register*, dated Spring 1992, after the death of Alex Haley. The text recalls his participation in a "Floating College" ("Going down the Mississippi"), organized by Ole Miss on a paddleboat, the *Delta Queen*, the previous spring. When it was his turn to speak, Haley spoke of the slave trade ("one of every four enslaved Africans died on the slave ships—'Their shrieks became part of the wind' "). He told the story of John Newton, who was captain of one of these ships but quit this shameful practice to devote himself to religion. Newton composed a number of hymns, the oldest of which, "the granddaddy of them all," was sung by Roy Yost, whom Haley introduced. Yost was a young Black working as a waiter and electrician on the *Delta Queen* whom Haley had met the day before when he got on the boat. "Haley mentioned that Yost's wife, Rebecca, a *Delta Queen* maid, hoped to be a lawyer. 'The South is changing,' Haley said, 'This is the new South.' "

•   •   •

My next example comes from a television program about Italian-Americans, produced by the IAMUS Association: Italian-Americans for a Multicultural United States. Among other topics, the program discussed Sacco and Vanzetti, the Rosenbergs, and Mumia Abu-Jamal, the Black journalist and writer accused of murdering a policeman who is now on death row despite the numerous discrepancies surrounding his case. I am not certain I remember the exact slogan of the association, but in my memory it goes like this:

Open heart + Open mind
Those who restore their heritage
And deplore conservatism.

In March 1996, one hundred and thirty parishioners in Thomasville, Georgia (all of them White), demanded that the little coffin of a baby, Whitney Elaine Johnson, be dug up and transferred somewhere else. "It's a hundred percent white cemetery here." Whitney's mother is White and her father is Black. "We don't allow blacks in our cemetery."

This kind of racism, an everyday, peaceful fascism that parades hand in hand with every virtue, is perhaps more terrifying than, for example, the formation of armed militia that prepare in the heartlands of the United States to wage a war for White supremacy and against the federal government. From the newspapers, we also learn that they enlist novice Black soldiers!

These are the ideas and realities that flow into the inextricable rush of the world, an inextricability that can be confronted, as William Faulkner has shown. It is expressible. It has the ocher color of wind in the grass. Is this not what we hear in the harsh humming of neon lights in storefronts on streets everywhere?

Inextricability: ethnic heritage and, at the same time, the multi-culture.

The coming together on a Mississippi boat of a writer and numerous other Africans, formerly loaded on other boats and thrown overboard, and a religious man who had been a trafficker in black flesh but composed hymns, and one hymn in particular, and a young man singing it while his wife no doubt listens, forgetting her work for a moment while the *Delta Queen* slowly paddles the waters of the Mississippi.

The despairing irony of an old militant who has given up part of himself in order to secure, in his mind, something of what remains.

Looking each other straight in the face, the sons of slaves and the sons of slave owners.

Here, in the distance and everywhere around, beyond the seas, the mountains, the deserts, and the cold sun, is the place that is neither community nor nation, where so many thoughts of the world meet up with so many other thoughts of the world. Where the one, fleeting, uncertain, and fragile world finally meets up with another one, that is just as uncertain, fragile, and fleeting.

During an evening screening of a lavishly produced historical film, a young English child asks a Moor, "Why are you black?" And the Moor responds, "Because Allah likes variety." A little later that same evening, answering questions on a television show, a film director states, "When staged, every truth is dead, much too beautiful. . . . If it is staged well, it appears affected, too perfect. Truth isn't like that, it flows."

It weaves in and out along the road, the trace.

Closed places are traversed by roads. The trace passes by everyone's territory without anyone taking offense. It leads into the Frontier and forecasts the Faraway. In its interconnected paths and uncertainties, it turns the world into an illuminated component of place. Every time I understand a thought of the world arising from another place or a place of otherness, I touch upon a place that belongs to everyone, a place of the world: which is not the graffiti that is in all places, nor the fleeting dissolution or mutual cancellation of these places. It is a network of their respective assumptions.

The unbounded openness of the work is such that anyone can find a suitable path among those Faulkner proposes without betraying or losing oneself. He is not one of those authors that squelch the imagination of those they reach, who from then on pathetically repeat the same old stories, supposedly inspired by masters.

The list is long of the writers, known and unknown, who, without feeling complacency or a novice's weakness, have been influenced at least partially by Faulkner's poetics. It is unfortunate not to be able to cite more than a few of the writers who have declared their relationship with him. Engaging with his works is a secret satisfaction, predisposed neither to mediocrity nor to uniformity.

The irreparable daily misery, chaotic streets, and uniformity that smother any suspense of life and permeate the minutest parts of reality: this is the art of Flannery O'Connor.

The dense thicket of prose, wound up in the river of Time, patiently going down through the ages to identify an improbable and unbearable point of origin: this is Alejo Carpentier's *The Lost Steps*.

The fraught ambiguity where hearts and minds are in conflict, the torment of haunting shadows all around, and a sort of pale clarity that grows from the struggle of wills and irresolutions: this is *Set This House on Fire* by William Styron.

The story that intensifies with more stories that meet and fuse into a dizzying circularity, forming or closing again and again around itself like a calamitous parchment—and the boat of time, stranded in banks of bottomless vegetation—this is *One Hundred Years of Solitude* by Gabriel García Márquez.

The curse that has come from a long time ago that, for some unknown reason, clings to one family and one family alone, a family marked by its own ghost. The ghost has been leached from a single misfortune and a single error, yet everyone finds meaning there: this is *Beloved*, by Toni Morrison.

Irreparability, Time, ambiguity, vertiginousness, malediction; these are all Faulknerian places, and sites of a style of writing. But this is not the moment for me to illustrate this.

McCaslin Edmonds—unless it was Ike McCaslin—thought that "no man is ever free and probably could not bear it if he were." (This is in *Go Down, Moses*, in the central chapter, "The Bear," at the most confusing time in the progression of inextricable generations of White and Black McCaslins whose traces and generations are recorded in old registries). But when he meets Fonsiba (Sophonsiba) again, who was from the Black side of the family and had fled to marry a worthless Black farmer who owned a rotten piece of land in Arkansas ("a single log edifice with a clay chimney which seemed in process of being flattened by the rain to a nameless and valueless rubble of dissolution in that roadless and even pathless waste of unfenced fallow and wilderness jungle"), he asks her, "Are you happy, Fonsiba?" she replies:

"I am free."

So many flowers have grown here, as they have elsewhere, so many varieties other than the flowers of the great Mansions: armfuls of flowers, whole fields in bloom, blossoms or tufts of cotton that are like flowers, but odorless and so difficult to smell and many of them impossible to pick, the silvery spears of sugarcane swaying in westerly winds, and vast expanses of the *color purple* where so much misery and so much hope have been invested. And when all of this has been carried away, when the stoves of the distilleries have rusted in every land, here, in the vast and sparkling shopping malls, we will have flowers of rotten steel and cement. Flowers of the Africans, the Aryans (called Caucasians in the United States of America), the Jews, the Arabs, and the Chinese whom Isaac McCaslin insulted when he met them. Flowers of the Native Americans, the East Indians, the mulattoes and mixed-bloods and all mixtures unforeseeable on the horizon. The ordinary sea flower, a composite flower, finally tossed up by an imperceptible wave onto a beach that was spared from a hurricane last night.

"Yes," she says, "I suppose there are many other ways to explain his works. For example, discourse about the epic and the tragic could have been backed up with character or plot analysis. I could get involved in a discussion like that."

"Not characters, but people who resist and wander. But, yes," I say, "there are many other possibilities. As long as one tries to justify and prove them, each can become the best."

"Neither prove nor justify. The best you can do is reach an approximation. But, yes," she says, "forever the best, the best each time."

GLOSSARY

Béké: White colonist of the French-speaking Caribbean.
To maroon (*marronner*): For the slaves who refused servile labor: to flee to the woods or into the hills.
Morne: Term for a hill or small mountain in the Antilles.
Quimbois: Objects and practices of West Indian sorcery or witchcraft.

Several methods of torture inflicted upon slaves:
    Suspension pole (*la brimballe*): You are suspended by your hands and whipped.
    Stake (*la cippe*): You are suspended by your armpits and whipped.
    Collar restraint (*le frontal*): Your head is constricted in an adjustable iron collar.
    Whipping bar (*le garrot*): You are tied around a pole and whipped.

SOURCES

PRINCIPAL TEXTS CITED

Absalom, Absalom!, New York: The Modern Library, 1951; *Collected Stories of William Faulkner*, New York: Vintage Books, 1977; *Essays, Speeches & Public Letters by William Faulkner*, edited by James B. Meriweather, New York: Random House, 1965; *Go Down, Moses*, New York: The Modern Library, 1955; *The Hamlet*, New York: Random House, 1964; *Intruder in the Dust*, New York: The Modern Library, 1964; *Light in August*, New York: Random House, 1950; *The Mansion*, New York: Random House, 1959; *Mosquitoes*, New York: Liveright, 1955; *Sartoris*, New York: Random House, 1956; *Selected Letters of William Faulkner*, edited by Joseph Blotner, New York: Random House, 1976; *Selected Short Stories of William Faulkner*, New York: The Modern Library, 1993; *Soldier's Pay*, New York: Liveright, 1954; *The Sound and the Fury*, New York: Vintage Books, 1956; *The Town*, New York: Random House, 1957; *The Unvanquished*, New York: Random House, 1938; *The Wild Palms*, New York: Vintage Books, 1964.

Joseph Blotner. *Faulkner: A Biography*, Vol. 1, New York: Random House, 1974.

Aimé Césaire. *The Collected Poetry*. Clayton Eshleman and Annette Smith, trans. Berkeley: University of California Press, 1983.

Frederick R. Karl, *William Faulkner, American Writer*. New York, Weidenfeld & Nicolson, 1989.

Saint-John Perse. *Eloges and Other Poems*, Bilingual edition, trans. Louise Varese. New York: Pantheon, 1956.

NOTES

1. THE ROAD TO ROWAN OAK

7–8. "the shabby church with its canting travesty of a spire." *Soldier's Pay*, 319.

19. "His voice had the proud tranquility of flags in the dust." *Sartoris*, 19.

2. THE FAULKNER DOSSIER

43. "boys riding the sheer tremendous tidal wave of desperate living." *Light in August*, 423.

3. IN BLACK AND WHITE

65. "with the grave and simple pleasure of his race"; "[w]ith his race's fine feeling for potential theatrics." *Sartoris*, 11, 3.

65. "When I came to this goddamn country . . . I thought niggers were niggers." "Ad Astra," in *Collected Stories*, 419.

65–66. "I need little; nothing the Negroes can't do." "There Was a Queen," in *Collected Stories*, 738.

66. "Afterward, Uncle Buck admitted that it was his own mistake, that he had forgotten when even a little child should have known: not ever to stand right in front of or right behind a nigger when you scare him; but always to stand to one side of him. Uncle Buck forgot that." *Go Down, Moses*, 18–19.

66. "Without changing the inflection of his voice and apparently without effort or even design Lucas became not Negro but nigger, not secret so much as impenetrable, not servile and not effacing, but enveloping himself in an aura of timeless and stupid impassivity almost like a smell." *Go Down, Moses*, 59–60.

66. "He thought, and not for the first time: *I am not only looking at a face older than mine and which has seen and winnowed more, but at a man most of whose blood was pure ten thousand years when my own anonymous beginnings became mixed enough to produce me.*" *Go Down, Moses*, 71.

69. "[H]e . . . Sambo . . . will even beat us there because he has the capacity to endure and survive." *Intruder in the Dust*, 204.

69. "[B]ecause he had patience even when he didn't have hope, the long view even when there was nothing to see at the end of it." *Intruder in the Dust*, 156.

69. "[T]hey can stand anything." *Intruder in the Dust*, 149.

70. "[H]e and his gang had beat up Negroes as a matter of principle. Not chastising them as individual Negroes, nor even, Charles's Uncle Gavin said, warring against them as representatives of a race which was alien because it was
of a different appearance and therefore enemy *per se*, but—and his Uncle
Gavin said Clarence and his gang did not know this because they dared not
know it was so—because they were afraid of that alien race." *The Mansion*,
299.

70. " 'No,' his uncle said. 'I only say that the injustice is ours, the South's. We
must expiate and abolish it ourselves, alone and without help nor even (with
thanks) advice. We owe that to Lucas." *Intruder in the Dust*, 204.

71. "himself his own battleground, the scene of his own vanquishment and the
mausoleum of his defeat." *Go Down, Moses*, 168.

71. "the old man of seventy who had been a negro for two generations now but
whose face and bearing were still those of the Chickasaw chief who had been
his father." *Go Down, Moses*, 164.

71. "the old bear, solitary, indomitable, and alone; widowered childless and absolved of mortality—old Priam reft of his old wife and outlived all his sons."
Go Down, Moses, 194.

71. "the old male bear itself, so long unwifed and childless as to have become its
own ungendered progenitor." *Go Down, Moses*, 210.

72. " 'Did you ever know anybody yet, even your father and Uncle Buddy, that
ever told him to do or not do anything that he ever paid any attention to?' "
Go Down, Moses, 168.

72. "In the boy's eyes at least it was Sam Fathers, the negro, who bore himself
not only toward his cousin McCaslin and Major de Spain but toward all white
men, with gravity and dignity and without servility or recourse to that impenetrable wall of ready and easy mirth which negroes sustain between themselves
and white men." *Go Down, Moses*, 170.

73. "They were both on a footlog across a slough—the Negro gaunt, lean, hard,
tireless and desperate; the Indian thick, soft-looking, the apparent embodiment
of the ultimate and the supreme reluctance and inertia." "Red Leaves," in *Selected Stories*, 123.

73. "This world is going to the dogs. It is being ruined by white men. We got along
fine for years and years, before the white men foisted their Negroes upon us." "Red
Leaves," in *Selected Stories*, 111.

74. " 'He probably never held it against old Doom for selling him and his mother
into slavery, because he probably believed the damage was already done before
then and it was the same warriors' and chiefs' blood in him and Doom both

that was betrayed through the black blood which his mother gave him."*Go Down, Moses*, 168.

80–81. "teaching him his manners, behavior—to be gentle with his inferiors, honorable with his equals, generous to the weak and considerate of the aged, courteous, truthful and brave to all." *Go Down, Moses*, 117.

84. "doubtless there were more than Akers who did not know that the language in which they and Sutpen communicated was a sort of French and not some dark and fatal tongue of their own." *Absalom, Absalom!*, 36.

85. *"Old Carothers got his nigger bastards right in his back yard and I would like to have seen the husband or anybody else that said him nay." Go Down, Moses*, 116.

90. "the three-hundred-dollar mule which he had stolen from not only his business partner and guarantor but actually from his own blood relation and swapped for a machine for divining the hiding-place of buried money." *Go Down, Moses*, 117.

91. "already alive when their father, Carothers McCaslin, got the land from the Indians back in the old time when men black and white were men." *Go Down, Moses*, 36–37.

91. "He listened as Lucas referred to his father as Mr. Edmonds, never as Mister Zack; he watched him avoid having to address the white man directly by any name at all with a calculation so coldly and constantly alert, a finesse so deliberate and unflagging, that for a time he could not tell if even his father knew that the negro was refusing to call him mister." *Go Down, Moses*, 114.

91. "in his father's face that morning, what shadow, what stain, what mark—something which had happened between Lucas and his father, which nobody but they knew and would ever know if the telling depended on them—something which had happened because they were themselves, men, not stemming from any difference of race nor because one blood strain ran in them both." *Go Down, Moses*, 115.

91. "[h]e even knew what it had been. *It was a woman,* he thought, . . . *My father and a nigger man over a nigger woman,* because he simply declined even to realise that he had even refused to think *a white woman.*" *Go Down, Moses*, 115.

91–92. "the face which was not at all a replica even in caricature of his grandfather McCaslin's but which had heired and now reproduced with absolute and shocking fidelity the old ancestor's entire generation and thought—the face which, as old Isaac McCaslin had seen it that morning forty-five years ago, was a composite of a whole generation of fierce and undefeated young Confederate soldiers, embalmed and slightly mummified—and he thought with amazement and something very like horror: *He's more like old Carothers than all the rest of us put together, including old Carothers. He is both heir and prototype simultaneously of all the geography and climate and biology which sired old Carothers and all the rest of us and our kind, myriad, countless, faceless, even nameless now except himself who fathered himself, intact and complete, contemptuous, as old Carothers must have been, of all blood black white yellow or red, including his own." Go Down, Moses,* 118.

95. "Then one day the old curse of his fathers, the old haughty ancestral pride based not on any value but on an accident of geography, stemmed not from courage and honor but from wrong and shame, descended to him." *Go Down, Moses,* 111.

"So he entered his heritage. He ate its bitter fruit." *Go Down, Moses,* 114.

95. "In 1865, . . . Abe Lincoln freed the niggers from the Compsons. In 1933, Jason Compson freed the Compsons from the niggers." *Compson Appendix: 1699–1945* in *The Sound and the Fury,* 423.

95. "two opposed concepts antipathetic by race, blood, nature and environment." *Sartoris,* 347.

104. "I do not believe there is a debatable point between us. We both agree in advance that the position you will take is right morally legally and ethically. If it is not evident to you that the position I take in asking for moderation and patience is right practically, then we will both waste our breath in debate." *Selected Letters,* 398.

105. "I speculated on time and death and wondered if I had invented the world to which I should give life or if it had invented me, giving me an illusion of greatness." Blotner, *Faulkner,* Vol. 1, 584.

4. THE TRACE

109. "Even his name was forgotten, his pride but a legend about the land he had wrested from the jungle and tamed." *The Hamlet,* 3–4.

109. "that appellation which those who came after him in battered wagons and on muleback and even on foot, with flintlock rifles and dogs and children and home-made whiskey stills and Protestant psalm-books, could not even read, let alone pronounce." *The Hamlet,* 4.

113. "Charles Stuart . . . was not expelled from the United States, he talked himself countryless, his expulsion due not to the treason but to his having been so vocal and vociferant in the conduct of it, burning each bridge vocally behind him before he had even reached the place to build the next one. . . . Fled by

night, running true to family tradition, with his son and the old claymore and the tartan." *Compson Appendix*, 406.

113. "Lena thinks, 'I have come from Alabama: a fur piece. All the way from Alabama a-walking. A fur piece.' Thinking *although I have not been quite a month on the road I am already in Mississippi.*" *Light in August*, 3.

113. " 'My, my. A body does get around. Here we aint been coming from Alabama but two months, and now it's already Tennessee.' " *Light in August*, 444.

115–116. "It's because we alone in the United States (I'm not speaking of Sambo right now; I'll get to him in a minute) are a homogeneous people. I mean the only one of any size." *Intruder in the Dust*, 153.

116. " 'And as for Lucas Beauchamp, Sambo, he's a homogeneous man too, except that . . ." *Intruder in the Dust*, 155.

118. " 'Oh-h-h, damn you! Damn you! You—you Sartoris!' " *Sartoris*, 75.

118. ". . . the best of all talking. It was of the wilderness, the big woods, bigger and older than any recorded document—of white man fatuous enough to believe he had bought any fragment of it, of Indian ruthless enough to pretend that any fragment of it had been his to convey." *Go Down, Moses*, 191.

119. "owned no property and never desired to since the earth was no man's but all men's, as light and air and weather were." *Go Down, Moses*, 3.

119. "their hold upon [the land] actually was as trivial and without reality as the now faded and archaic script in the chancery book in Jefferson which allocated it to them and that it was he, the boy, who was the guest here and Sam Fathers's voice the mouthpiece of the host." *Go Down, Moses*, 171.

119. "his elder cousin, McCaslin Edmonds, grandson of Isaac's father's sister and so descended by the distaff, yet notwithstanding the inheritor, and in his time the bequestor, of that which some had thought then and some still thought should have been Isaac's . . ." *Go Down, Moses*, 3.

120. This land which man has deswamped and denuded and derivered in two generations . . . where white men rent farms and live like niggers and niggers crop on shares and live like animals, where cotton is planted and grows mantall in the very cracks of the sidewalks, and usury and mortgage and bankruptcy and measureless wealth, Chinese and African and Aryan and Jew, all breed and spawn together until no man has time to say which one is which nor cares." Go Down, Moses, 364.

120. ". . . the surrey moving through the skeleton stalks of cotton and corn in the last of open country, the last trace of man's puny gnawing at the immemorial flank." *Go Down, Moses*, 195.

120. "the old wild life which the little puny humans swarmed and hacked at in a fury of abhorrence and fear like pygmies about the ankles of a drowsing elephant." *Go Down, Moses*, 193.

120. "an unforgettable sense of the big woods—not a quality dangerous or particularly inimical, but profound, sentient, gigantic and brooding." *Go Down, Moses*, 175.

120. "the wilderness . . . seemed to lean, stooping a little, watching them and listening, not quite inimical . . . but just brooding, secret, tremendous, almost inattentive . . ." *Go Down, Moses*, 177.

120. "It seemed to lean inward above them, above himself and Sam and Walter and Boon in their separate lurking-places, tremendous, attentive, impartial and omniscient . . ." *Go Down, Moses*, 181.

120–121. ". . . and in the following silence the wilderness ceased to breathe also, leaning, stooping overhead with its breath held, tremendous and impartial and waiting." *Go Down, Moses*, 182.

121. ". . . it was still no living creature but only the wilderness which, leaning for a moment, had patted lightly once her temerity." *Go Down, Moses*, 199.

121. "not white nor black nor red but men, hunters, with the will and hardihood to endure and the humility and skill to survive." *Go Down, Moses*, 191.

122. "and a cook who was hidden under the mess stuck his arm out and shot Bayard in the back with a derringer." *Sartoris*, 17.

123. "on the next night . . . discovered by a neighbor in bed with his wife and . . . shot to death." *Absalom, Absalom!*, 276.

123. "Bedford Forrest while he was still only a slave-dealer and not yet a general." *Go Down, Moses*, 263.

124. "The first sane Compson since before Culloden and (a childless bachelor) hence the last." *Compson Appendix*, 420.

125–126. "not denying, declining the name itself, because he used three quarters of it; but simply taking the name and changing, altering it, making it no longer the white man's but his own, by himself composed, himself selfprogenitive and nominate, by himself ancestored, as, for all the old ledgers recorded to the contrary, old Carothers himself was." *Go Down, Moses*, 281.

126. "An Isaac born into a later life than Abraham's and reputing immolation: fatherless and therefore safe declining the altar because maybe this time the exasperated Hand might not supply the kid." *Go Down, Moses*, 270–71.

126. "The last. Candace's daughter. Fatherless nine months before her birth, nameless at birth and already doomed to be unwed from the instant the dividing egg determined its sex." *Compson Appendix*, 424.

127. "born merely a subchief, a Mingo, one of three children on the mother's side of the family." "Red Leaves," in *Selected Stories*, 105.

127. "the chief, the Man, the hereditary owner of that land which belonged to the male side of the family." "Red Leaves," in *Selected Stories*, 105.

132. "darting from beneath his hidden face covert, ceaseless glances quick and darting, all-embracing as those of an animal." In *Sartoris*, 156.

136. "might be Clytie's, got by its father on the body of his own daughter." In *Absalom, Absalom!*, 163.

141. "a damned highnosed impudent Negro who even if he wasn't a murderer had been about to get if not about what he deserved at least exactly what he had spent the sixty-odd years of his life asking for." *Intruder in the Dust*, 151.

144. " 'Dont you see?' he cried. 'Dont you see? This whole land, the whole South, is cursed, and all of us who derive from it, whom it ever suckled, white and black both, lie under the curse? Granted that my people brought the curse onto the land . . .' " *Go Down, Moses*, 278.

146. "that unmistakable way in which an open door stands open when nobody lives in the room any more . . . [odor] filling the room, the dusk, the evening." *The Unvanquished*, 239.

146–147. "Some bush or shrub starred with white bloom—jasmine, spiraea, honeysuckle, perhaps myriad scentless unpickable Cherokee roses." *Absalom, Absalom!*, 294–95.

5 . THE REAL—THE DEFERRED

149. "They were Protestants and Democrats and prolific; there was not one Negro landowner in the entire section." *The Hamlet*, 4–5.

149. "to look quietly at the cold embers of a lynching." *The Hamlet*, 28.

151. "Jones grew up in a Catholic orphanage, but like Henry James, he attained verisimilitude by means of tediousness." *Soldier's Pay*, 231.

153. "And as for Lucas Beauchamp, Sambo, he's a homogeneous man too, except that part of him which is trying to escape not even into the best of the white race but into the second best—the cheap shoddy dishonest music, the cheap flash baseless overvalued money." *Intruder in the Dust*, 155.

153–154. " . . . the darkness and the heat thicker, making thicker the imminence of sex after harsh labor along the mooned land; and from it welled the crooning submerged passion of the dark race. It was nothing, it was everything." *Soldier's Pay*, 319.

155. "the motionless uprush of the main ridge and the strong constant resinous downflow of the pines where the dogwood looked indeed like nuns now in the long green corridors." *Intruder in the Dust*, 150–51.

155. "unfolding beneath him like a map in one slow soundless explosion: to the east ridge on green ridge tumbling away toward Alabama and to the west and south the checkered fields and the woods flowing on into the blue and gauzed horizon beyond which lay at last like a cloud the long wall of the levee and the great River itself flowing not merely from the north but out of the North circumscribing and outland—the umbilicus of America . . . " *Intruder in the Dust*, 151.

157–158. " 'You aint got any complaints about the way I farm my land and make my crop, have you? . . . Long as I do that, I'm the one to say about my private business. . . . Besides, I will have to quit hunting every night soon now, to get my cotton picked. Then I'll just hunt Saturday and Sunday night.' Up to now he had been speaking to the ceiling apparently. Now he looked at Edmonds. 'But them two nights is mine. On them two nights I dont farm nobody's land, I dont care who he is that claims to own it.' " *Go Down, Moses*, 120–121.

158. "[S]ince He had created them, upon this land this South for which He had done so much with woods for game and streams for fish and deep rich soil for seed and lush springs to sprout it and long summers to mature it and serene falls to harvest it and short mild winters for men and animals and saw no hope anywhere." *Go Down, Moses*, 283.

160–161. " 'Them convicts. A mule's got twice as much sense.' " " 'A mule's got twice as much sense as anything except a rat,' the emissary said in his pleasant voice." *The Wild Palms*, 326.

161. "[I]t crawled and lurked: the old one, the ancient and accursed about the earth, fatal and solitary and he could smell it now: the thin sick smell of rotting cucumbers and something else which had no name, evocative of all knowledge and an old weariness and of pariah-hood and of death." *Go Down, Moses*, 329.

172. "For twenty years . . . while others of his race sweat in the fields, he served the Man in the shade. Why should he not wish to die, since he did not wish to sweat?" "Red Leaves," in *Selected Stories*, 114.

173. "Maybe you will, since you don't seem to want to know as much as you want something new to be uncertain about." "Beyond," in *Collected Stories*, 787.

173. " 'Mr. de Montigny! From Louisiana!' she screamed, and saw the grandmother, without moving below the hips, start violently backward as a snake does to strike." "Elly," in *Collected Stories*, 211.

173. "Not contented with deceiving your parents and your friends, you must bring a Negro into my son's house as a guest." "Elly," in *Collected Stories*, 217.

173. "He sprang, still seated even, flinging himself backward onto one arm, awry-haired, glaring. Now he understood what it was she had brought into the tent with her, what old Isham had already told him by sending the youth to bring her in to him—the pale lips, the skin pallid and deadlooking yet not ill, the dark and tragic and foreknowing eyes. 'Maybe in a thousand or two thousand years in America,' he thought. 'But not now! Not now!' He cried, not loud, in a voice of amazement, pity and outrage: 'You're a nigger!' " Go Down, Moses, 360–361.

173. "[S]he knew at once that he was a Jew, and when he spoke to her her outrage became fury and she jerked back in the chair like a striking snake, the motion strong enough to thrust the chair back from the table. 'Narcissa,' she said, 'what is this Yankee doing here?' " "There Was a Queen," in Selected Stories, 223.

173. "Percy . . . was suffering the terrible tragedy of having been born not alone too late, but not late enough to have escaped firsthand knowledge of the lost time." Light in August, 394.

173. " 'He went to the West Indies." Absalom, Absalom!, 239.

174. "the . . . blood . . . seemed to rush out of his pale body like the rush of sparks from a rising rocket; upon that black blast the man seemed to rise soaring into their memories forever and ever." Light in August, 407.

174. "Yet, leaning forward in the window, his bandaged head huge and without depth upon the twin blobs of his hands upon the ledge, it seems to him that he still hears them: the wild bugles and the clashing sabres and the dying thunder of hooves." Light in August, 432.

176. "whereupon once more his uncle spoke at complete one with him and again without surprise he saw his thinking not be interrupted but merely swap one saddle for another." Intruder in the Dust, 153.

177. "the purpose of this note is simply to notify the reader that the author has already found more discrepancies and contradictions than he hopes the reader will." The Mansion, prefatory note.

182. "You are my brother." "No I'm not. I'm the nigger that's going to sleep with your sister. Unless you stop me, Henry." Absalom, Absalom!, 357–58.

182–183. " . . . and then Wash Jones sitting that saddleless mule before Miss Rosa's gate, shouting her name into the sunny and peaceful quiet of the street, saying, 'Air you Rosie Coldfield? Then you better come on out yon. Henry has done shot that durn French feller. Kilt him dead as a beef." Absalom, Absalom!, 133.

186. "Her eyes . . . were darkest hyacinth, what I have always imagined that Homer's hyacinthine sea must have had to look like." The Town, 192.

186. "I am happy I was given the privilege of meddling with impunity in other peoples affairs without really doing any harm by belonging to that avocation whose acolytes

have been absolved in advance for holding justice above truth I have been denied the chance to destroy what I loved by touching it." The Mansion, 363.

186. "It was because I not only believe in and am an advocate of fate and destiny, I admire them; I want to be one of the instruments too, no matter how modest." *The Mansion.* 368.

188. "To be unschooled, untraveled, and to an extent unread, Ratliff had a terrifying capacity for knowledge or local information or acquaintanceship to match the need of any local crisis." *The Mansion,* 381.

188. "rural bucolic grass-roots philosopher and Cincinnatus." *The Mansion,* 356.

189. *"[T]he majesty of Fate become contemptuous through ubiquity and sheer repetition."* Mosquitoes, 8.

192. "[N]ot held fast in earth but free in earth and not in earth but of earth, myriad yet undiffused of every myriad part, leaf and twig and particle, air and sun and rain and dew and night, acorn oak and leaf and acorn again, dark and dawn and dark and dawn again in their immutable progression and, being myriad, one." *Go Down, Moses,* 328–29.

192. "[H]imself among them, equal to any, good as any, brave as any, being inextricable from, anonymous with all of them: the beautiful, the splendid, the proud and the brave, right on up to the very top itself among the shining phantoms and dreams which are the milestones of the long human recording— Helen and the bishops, the kings and the unhorned angels, the scornful and graceless seraphim." *The Mansion,* 435–36.

6. THE DEFERRED—THE WORD

199. "circular mail matter and mail order catalogues and government bulletins of all kinds. In one corner, on an up-ended packing-box, sat a water cooler of stained oxidized glass, in another corner leaned a clump of cane fishing poles warping slowly of their own weight; and on every horizontal surface rested a collection of objects not to be found outside of a second-hand store—old garments, bottles, a kerosene lamp, a wooden box of tins of axle grease, lacking one; a clock in the shape of a bland china morning-glory supported by four garlanded maidens who had suffered sundry astonishing anatomical mishaps." *Sartoris,* 102.

200–201. We could hear the roof and the fire, and a snuffling outside the door.
"Where was he going to get a frog in November," Father said.
"I dont know, sir." Quentin said.

We could hear them.

"Jason," Father said. We could hear Jason.

"Jason," Father said. "Come in here and stop that."

We could hear the roof and the fire and Jason.

"Stop that now," Father said. "Do you want me to whip you again." Father
lifted Jason up into the chair by him. Jason snuffled. We could hear the fire
and the roof.

Jason snuffled a little louder.

"One more time," Father said. We could hear the fire and the roof.

The Sound and the Fury, 82–83.

201. "and now the boy made one—himself and his cousin McCaslin and Tennie's
Jim and Major de Spain and General Compson and Walter Ewell and Boon
and old Uncle Ash to do the cooking, waiting for them in Jefferson with the
other wagon, and the surrey." *Go Down, Moses*, 175.

201–202. "the boy and Sam and Uncle Ash in the wagon with the dogs, his cousin
and Major de Spain and General Compson and Boon and Walter and Tennie's
Jim riding double on the horses." *Go Down, Moses*, 202.

202. "the ringing heroic catalogue: Ball: McCudden: Mannock: Bishop: Barker:
Rhys Davies: and above all, simply: England." *A Fable*, p. 88.

203–204. *Caddy*

Dont touch me just promise

If you're sick you cant

Yes I can after that it'll be all right it wont matter dont let them send him to Jackson
promise

I promise Caddy Caddy

Dont touch me dont touch me

What does it look like Caddy

What

That that grins at you that thing through them

The Sound and the Fury, 139.

205. "so that he had been robbed not only of his thievings but his savings too,
and by his own victim; he had been robbed not only of the four thousand dollars
which he had risked jail to acquire but of the three thousand which he had
hoarded at the price of sacrifice and denial, almost a nickel and a dime at a
time, over a period of almost twenty years: and this not only by his own victim
but by a child who did it at one blow, without premeditation." *The Sound and
the Fury*, 425–26.

206. "what would be known afterward as the First Battle of the Somme—a matter
which would give even those who had survived to remember Loos and the

Canal not only something to blench for, but the discovery something even remained to blench with." *A Fable*, 140.

207. "Or maybe he just didn't know he had a reason for Jefferson. Or maybe married men dont even need reasons, being as they already got wives. Or maybe it's women that don't need reasons, for the simple reason that they never heard of a reason and wouldn't recognize it face to face, since they don't function from reasons." *The Mansion*, 107.

212. "a place called the West Indies to which poor men went in ships and became rich, it didn't matter how, so long as that man was clever and courageous." *Absalom, Absalom!*, 242.

212. "Loving all of it even while he had to hate some of it because he knows now that you dont love because: you love despite; not for the virtues, but despite the faults." *Essays*, 42–43.

213. "*ubiquitous as undertakers, cunning as pawnbrokers, confident and unavoidable as politicians. They came cityward lustful as country boys, as passionately integral as a college football squad.*" *Mosquitoes*, 8.

214. "I thought it would be interesting to imagine the thoughts of a group of children on the day of their grandmother's burial." Faulkner in conversation with Maurice Coindreau as quoted by Raymond Queneau in his preface to the Collection Points edition of *Mosquitoes* (Paris: Le Seuil, 1980).

214. "he violated all the rules of decency and honor and pity and compassion, and the fates took revenge on him. That's what the story is." *William Faulkner: American Writer*, 549.

215. "He could have written *I have everything. You trusted me. You chose to let me find you murdered your so-called father rather than tell me a lie.* He could, perhaps, should have written *I have everything. Haven't I just finished being accessory before a murder.* Instead, he wrote *We have had everything.*

" 'No,' she said.

"He wrote *Yes.*

" 'No,' she said.

"He printed YES this time in letters large enough to cover the rest of the face of the tablet and erased it clean with the heel of his palm and wrote . . ." *The Mansion*, 425.

7. THE FRONTIER—THE BEYOND—BACK ON THE TRACE

234. "bourne . . . for the implicated, the insolvent or the merely hopeful." *The Town*, 6.

235. "Gowrie and McCallum and Fraser and Ingrum that used to be Ingraham and Workitt that used to be Urquhart." *Intruder in the Dust*, 148.

236. "He had quite possibly been a foreigner, though not necessarily French, since to the people who had come after him and had almost obliterated all trace of his sojourn, anyone speaking the tongue with a foreign flavor or whose appearance or even occupation was strange, would have been a Frenchman regardless of what nationality he might affirm." *The Hamlet*, 3.

237. "It was 1940 now. The Nibelung maniac had destroyed Poland and turned back west where Paris, the civilized world's eternal and splendid courtesan, had been sold to him like any whore." *The Mansion*, 233.

237. "Called 'l'Homme' (and sometimes 'de l'homme') by his foster brother, a Chevalier of France, who had he not been born too late could have been among the brightest in that glittering galaxy of knightly blackguards who were Napoleon's marshals." *Compson Appendix*, 403.

237–238. "[who] had come all the way from Martinique." *Absalom, Absalom!*, 39.

238. "the little grim harried foreigner had singlehanded given battle to and vanquished Sutpen's fierce and overweening vanity or desire for magnificence or for vindication or whatever it was (even General Compson did not know yet) and so created of Sutpen's very defeat the victory which, in conquering, Sutpen himself would have failed to gain." *Absalom, Absalom!*, 38–39.

239. "Wait . . . for Christ's sake wait. You mean that he—" *Absalom, Absalom!*, 289.

241. "Old Ben and the mongrel Lion were taintless and incorruptible." *Go Down, Moses*, 191.

241. "Now the white man leaned in the window, looking at the impenetrable face with its definite strain of white blood, the same blood which ran in his own veins, which had not only come to the negro through male descent while it had come to him from a woman, but had reached the negro a generation sooner—a face composed, inscrutable, even a little haughty." *Go Down, Moses*, 70–71.

242. "sitting on the saddleless mule in the street before the gate, shouting, 'Hello, Hello,' at intervals until she came to the door, whereupon he lowered his voice somewhat, though not much. 'Air you Rosie Coldfield?' he said." *Absalom, Absalom!*, 87.

248. "From the V strut out each wing tipped and swayed, and he jockeyed the thing carefully on, gaining height. He realized that there was a certain point beyond which his own speed was likely to rob him of lifting surface. He had about two thousand feet now and he turned, and in doing so he found that

aileron pressure utterly negatived the inner plane's dihedral and doubled that of the outer one, and he found himself in the wildest skid he had ever seen since his Hun days." *Sartoris*, 366.

255. "no man is ever free and probably could not bear it if he were." *Go Down, Moses*, 281.

255. "a single log edifice with a clay chimney which seemed in process of being flattened by the rain to a nameless and valueless rubble of dissolution in that roadless and even pathless waste of unfenced fallow and wilderness jungle." *Go Down, Moses*, 277.